AYATULLAH IBRAHIM AMINI

Self Building An Islamic Guide For Spiritual Migration Towards God

Copyright © 1997 by Ayatullah Ibrahim Amini

All rights reserved. No part of this publication may be reproduced, stored or transmitted in any form or by any means, electronic, mechanical, photocopying, recording, scanning, or otherwise without written permission from the publisher. It is illegal to copy this book, post it to a website, or distribute it by any other means without permission.

First edition

Contents

Translator's Foreword	1
Biography of Ayatullah Ibrahim Amini	7
Preface	10
An Important Reminder	11
Self Purification - The Main Goal of Divine Messengers	13
Self-Awareness and Self-building.	17
Human-soul and Animal-self	20
Human Virtues	24
Esoteric Life	30
What to Be?	36
The Heart in Quran	42
Heart in Traditions	53
Hard-heartedness	57
Heart's Physicians	59
Refinement and Perfection of Self	62
Self-refinement	65
Negligence from the Disease	67
Diagnosis of Self-sickness	68
Decision for Treatment	81
Control and Domination of Self	84
Self-Struggle	88
Greater Struggle (Jihad-e-Akbar)	90
Struggle and Divine Assistance	93
Man -His own Physician	95
Prevention	97
Sudden Renunciation	99

Gradual Renunciation	105
Meditation	106
Reward and Punishment	106
Dignity of Human Essence and Strengthening Human Virtues	109
Renunciation of Bad Company	111
Avoiding Potential Blunders	113
Egotism -the Root of all Evils	115
Worldliness -the Source of all Sins	118
What is World?	120
World's Reality	124
The Next Worlders	126
The Worldly Beings	129
The Worldly and Next Worlders	131
Piety -the Most Important Factor for Purification	134
Piety -Objective Behind the Divine Commands	137
Definition of Piety	139
Piety and Seclusion	142
Piety and Insight	142
Piety and Victory over the Difficulties	145
Piety and Freedom	148
Piety and Treatment of Diseases	149
The Characteristics of Pious (Sermon of Hammam)	151
Supervision -the Most Important Factor for Self- restraint	156
Recordings of Deeds	156
Accounting on the Judgment Day	158
Self-scrutiny Before the Judgment Day	161
How to Scrutinize?	164
Repentance and Self-cleansing	175
The Need for Repentance	176
Acceptance of Repentance	179
What is Repentance?	181
Things which Require Repentance	183
Nourishment and Perfection of Self (Tahliyeh)	186

God's Nearness	186
Meanings of God's Nearness	189
Faith -the Foundation of Spiritual Perfection	193
The Means of Perfection and God's Nearness	196
First Means -God's Remembrance (Dikhr)	196
The Effects and Indications of Invocation (Dhikr)	213
Commitment for God's Obedience	213
Humility	214
Excitement for worshiping	215
Tranquility and Assurance	215
God's Attention towards the Servant	217
God's Love towards the Servant	218
The Most Important Effects	219
The Means of Attainment	221
Meditation and Reasoning	221
Deliberations over the Quranic Verses	222
worshiping	224
Invocations and Supplications	225
Instructions	230
Instructions of the Commander of the Faithful Imam ' Ali (A):	234
Instructions of Imam al-Sadiq (A)	238
Instructions of Allameh Majlisi (R.A.)	242
Letter of Akhund-Mulla Hussein Quli Hamdani	243
Instructions of Mirza Javad Agha Malaki Tabrizi (R.A)	248
Instructions of Sheikh Najmuddin (R.A)	252
Obstacles of the Path	256
Second Means -Nourishment of Moral Virtues	267
Third Means -the Righteous Deeds	269
The Sincerity	272
Some Righteous Deeds	280
First -Obligatory Prayers	280
Second -Supererogatory Prayers (Nawafil)	296

Third-Night Prayer (Namaz-e-Shab)	299
Fourth Means -Crusade (Jihad) and Martyrdom (Shahadat)	307
Fifth Means -Benevolence and Service to Humanity	312
Sixth Means - Supplications (Dua)	315
Seventh Means -Fasting (Sawm)	321
Role of Fasting in Self-Building	324
A Mystical Poem (Ghazal-e-Irfani) of Imam Khomeini (R.A.)	331
Supplication of the Holy Month of Sha'ban (Munajat-...	336
A Prayer	345

Translator's Foreword

*I*n the Name of God the Beneficent, The Merciful

The human being is the most complicated and astonishing creation of God-Almighty, the creation who in addition to having its primordial animalistic desires also possesses their peculiar nature and spiritual personality. The creation that has been assigned the Divine Viceregency upon earth,[1] accepted the Divine Trust[2] when heavens, the earth and the mountains shrank from bearing it, and in its upward heavenly ascent[3] even surpassed the God's Favorite Angels.

A creation that selects and thinks, and through combination of his mental power and physical endeavors is capable of removing all obstacles from his path for betterment of his life. The one who creates his own life history through enrichment of knowledge inherited from his predecessors and makes, the path smoother for further advancement by the coming generations in the future.

---

[1] *And when thy Lord said unto the angels: Lo! I am about to place a viceroy in the earth.* -the Holy Quran (20: 30)

[2] *Lo! We offered the trust unto the heavens and the earth and the hills, but they shrank from bearing it and were afraid of it. And man assumed it.* -the Holy Quran (33: 72)

[3] *When he was on the uppermost horizon Then he drew nigh and came down Till he was (distant) two bows' length or even nearer And He revealed unto His slave that which He revealed.* -the Holy Qur-an (53: 7-10)

But unfortunately, in the midst of man's struggle with nature for improving the quality of his living environment, the most precious reality that has been forgotten is the self and the jewel of human personality. Or in other words, what has been forgotten is the man himself, his training and self-purification and making him an ideal or perfect human being. A human being who has been called by the God-Almighty, the Most Superior Creation, [4] and about whose identification the authentic commentators of the revelations have said:

"Whoever has recognized his self -in reality has recognized his Creator." [5]

Self-forgetfulness, negligence shown towards recognizing the infinite dimensions of human celestial soul and under estimation of human inner potential for attaining self-purification or moral perfection is the pain which has inflicted plenty of suffering upon the modern human societies. The domination of technology, fast pace of modern life, usurpation of power by materialists and world-worshippers over vast regions of the world on one hand and the failure and incompetency of various school and ideologies in presenting a clearly illuminated path and satisfactory interpretation of human being on the other hand have made this journey of retrogression and self alienation further complicated.

But in the Islamic Ideology, the greatest aim in the life's struggle is to become victorious over the self. In the Holy Quran the God Almighty after repeated oaths has emphasized the importance of spiritual purification as follows:

"He is indeed successful who causeth it to grow, (the self) And he is indeed a failure who stunteth it." -the Holy Quran (91: 9-10)

In accordance with Divine Islamic Ideology, the most exalted aim is training and guidance of human beings in their spiritual journey from the earthly temporary abode towards the Celestial Kingdom. The aim consists

---

[4] *So blessed be God, the Best of Creators!* -the HolyQuran (23: 14)

[5] A narration from the Infallible Imams (A) of the Holy Prophet's (S) Ahlul Bayt.

of creation of a society and environment where only God-Almighty is worshipped; in which the light of servitude, devotion, and manifestation of faith towards the unseen will destroy the darkness of selfish whims and passions, thus, enabling the human eyes to witness God's Infinite Glory all over upon his existence and introducing the rule of Monotheism (*Towheed*) and its relevant vast dimensions over all human relations and transactions. Of course, this is not possible without self-purification.

The Western people and the Muslim immigrants now settled in Western countries in general are curious to know more about Islamic Mysticism or Gnosticism (*Irfan*). Therefore, I had always desired to translate a suitable book dealing with the Islamic Gnosticism. Thanks God-the Almighty that He bestowed upon this humble servant His Special Grace for completing this translation of Ayatullah Amini's Persian Book

–*Khud Sazi, Tazkiyeh wa Tehzibe Nafs.*

The book presents a detailed description of special deeds as per formed by God's most devoted sincere servants during their lives, the self-restraint and asceticism practiced by them during these worships, and the spiritual purification achieved by them. In their spiritual migration towards God-Almighty the more they endeavored to advance for-ward the more nearer they reached to God's Countenance (*Laqa*).

In Islamic Mysticism [6] the gnostic journey is called '*sayr wa saluk*' and the wayfarer who undertakes this journey is called '*salik*', who strives to utilize all his energy, strength and courage in his spiritual migration towards God-Almighty; takes all necessary precautions to remain purified in his march; is not tired of restrictions and limitations; guards his breaths day and night lest he transgresses and becomes deviated; strictly supervises all entries leading to heart's domain lest illicit desires, forbidden thoughts make their entries thus, making his beloved's promises contaminated with

---

[6] In order to provide a further glimpse of Islamic Mysticism, the translation and commentary of a famous mystical verse of Imam Khomeini (RA) –the most eminent gnostic of our time, has been included at the end of this book.

alien's presence. The most famous mystic poet of Iran, Hafiz-e-Shirazi [7] has so beautifully summarized the wayfarer's above mentioned endeavors in his following verse:

"I remained vigilant guarding the heart's premises every night. So that no alien thought (except my beloved's) could make its entry."

After endeavoring the hardships of his gnostic journey, those who succeed attain the nearness of their beloved (i.e. God-Almighty); the Commander of the Faithful Imam 'Ali (A) have described this gnostic stage in the following tradition:

"Truly when a wayfarer (salik) succeeds in making his wisdom alive and in letting his self die, his body becomes gradually weaker and thinner, his heaviness turning into slimness. A Divine illumination whose manifestation was intermittent becomes clearly visible for him, thus making his path clearly brightened, guiding and moving him through it; passing through various gates (of

---

[7] Khuwaja Shamsuddin Hafiz-i-Shirazi the most eminent mystic poet of Iran, was born in the year 726 A.H. in Shiraz. All the Gnostics of the world humble themselves before the exaltedness and sacredness of Hafiz who is considered as their Qibleh-Gah (patron). His contentment, sur-render, absolute freedom from wants, and truthfulness had bestowed a unique sacredness upon his poetry. After passage of more than six hun-dred years his poetic work Diwan of Hafiz is widely used for Estekhara (consultation), but only those who have purified their souls thoroughly may receive guidance from his poetry. Following are some examples of his poetry:

"Thanks God whatever I requested from God, eventually my wishes were granted."

"Each treasurer of prosperity which was bestowed upon Hafiz by God was due to the blessings of night prayer and dawn supplications."

Upon knowing Hafiz, Goethe wished to be one of his disciples. He said: Oh Hafiz, your word is as great as eternity for it has no beginning and no end. Your word as the canopy of heaven solely depends upon it-self. It is all signs, beauty and excellence."

After studying the lyric poems of Hafiz, Hitche wrote:

"O Hafiz, you have created a tavern of philosophy greater than any worldly palace. In it you provided a wine of grace and world beyond the capacity of the world to drink. The highest pinnacle of any amount is but a sign of your great-ness and the unfathomable depth of any vortex is just a mark of your perfection, and the excellence of your world."

Hafiz, after blessing the humanity with precious gift of his poetic works died at the age of 65 years in the year 791 A.H. His tomb is located in Shiraz. His verses like immortal sign still show light to the world's de-viated ones whose hearts are full of intense darkness.

asceticism) he eventually reaches to the permanent abode of prosperity and with a tranquil and contented heart places his feet in a place of ease and comfort. This is because, he had utilized his reason properly and had made his Creator pleased."

-Sharhe Nahjul Balagha, Ibne abi al-Hadid, p.111-127

A gnostic after attaining God's Learning (*marefah*) becomes some one whose physical body is with the people but his heart is always engaged in God's Remembrance. A gnostic is the trustee of God's Trust and is the treasurer of Divine-Mysteries; is the source of His Light and proof of His Blessings upon the mankind; is the carrier of Divine Knowledge and Scale of Divine Mercy and Justice; is needless of mankind, desires and world; does not have any other companion except God-Almighty; and does not have any indication, speech and breathing but by means of God, for the sake of God, from the God and with the God.

The main contents of the book as mentioned earlier are the etiquette and instructions of gnostic journey, ways and manners of servitude, detailed descriptions of deeds and worships that must be performed by a wayfarer, and what sort of behaviors and restrictions they must practice in order to attain the desired results. The book consists of preface and three parts covering the following topics:

Self-purification, Human Virtues, What to Be?, Heart in Quran, Hard-heartedness, Self-refinement, Self-struggle, Egotism, Wordliness, Piety, Characteristics of the Pious, Repentance or Self-cleansing, Training and Perfection of Self, Faith, Means of Achieving Perfection and God's Nearness, Invocations, Instructions, Obstacles of the Path, Nourishment of Moral Virtues, Righteous Deeds etc. The most prevalent misunderstanding[8] about Islamic Mysticism which must be clarified is that relinquishment of worldly involvement, seclusion, and monasticism are not prerequisites for undertaking a spiritual migration towards God-Almighty; on the contrary,

---

[8] Regarding these misunderstandings Imam Khomeini (RA) in his last testament writes:
    "Among the noticeable conspiracies during the present century and especially during the last few decades and since the victory of the Islamic Revolution is the vast world wide propaganda for dismaying nations and especially the self-sacri-ficing people of Iran with a view to making them lose their confidence in Islam and eventually renounce it.*

as it would be shown in the later part of this book, Islam demands from its followers that while living among the people a normal social life discharging the individual and collective obligations, they should not be negligent of their own selves and must pay special attention towards their spiritual purification.

I wish to thank all those who have contributed to the realization of this translation. I am indebted to Ayatullah Ibrahim Amini and Mr. Ansariyan for support, valuable suggestions, and guidance. I am sincerely indebted to my wife Fatimah Razavi for proof reading Arabic text and Mr. Soulat Parviz for his painstaking efforts in type-setting. For the sake of convenience of readers who are not familiar with Arabic language the recital of important supplications have been written in English. Elucidatory footnotes and chapters added by the translator are identified with [Tr]. Due to pressure of time, as I am leaving tomorrow for Hajj pilgrimage there might be errors and omissions for which I apologize to my readers, and welcome their suggestions and comments.

Sayyid Hussein Alamdar Dhiqadh, 23,1417 A.H.
April 2, 1997 Tehran

Sometimes they do it directly, albeit crudely, suggesting, for example, that the edicts of Islam which were established one thousand and four hundred years ago cannot possibly be relied on as laws on the basis of which to administer countries in the present century, that Islam is a reactionary religion opposed to every in-novation and to the manifestation of modern civilization, or that in the present era the countries in the world cannot discard the world's civilization and its manifestations.

And similar foolish and occasionally malicious and vicious propaganda nicely wrapped and offered in the form of pro-Islamic propaganda and under the pre-text of support for the sanctity of Islamic ways, among other things, that Islam and other divine religions are concerned about the spiritualities, about the moral rectification of mankind, that they invite them to resign earthly pursuits, that they invite man to renounce the material world and engage himself in acts of worship, saying prayers and devotions which, they argue, bring man nearer to God and distance him from the material world; that involvement in the adminis-tration of state and government and politics is against that lofty and spiritual goal because the latter activities are solely for this material world, which is against the teachings of the great prophets."

Imam's Final Dis-course, pp. 22-23.

Biography of Ayatullah Ibrahim Amini

He was born in 1925 in the City of Najafabad in the Province of Esfahan. Having finished his primary studies in Najafabad, he joined the Religious Learning Center of Esfahan in 1942. After completing his curriculum of religious studies in Esfahan, he joined the most famous Religious Learning Center of Qum in 1947, where he learned Dars-e-Khar-ij[9], Jurisprudence and principles, under the tutorship of most eminent religious scholars of that period. He studied the Philosophy books: Man-zoomeh of Hakim Sabzavari, Isfar of Sadar al-Mutaleheen and Shifa of Avicena, under the tutorship of most eminent philosophers of that period. Also, he studied the religious sciences of Kalam (Discourse) and Taf-seer (Commentary) during his stay over there.

While, pursuing his religious studies at Esfahan and Qum he also taught Literature, Jurisprudence and Philosophy. Because of his special attitude and inclination towards the sciences namely: Psychology, Child-Psychology, Education and Training, Family-rights, Family-ethics, and Traditions of Holy Prophet (S) and Infallible Imams (A), he pursued advance studies and research in these areas.

Ayatullah Amini from the very beginning was interested in writing and

---

[9] Dars-e-Kharij: The highest level of theological education related to jurisprudence in the form of lectures, beyond the limited boundaries of textbooks.

academic research and therefore, since the year 1945 he has been engaged intensively in writing and research. Following is a list of some of his published works:

1. Dad-Gustar -e-Jahan (World Administer of Justice) about the life of Imam al-Mahdi (A).
2. Barrasi Masail-e-Kulli Imamat (Over all review of affairs related to Divinely Appointed Viceregency).
3. Aayeen-e-Hamsar Dari (the Code of Marital Relationship).
4. Aayeen-e-Tarbiyat dar Tarbiyate-Kudak (The Code of Child-training).
5. Islam wa Talim wa Tarbiyat (Education and Training in Islam).
6. Intekhab-e-Hamsar (Selection of Spouse).
7. Bano-e-Namuna-e-lslam (The Ideal Women of Islam), about the life of Fatimeh az-Zahra (SA) the daughter of the Holy Prophet (S).
8. Khud Sazi dar Akhlaque (Moral Self-building).
9. Aamuzish-e-Din (Religious-Education): Roots and Branches of religion, explained in simple language, consisting of seven volumes, are in-cluded in the curriculum of Primary Education.
10. Droos min al-Saqafateh al-Islamiyah: A complete course of Roots and Branches of Religion of Intermediate level.
11. Aashnai ba Masail-e-Kulli Islam (Acquaintance with over all Islam-ic Affairs).
12. Hame Bayad Be Danand (Everybody should know); A small book-let containing the details of Roots and Branches of the Religion for younger people.
13. Islam wa Tammudan-e-Gharb (Islam and Western Civilization): Translation from Arabic into Persian of Moududi's Book: Nahn wa al-Hazarate al-Gharbiyeh.
14. A lot of miscellaneous articles written on various: Ideological, Political, Social, Ethical and Educational topics for presentation at Na-tional and International Seminars and Conferences. The above listed books were written in Persian but so far many of them have been trans-lated into various foreign languages.

Ayatullah Amini, an eminent scholar and jurisprudent is a professor at the Religious Learning Center at Qum where he is involved in teaching,

writing and research activities. He very frequently represents the Islamic Republic of Iran at various international conferences. In addition to his teaching responsibilities he also holds many important national positions as follows:

Member and Vice President of Assembly of Experts (*Majlis-e-Khubrigan*), Secretary-General of Office and Educational Research Center of Assembly of Experts, Member Academic Council of Religious Learning Center of Qum, and Chief of Cultural Affairs, Member Board of Trustees of World Center for Islamic Sciences, Member, board of Trustees Imam al-Sadiq University in Tehran and Member Supreme Council of World Assembly of Ahlul Bayt (A)

Preface

In the Name of God the Beneficent and Merciful

Praise to the Lord of the Worlds, salutations and greetings be upon the most noble messenger and prophet, God's beloved, Abi al-Qasim Muhammad (S), who was appointed, to be a blessing for the mankind, to help them attaining spiritual purification, to teach them the book and wisdom and salutations be upon his Holy Household, Ahlul-Bayt (A)

Oh God! Please guide us towards the straight path leading to perfection: enlighten our darken hearts with the light of faith and Your Knowledge; remove the dark intense veils of egotism, selfishness, whims and passions of self; open our exoteric heart's eyes for witnessing Your Unique Beauty; strengthen us on the path of self-building and self-purification, remove from our hearts the love and desires of other than You; remove the veils of negligence and satisfy our thirst with the pure fountain of your Love and Nearness. Oh God! Please enlighten our hearts with the heavenly light of faith and certainty by awakening us from the deep sleep of ignorance, so that we may discover our lost selves and do not waste our precious lives in ignorance like before.

Any how, this servant of God, confused, bewildered, entangled, captive of selfish whims and passions, ignorant of the existence of various spiritual stations of perfection and stages of mystical journey towards God-Almighty was suddenly inspired to move his feet inside this vast arena of spiritual fields dealing with self-building, refinement, and purification of human self. By utilization of enlightened verses of the Holy Quran and instructions given by Holy Prophet (S) and infallible Imams

1. of his Holy Progeny (Ahlul Bayt) [10] abstraction of the overall basic principles of self-purification and spiritual mystic journey towards God-Almighty was accomplished. May be these efforts would be of some help, and guidance for the truth seekers and wayfarers in their march on this road of spiritual perfection.

May Merciful God accept this insignificant work and may hold the hand of this deprived servant, leading from the intense darkness of ignorance and egotism towards the illuminated valley of invocations, love, enlightenment, and countenance of God-Almighty. And if it happened, may be it will compensate the omissions of the past for the coming life (if there is any left) of this servant.

An Important Reminder

Before entering into discussion, it must be emphasized that the monasticism, renunciation of worldly affairs, and unacceptance of social responsibilities are not pre requisite for undertaking a self-purification program, on the contrary, as will be shown in the book later on that seclusion and relinquishment of individual and social responsibilities are inconsistence with the spiritual self-building and self-purification program.

---

[10] Ahlul Bayt (A): It refers to the immediate descendants of a family or such a family of the same house or bayt. In this compound form, Ahlul Bayt is used in the Holy Quran especially in reference to the immediate family of Muhammad (S). In verse 33: 33 we hear:
"**And God only wishes to remove from you all kind of uncleanliness, O members of the family (of Muhammad) and thoroughly purify you.**"
All the commentators of the Holy Quran are unanimous in the opinion that the term Ahlul Bayt in this verse refers to Muhammad's daughter Fatimah, his cousin and son in-law 'Ali, and his two beloved grandsons, Hasan and Husayn [Tr].

Islam demands from Muslims that simultaneous to living among the people and discharging their social obligations they should not be ignorant about their spiritual requirements and therefore, should pay special attention towards their self-building and self-refinement.

Ibrahim Amini March, 1984 Qum, I.R. IRAN.

Self Purification – The Main Goal of Divine Messengers

The greatest aim of Divine Messengers was to emphasize the importance of refinement, purification, and training of human selves. God-Almighty said in the Holy Quran:

"God did confer a great favor on the believers when he sent among them an apostle from among themselves rehearsing unto them the signs of God, sanctifying them and instructing them in scripture and wisdom, while before that, they had been in manifest error."-the Holy Quran (13: 164)

Therefore, it is obvious that the subject of human education and training was of such vital importance that God-Almighty sent Divine Messengers especially for this purpose thus, conferring a great favor ul1on the believers. The individual as well as collective personality, prosperity or cruelty (of this world and Hereafter) of a human being depends upon how much efforts he had already made or is still making for self-building. It is from this consideration that self-building is regarded something of such vital importance because it determines ones eventual destiny.

The Divine Messengers came to teach human beings regarding the path of self-building, nourishment, and perfection of self, as well as to accompany them as their guide and helper in this vital and determinant task.

They came for cleansing and sanctifying human selves from their indecent moral characteristics and animal instincts, and bestowing upon them superior spiritual virtues. The prophets lectured human beings about the self-building program, acted as helper and knowledgeable guides in identifying the ugliness in their moral conducts, and showed them the ways and means for self-control against their selfish whims and passions. By timely issuance of warning and intimidating they succeeded in sanctifying the human selves from the moral obscenities and indecencies. They came for plantation of sapling of higher moral virtues within human souls, nurtured and protected it for its eventual blooming, and in doing so acted as guides, friends, and helpers of the people by encouraging and pursuing them towards the desired sublime' objectives. The Holy Prophet(S) has said:

"I emphasize the importance of good morals for you because God-Almighty has sent me especially for this purpose." -Bihar al-Anwar vol. 69, p-375.

He further said:

"I was appointed for the Prophethood so that I may accomplish the important task of moral perfection within human souls." —Al Mustadarak, vol. 2, p-282.

Imam al-Sadiq [11] (A) said:

---

[11] Imam Ja'far al-Sadiq (A): The sixth Imam, Ja'far, known as al-Sadiq (A) was born in Medina on Monday, 17th Rabi-ul-awwal 83 A.H. The son of the fifth Imam, he lived in an increasingly favorable climate and was able to teach openly in Median. Large numbers of scholars gathered around him to learn, including such famous Sunni figures as Abu Hani-fa, the founder of the one of the four Sunni schools of Law. Towards the end of Imam Ja'far's life severe restrictions were placed upon his activities, as a result of growing Shi'ite unrest. More traditions are recorded from him than from all the other Imams together. He is so important for Twelve-Imam Shi'ite law that it is named the Jafri School after him. He is buried in the Baqi cemetery in Medina.

Ja'far's fame for religious learning was great, greater than that of his father or of any other Twelver Imam except for 'Ali bin Abu Talib (A) himself. perhaps the earliest historical reference presenting Ja'far as one of the most respected and highly esteemed personalities of his epoch, and as having profound knowledge and learning, is Ya'qubi's statement that it was customary for scholars who related anything from him to say: "The Learned One informed us".

"God-Almighty appointed prophets with good morals; therefore, whoever discovers these virtues within himself should be thankful to God for this bounty, whoever lacks these virtues must pray, cry, and shed tears 1before God Almighty asking for such blessing."

-al Mustadarak, vol. 2, p-283.

The commander of faithful Imam Ali [12] (A) said:

"Supposedly, if neither there was any desire for Paradise nor there was any fear of Hell, and also there would have not been any belief about the reward and punishment in the Next World; even then it would have been be fitting to strive

---

Even the famous jurist of Medina, the Imam Malik b. Anas, is reported to have said, when quoting Ja'far's traditions: "The Thiqa (truthful) Ja'far b. Muhammad himself told me that...." Similar compliments for Ja'far are attributed to the Imam Abu Hanifa, who is also reported to have been his pupil. Al-Sadiq's (A) knowledge was great in religion and culture, he was fully informed in philosophy, he attained great piety in the world, and he abstained entirely from lusts. He lived in Medina long enough to greatly profit the sect that followed him, and to give his friends the advantage of the hidden sciences. He died at the age of 65, in Medina on Monday, 25th Shawwal 148 H.; poisoned by al-Mansur ad-Dawaniqi, the Abbasid Caliph.

[12] "The Commander of the Faithful' Ali ibn Abu Talib (A): Was the first perfect exemplar of the teachings of the Most Noble Messenger (S) 'Ali was raised by him from early childhood and followed him like a shadow until the very end of the latter's life. He was like a moth before the prophetic flame; the final moment when he was separated from the Most Noble Messenger (S) was when he embraced his corpse and laid it to rest. 'Ali (A) was the first person after the Most Noble Messenger (S) to approach spiritual realities in the manner of philosophical reflection, that is, by free exercise of reason. He used many technical terms and laid out and organized the rules of Arabic grammar in order to protect the Holy Quran from copyist's errors. The exact scholarship, spiritual culture, and consideration of ethical, social, political, and even mathematical problems shown in' Ali's (A) discourses, letters, and other documents that have reached us are astonishing.

The wealth of these documents makes ' Ali (A) the best known individual among Muslims to have a full realization of the sublime goals of the Holy Quran and the critical and practical concepts of Islam as they should be realized. They testify to the soundness of the Prophetic saying, 'I am the city of knowledge and Ali is its gate'. Furthermore, he combined this knowledge with action. In short, ' Ali's outstanding character is beyond description, and his virtues are innumerable. Never in history has someone's character drawn the attention of the world's scholars and thinkers to such an extent.

-R. Compbell, Allameh Sayyed Mohammad Hosayn Tabatabai, Islamic teachings pp.123-127.

for moral perfection, because, good morals are the path towards prosperity and victory."

-Al-Mustadarak,

vol. 2, p-283.

Imam Baqir [13] said:

"The most perfect believers from the point of view of faith are the ones who excel in moral conduct." -Al-Kafi, vol. 2, p-99.

The Holy Prophet (S) said:

"There is nothing better than good moral conduct which could be written on the "Letter of Deeds" on the Day of Resurrection." -Al-Kafi, vol. 2, p-99.

And said

"My Ummah will enter into Paradise mostly on the basis of piety and excellence in moral conduct." -Al-Kafi,vol. 2, p-100.

and the following narration:

"A man approached the Holy Prophet (S) and asked: 'What is religion?' The Holy Prophet (S) replied: 'Good moral conduct.' The man asked the same questions from the Holy Prophet (S) alternatively by appearing from right, left, and behind the Messenger. Finally the Holy Prophet (S) took a deep look at him and said: 'Why don't you understand?' Religion is defined as never to get angry." -Mohajateh Al-Baiza, vol. 5, p-89.

Islam has attached special importance for moral ethics, and because of these consideration the Holy Quran contains relatively more verses regarding ethics as compared verses related to obligation. Inside the books of narrations, one may finds thousands of narrations regarding ethics as compared to narrations dealing with other topics; if this number is not regarded greater in quantity, certainly it is not smaller either. The rewards and promises mentioned for good moral deeds are certainly not lesser than

---

[13] The Fifth Imam, Muhammad, known as al-Baqir (57/675-114/732) The son of the fourth Imam, he was present at Karbala at a young age. Because of changing political and religious conditions, among them the general revulsion following the events at Karbala, many people came to Medina to learn the religious and spiritual sciences from him. He trained numerous well-known men of religion, and mainly for this reason is the first Imam after' Ali from whom large numbers of traditions are recorded. He buried in the Baqi' cemetery in Medina.

the rewards prescribed for other actions, and likewise the warnings and punishments described for indecent moral actions are certainly not less than the punishments for other actions.

Therefore, in Islam, ethics constitutes the basics and should not be treated simply as secondary religious obligations or something related to the beautification and decoration of religious persons. If religion has defined do's and don'ts for obligations, it has defined the same for ethics. If encouragement, persuasion, rewards, punishment, and warnings have been utilized for obligations, the same approach has been applied for ethics as well as. Therefore, there exists no difference between ethics and obligations as for as religious recommendations are concerned, and in order to achieve perfection and prosperity one cannot remain ignorant of ethical matters.

The moral obligations cannot be ignored by taking the excuse of treating them simply as moral obligations, likewise forbidden moral acts should not be performed either. If performance of daily-prayers is compulsory and their non-performance is prohibited and brings Divine-Punishment, equally important is the fulfillment of a promise and its breach is prohibited and brings Divine-Wrath. The real religious and prosperous is some one who is committed to his religious obligation as well as is honest in fulfillment of his moral commitments. On the contrary ethics play an important role for achieving prosperity and spiritual perfection that will be explained in the book later on.

Self-Awareness and Self-building.

Although a human being is not more than a single reality, but is the possessor of different dimensions within his single existence –the existence which starts from the insignificant dusty material lacking any sort of sense and feelings and ultimately terminates into a precious celestial jewel.

God-Almighty said in the Holy Quran:

"Who made all things good which He created, and He began the creation of man from clay, then He made his seed from a draught

of despised fluid; then he fashioned him and breathed into him of his spirit; and appointed for you hearing and sights and hearts; small thanks give ye" -the Holy Quran (32: 7-9)

A human being is the possessor of various facts and parameters within his existence. From one aspect he is the possessor of physical body and a name, while from another aspect he is possessor of animal instincts as well as. Eventually overall, he is a human being possessing superior human virtues which are not found in other animals.

Therefore, human being is a single reality, a reality that possesses various dimensions and facts within his single existence. When it is said: My weight and my face, it is indicative of his body and name; when it is said: My food and my health, it is also related to his body; when it is said: movement, anger, and sexual passion, it indicates his animal self; and lastly when it is said; my wisdom, my thinking and my thoughts, it indicates to his superior human virtues. Therefore, a human being possesses different kinds of selves namely; self related to his physical body, self related to his animal instincts, and the human-self, but the most valuable and precious self is his human-self. What had made human beings, "Vicegerent of God" upon earth and has distinguished them over other creatures is nothing but the single heavenly "Spirit" blown into his existence by the God-Almighty, called Human Soul. The wise God has explained the creation of human beings in the Holy Quran as follows:

> *"Verily we created man from a product of wet earth; then placed him as a drop (of seed) in a safe lodging; then fashioned we the drop a clot, then fashioned we the little lump bones, then clothed the bones with flesh,. and then produced it as another creation. So blessed the God, the Best of Creators." -the Holy Quran (23:12-14)*

It is about the creation of human being that God-Almighty has said:

> "So blessed the God -the Best of Creators." -the HolyQuran (23:14)

It was because of this Heavenly Spirit that human being reaches to an exalted position that God-Almighty orders the angels as follows:

> "So when I have made him and have breathed unto him of My Spirit, do ye fall down prostrating yourself unto him." -the Holy Quran (15: 29)

If, human beings were bestowed distinction over other creatures and God-Almighty said about them as follows:

> "Verily, we have honored the children of Adam. We carry them on the land and the sea, and have made provision of good things for them, and have preferred them above many of those whom we created with a marked preferment." -the Holy Quran (17: 70)

Therefore, if a human being should strive for self-building he must build his human-self and not his animal or physical-self. The aims of prophets had been to strengthen the human beings in their endeavors for perfecting their human selves. The Prophets said to the human-beings:

Don't forget that your self is your human-self; in case you sacrificed your human-self for the sake of whims and passions of your animal-self; you will inflict upon yourself a terrible loss.

The God-Almighty has said in the Holy Quran:

> "Say: the losers will be those who loose themselves and their house folk on the Day of Resurrection. Ah, that will be the manifest loss." -the Holy Quran (39:15)

Those who never think about any thing except their animal existence have indeed lost their human personality and are not striving for their recovery either. The Commander of the Faithful Imam 'Ali (A) has said:

"It is indeed strange to see someone so desperately looking for lost personal things, while making absolutely no efforts to find his lost (human) self." -Gharar al-Hukm p-495.

There can not be more severe and painful loss than some one's loosing his human personality and real self; for such a person nothing is left except animalism.

Human-soul and Animal-self

The verses of the Holy Quran and narrations about human-self could be divided into two categories. Some of the verses define human-self as a precious valuable jewel possessing Heavenly excellence, descended from Heaven, which is the source of all superior characteristics and human virtues. These verses recommend that human beings must strive for achieving self-refinement and self-perfection through training, and must be careful for its protection, never to loose such a precious Heavenly gift. For example God-Almighty in Holy Quran defines this precious jewel as follows:

> "They will ask the (of Muhammad) concerning the spirit. Say: The spirit is by command of my Lord, and knowledge ye have been vouchsafed but little." -the Holy Quran (17:85)

In the above verse the spirit has been defined as an existence belonging to the celestial world that is superior than the material world. The Commander of the Faithful Imam Ali (A) about the self said:

"Self is like a precious jewel, whoever strives for his protection, he will help him attaining exalted positions, and whoever acted negligently in his protection he shall pull him towards humiliation." -Gharar al-Hukm, p-226.

And said:

"Whoever knows the worth of his self will never allow himself to be indulging into passing worldly amusements and shameful deeds." -Gharar al-Hukm, p-669.

And said:

"Whoever discovers the nobility of self shall guard him against lowness of passions and false desires." -Gharar al-Hukm, p-710.

And said:

"Whoever possesses the nobility of self will have more compassion."
-Gharar al-Hukm, p-638.

Also said:

"Whoever possesses the nobility of self will become free from Wants." -Gharar al-Hukm, p-669.

From the above quoted verses and narrations whose examples are frequent, it can be derived that human self is a valuable and precious jewel which should be carefully guarded protected and nourished.

The second category of verses and narrations defines the self as something wicked and dangerous enemy responsible for all sort of evils, against whom we are supposed to wage a great struggle (Jihad-e-Akbar) till it becomes completely submissive, otherwise it will inflict terrible misfortune and cruelty upon the defeated person.

Following are some examples:

> "But as far him who feared to stand before his lord and restrained his soul from lust, Lo ! The garden will be his home."
> -the Holy Quran (79:40-41)

The Holy Quran quotes from Prophet Joseph (A):

> "I don't exculpate myself Lo! the (human) soul enjoineth unto evil, save that whereon my Lord hath mercy. Lo! My Lord is Forgiving, Merciful." -the Holy Quran (12: 53)

The Holy Prophet (S) said:

"Your's greatest enemy is your self, which is located between your two sides."
-Bihar al-Anwar,

vol. 70, p-64.

Imam 'Ali (A) said:

"Self commands you continuously to indulge into evil deeds, therefore, whoever trusted his self -he will deceit him, whoever believed his self -he will destroy him; and whoever is satisfied with his self —he will lead him to face worst kind of disasters."

-Gharar al-Hukm, p-226.

He further said:

"Trusting the self provides the most dependable opportunities for devil's entrance"

-Gharar al-Hukm, p-54.

Imam al-Sajjad[14] (A) said:

"Oh God! I do complain to you against the self —which continuously commands; to indulge into sinful acts and deviations,. Stands up against Your wrath and punishment; and pulls me towards the path of absolute destruction."

-Bihar al-Anwar, vol. 94, p-143.

From the above quoted verses and narrations whose examples are frequent, it can be derived that human self constitutes an evil existence which is the source of all sort of sins and therefore, should be made submissive through efforts and waging greater struggle (*Jihad-e-Akbar*). Here it is quite possible that some may consider that these two categories

---

[14] Imam al-Sajjad (A): The son of Imam al-Husayn by the daughter of Yazdigird the last Sassanid king of Iran was born in Medina on Saturday, 15th Jamadi al-Ola 36 A.H. He participated in Imam al Husayn's uprising and accompanied his father to Karbala being a tragic witness to the tragic event. After his father's martyrdom he was made captive and taken from Karbala to Kufa and from Kufa to Damascus. His speeches and protests on necessary occasions made manifest the worthiness and glory of Ahlal Bayt (A), the cruel injustice suffered by his father, and the enormities perpetuated by the Yazid's Ummayad regime.

Imam al-Shafi considered Imam' Ali ibn al-Husayn (A) as the most su-preme jurist of all the people of Medina. His book. Al-Shaifah Al-Saj-jadiyyah" represents and stands out as a profound social work of the time and a reflection of a supreme endeavor to meet the exigencies of spiritual ordeals facing the society at the time of Imam. He died at the age of 58 in Medina; poisoned by al-Walid ibn Abdul Malik ibn Marwan on 25th Muharram 95 A.H., and is buried in Jannatu'l Baqi Cemetery in Medina [Tr].

of verses and narrations are incompatible and contradict each other; or one might imagine that a human being possesses two selves, namely: human-self which is the source of all goodness and blessing, and the other one animal-self which is the source of all evil and sinfulness.

Both of the above mentioned interpretations are incorrect because firstly there exists no conflict between the above mentioned verses and narrations of two categories; secondly, the sciences had already proved that a human being is not more than a single reality possessing a single self and it is not such that his animalism and humanism are separate from each other.

But human self comprises of two stages and two dimensions of his single existence. At lower the stage, self is an animal possessing all anim-alistic characteristic, while at higher stage, the self is a human possessing Divine-spirit -descended from the Celestial Heavenly Kingdom. When it is said: Self is noble, precious, source of all virtues and blessings; one must endeavor for his nourishment and perfection -here the higher stage of self has been indicated.

But when it is said: Self is your greatest enemy; don't trust him because he will lead you to eventual destruction, control and make him submissive through greater struggle -here his animal and lower stage have been pointed out. If it is said: Nourish and strengthen your self here the human dimension of the self is meant. When it is said: Wage greater struggle for his total submission, here the animal dimension of the self is meant.

There exists a continuous confrontation between these two selves or two stages of human existence. The animal self continuously strives to dominate by keeping human being amused with whims, passions and lower animal desires, thus, closing the path of advancement perfection, exaltation and movement towards God-Almighty and making a human being captive of his animal self. While on the contrary his human self or the higher stage of his existence continuously strives for attaining the higher sublime spiritual stations of human perfection leading towards God's Countenance, and in order to accomplish his cherished goal, tries to control, and forces the animal-self for his absolute submission. This internal struggle, within the human existence continues until one of the combatant becomes victorious defeating his opponent.

If the human or celestial-self gets upper hand -the human values become alive, thus, leading human being towards the road of spiritual excellence and perfection ultimately achieving the highest position of God's Countenance. But, on the contrary if the animalself becomes victorious -he turns off the light of wisdom, thus, throwing the human being into the deepest valley of darkness confusion and deviation. It was because of this internal confrontation within human existence that Divine Prophets came to help guide and support the human beings in their holy struggle which ultimately determines their destiny.

Human Virtues

A human being possesses two types of selves: the human self and the animal self, but the value of a human being is related to his human-self and has nothing to do with his animal self. The animal-self may be regarded some sort of parasitic existence, or like an uninvited guest, and in reality is the unconscious-self. Although, a human being is an animal and is obligated to fulfill his animalistic requirements, but he has not been created to live in this world like an animal, instead he has been created with the aims and objectives of utilizing and commissioning his animal existence for perfecting his human existence.

A human being have some genuine requirements incorporated within his inner existence for the sake of his animal as well as human existence. Since he is an animal, he requires food, water, clothing and shelter in order to motivate him for making serious endeavors for their search, feelings of thirst and hunger have been incorporated within his existence.

Similarly, for the sake of continuation of human race, sexual desires and love for female partner have been incorporated within his nature.

Since men like to live and in order to sustain his life he has no other choice except to take care of means of living required for his animal existence. When he sees food he feels hungry and desires to eat and therefore, he tells himself: I must arrange food for my own consumption and whatever obstacles are encountered in this path I must try to remove them. Of course, these feelings are not bad because for sustenance of life one must work, eat and drink. In Islam not only this has not been forbidden, on the contrary it has been recommended and encouraged. But parallel to that it must be clearly understood that the animal life is a preliminary and not the desired goal. Or in other words, the animal life is not the main guest rather some one accompanying him.

Therefore, if some one assigns authenticity to animal existence, strives and endeavors seriously day and night to fulfill his animal lower desires and passions; considers the aims of life simply eating, drinking, sleeping, and reproducing -has indeed fallen into intense darkness of deviation and wanderness. Because, he has removed the human wisdom and Heavenly spirit from the position of power and have confined them into a forgotten place. Such an individual does not deserve to be called as a human being -rather he is an animal with a human face. He possesses

wisdom but by his perverted deeds has become so isolated that he can no longer recognize and follow the superior human virtues and characteristics. In spite of having eyes he is unable to see the realities; in spite of possessing ears he cannot hear the facts. the Holy Quran considers such an individual as an animal and even worse and more deviated than the animals because animal lacks wisdom and does not understand, while the above mentioned person in spite of having wisdom does not understand.

The Holy Quran describes such individuals, as follows:

> *"And if they answer thee not, then know that what they follow is their lusts. And who goes farther astray than he who followeth his lust without guidance from God? Lo! God guideth not wondering folk." -the Holy Quran (28:50)*

And further said:

> *"Already have we urged unto Hell many of the Jinn and hu-*

mankind, having hearts wherewith they understand not, and having eyes wherewith they see not, and having earswherewith they hear not. These are as the cattle -nay but they are worse! These are the neglectful." -the Holy Qur-an (7: 179)

The Holy Quran further defines these creatures as follows:

"Hast thou seen him who maketh his desire his god, and God sendeth him astray purposely and sealeth up his hearing and his heart, and setteth on his sight a covering ? Than who will lead him after God (hath condemned him) ? Will you not then heed ?"
-the Holy Qur-an (45: 23)

How unfortunate and losers are those who have sacrificed their heavenly-self, prosperity, and human perfection for the sake of passions and desires of their animal existence? They have exchanged their human self with their animalistic pleasures. [15]

The Commander of the Faithful Imam' Ali (A) said:

"Whoever becomes involved into world's allurements, thus giving up his gains from his immortal life in the Next World -has indeed been cheated."

-Gharar al-Hukm,vol. 1, p-88.

He also said:

"Restrain your self from indulgence into lower shameful deeds no matter how attractive or appealing they might appear because, in this exchange or trade you do not receive the genuine value of your self Do not allow yourself to be slave of other because, God has created you as free. The goodness which cannot be obtained except through the evil is not goodness. Also a thing acquired except with serious efforts would not be easy to retained."

---

[15] The Commander of the faithful Imam' Ali (A) has said:
"This world is not a place of permanent settlement, it is passage, a road on which you are passing. There are two kinds of people here; those who have sold their souls for eternal damnation, the other type are those who have purchased their souls and freed them from damnation." -Nahjul-Balagha, S.M. A Jafri p-543 [Tr].

-Nahjul-Balagha, Sabhi Saleh, vol. 31, p-401.

And said:

"What a bad trade it is that one exchanges his self for this world instead of trading it with whatever is available with God-Almighty (in the Next World)."

-Nahjul-Balagha, sermon 32.

But, a human being cannot be summarized only into animal self, because he also possesses a human self, and on account of this merit he is an abstract and Celestial Jewel, descended from the Heavenly Kingdom, cherishing values other then animalistic desires. If a human being ponders deeply into his Inner existence and really recognized himself; he will discover that he has arrived from the kingdom of power, wonder, knowledge, blessing, benevolence, illumination, goodness, justice, and in one sentence from the kingdom of absolute perfection, and is originated and belonged to it.

It is here that a human being discovers another prospective and looks beyond the limit boundaries of created world -towards the supreme source of absolute perfection and feels attracted towards his higher values. Hence being committed for aspiration of those cherished values,

accordingly he changes the movement of his self from the animalistic course towards the exalted path of perfection -which ultimately leads him towards the highest spiritual station of God's Nearness.

When this internal revolution within him occurs the importance of higher and moral ethical values becomes explicit. Therefore, if a human being desires values such as knowledge, favor, welfare, sacrifice, justice, benevolence, defense of deprived and destitute, truth, goodness, and honesty-it is because, he considers him belonging to the World of Absolute Perfection and regards such virtues worthy of his exalted human position. It is because, of these feelings that he admires them to the extent, that he is ready to sacrifice his animal self and its desires for the sake of those cherished higher virtues.

Good morals, etiquette, and ethics are defined as a series of spiritual and meaningful perfection, whose proportion for his own spiritual perfection need, is clearly understood by the human celestial soul. The soul admits to himself: "I must do these things."

The ethical musts are derived from the degree of perfection and nobleness within the self and are utilized for achieving exaltation of essence and spiritual perfection. When he says: "I must offer sacrifice on this righteous path." Because, he understands that sacrifice is useful for achieving the perfection and exaltation of essence, and therefore, desires to do that. As for as the path and means of spiritual perfection are concerned they are the same for all human beings. Similarly, all of them have been created identical as for as their sense for recognition of values and anti values is concerned.

If a human being ponders deep into his own perfection seeker pure nature, away from the whims and passions of self, he might discover the moral and ethical virtues as well as the moral vices. All human beings of all times were created such by the God-Almighty. And if some, of them become deprived of this sacred sense of identification, it was because their whims, passions, and intense animalistic desires, silenced the light of their wisdom, leaving them like a sole rider in the fields of self-struggle.

The Holy Quran about the recognition of virtues and vices by the pure human nature as follows:

> *"And a soul and Him who perfected it and inspired it (with conscience of) what is wrong for it and what is right for it. He is indeed successful who causeth it to grow."*
> *-the Holy Qur-an (91:7-9)*

The Prophets came with the intention of awakening human nature and to charge their unconscious-self into conscious-self; they came to help, support, and guide human beings in recognizing and paying attention to higher moral values, and utilizing them for attaining God's-Nearness; they came to remind human beings about their exalted human position and need for safe guarding and motivating the superior human virtues; they came to emphasize the important point that: You are not animals instead are humans and possess the potential of being superior than the angels. World affairs and animalistic manifestations are far below before your exalted celestial dignity and therefore, you should not sell yourself for them.

Imam al-Sajjad (A) was asked:

"Who is the most exalted and most noble person?"

"The one who does not regard the world worthy of greatness of his self." Replied the Imam.

-Tohf al-Aqul, p-285.

If man really identifies his true human personality and if his human self indeed gets upperhand, then good morals and ethics become alive and dominate over the moral vices and rascalities. And when it occurs, a man is no longer permitted to ignore human values and follow vices for example, Ignoring truth and speaking lies, disregarding honesty and practicing treachery, not care about the honor of self and indulging into sinful deeds; and ignoring favor and practicing human persecution etc.

The Commander of Faithful Imam Ali (A) said:

"Whoever consider his self honorable will regard selfish passions low and mean."

-Nahjul al-Balagha,

saying 449.

The prophets continuously strived for awakening the upright human nature so that. they could learn about their jewel of existence and could discover their dependence and link with God-Almighty; thus spending everything in their possession for attaining the position of nearness and pleasure of the Lord of the worlds to the extent that their eating, drinking. Sleeping, seeing, speaking, working, living, and dying become sacred and ethical. Truly, when men become God's servant and do not cherish for any other goal except his pleasure everything become ethics, worship and virtue.

The Holy Quran said:

> **"Say: Lo! My worship and my sacrifice, and my living, and my dying are for God, the Lord of the worlds." -the Holy Quran (6:162)**

Therefore, because of the above mentioned reasons, recognition of self in Islam has been assigned a special importance. The Commander of the

Faithful Imam' Ali (A) has said:

"Self-consciousness is one of the most profitable assets of a person."
-Gharar al-Hukm, p-768.

And said:

"Whoever succeeds in self -his affairs will be improved." -Gharar al-Hukm, p-628.

What is meant with self recognition is not the particulars of one's identify card rather it means –man's realization of his true position with-in the created world; an understanding that he is not simply an earthly animal rather is a reflection of heavenly illumination from the Celestial Kingdom; is the Trustee and Vicegerent of God-Almighty upon earth. A celestial being who has been created conscious, empowered and free, is capable of upward ascent towards the absolute perfection, and his special creation has been assigned the responsibility of nourishment and perfection of the self. It is because of this realization that man feels a sense of greatness and perfection; discovers the sacredness and virtues within his inner existence and morals and ethics become valuable and meaningful for him. In that case he get relieved from the feelings of hopelessness, depressions, vainness, nonsense, aimless repetitions, and instead life becomes sacred, precious beautiful, and objective.

Esoteric Life

Man in this world has an outwardly life related to his body. He eats, drinks, sleeps, moves, and walks but at the same time also possesses a spiritual life in his inner essence. While he lives in this world, at the same time within his inner essence either journeys towards prosperity, perfection and enlightenment, or moves towards adversity, cruelty and intense darkness; either journeys on the righteous path of humanity and ascends towards God, or deviates from the righteous path heading towards darkest valleys where he wanders in darkness becoming eventually lower than animals; either marches up on the steps of perfection towards enlightenment, joy, perfection, and God's Countenance or falls into intense darkness for eternal punishment.

Although, majority of people are ignorant of this reality but it does exist. God-Almighty said in Holy Quran:

"They know only some appearance of the life of the World, and are needless of the Hereafter." -the Holy Quran (30: 7)

But being knowledgeable or ignorant does not change the reality on the Day of Resurrection when the dark curtain of materialism are rolled up from the human eyes thus, enabling him to witness the reality and his own state of affairs.

The God-Almighty said in Holy Quran:

"(And unto the evil-doer it is said): Thou wast in needlessness of this. Now we have removed from thee thy covering and piercing is thy sight this day."
-the Holy Quran (50:22)

Therefore, from the above quoted verses it may be inferred that affairs related to the Next World all along did exist within human inner essence right here in this world, but unfortunately man was ignorant to realize it. However, since in the Next World all the materialistic curtains of ignorance shall be removed from his sight, he will be forced to see these realities clearly over there. We may therefore, conclude from the above mentioned verses and traditions that the human-self earns things while living in this world, and these earning shall remain with him eventually determining his ultimate destiny in his eternal abode. Following are some examples:

God-Almighty said in the Holy Quran

"Every soul is a pledge for its own deeds." -the Holy Quran (74:38)

And said:

"Then every soul will be paid. in full what it hath earned; and they will not be wronged."
-the Holy Quran (3:161)

And said:

"God will not take you to task for that which is unintentional in your oaths. But He will take you to task for that which your hearts have garnered. God is forgiving, clement."-the Holy Quran (2:225)

And said:

"God tasketh not a soul beyond its scope. For it (is only) that which it hath earned, and against it (only that which it hath deserved." –the Holy Quran (2:286)

And said:

"On the Day when every soul will find itself confronted With all that it hath done of good and all that it hath done of evil (every soul) will long there might be a mighty space of distance between it and that evil." -the Holy Quran (3:30)

And said:

"Whoso doth right, it is for his soul. and whoso doth wrong, it is against it. And afterward unto your Lord ye will be brought back". -the Holy Quran (45:15)

And said:

"And whoso doth good an atom's weight will see it then, and whoso doth evil an atom's weight will see it then." -the Holy Quran (99:7-8)

And said:

"And that man hath only that for which he maketh effort and that his effort will be seen." -the Holy Quran (53: 39-40)

And said:

> "And whatever of Good ye send before (you) for your souls, ye will find it with God."
> -the Holy Qur-an (2:110)

And said:

> "The day when wealth and sons avail not (any man). Save him who bringeth unto God a whole heart." -the Holy Quran (26: 88-89)

The Holy Prophet (S) said .to one of his companions:

"Oh Qais! You will have no other choice except to live with a companion in your grave. He is alive and you will be buried with him. If he is good and honorable, will make you honorable, and if he is low and mean, you will become low and mean as well. After that on that on the Day of Resurrection you will be associated with him and will be reprimanded. Therefore, be careful and try to select a righteous companion for yourself; because if he is righteous -you will develop affection for him. If he is corrupt be assured that all the fear and punishment inflicted upon you will be through his existence. That companion is nothing but your actions and deeds in this life." -Jameh al-Sadat,vol. 1, p-17.

A human being in this same world is continuously occupied in nour-ishing his self as well as accumulating the provisions of his life in the Next World. Through his belief and thoughts, habits and virtues, love and liking, interests and desires and by means of actions which affects his self -he gradually nourishes, trains, and builds himself. His ultimate outcome is all related to the above mentioned factors, learning and right-eous belief, ethics and good morals, love and association with God-Almighty, obedience and seeking God's Pleasure, and performance of righteous deeds in accordance with Divine Commands etc. are things which are responsible for the ascension of human Celestial Soul towards the stages of perfection, ultimately achieving the highest spiritual station of God's Nearness. A human by means of faith and performance of righteous deeds in this very world discovers a new life and purity which would be manifested in the Next World.

God-Almighty said in the Holy Quran:

"Whosoever doth right, whether male or female, and is a believer, him verily We shall quicker good life." -the Holy Quran (16: 97)

Man in this world in addition of utilizing material blessings for his bodily pleasures could also utilize spiritual blessings for the growth, training and perfection of his soul and innerself, thus, building his Next World's life in such a manner that the desired result would be manifested in the Hereafter.

Imam al-Sadiq (A) said:

God-Almighty says to his servants:

"Oh my righteous servants! Utilize My worship's blessing in this world so that you could be benefited with them in the Next World as well." -Bihar al-Anwar, vol. 70, p-253.

The Commander of the Faithful Imam 'Ali (A) said:

"Continuation of invocation (dhikr) is the nourishment of human souls." -Gharar al-Hukm, p-764.

He also said:

"Don't forget invocation (dhikr) of God-Almighty because, it is the illumination of Hearts."

-Gharar al-Hukm, p-479.

Paradise and its blessings or hell and its punishments for a human being are decided in this same world through his beliefs, morals and deeds, even though he might be ignorant of them; but in the next world when the materialistic curtains are rolled up, this reality will be manifested.

Imam al-Sajjad (A) in a narration speaks as follows:

"Be aware! That whoever bears enmity with the prophets and saints; accepts religion other than God's religion; disregards Divine Obligations by following his own whims and passions; is indeed engulfed with eternal flames which consumes human bodies -the bodies who have given up their spirituality through domination of cruelty over their inner existence. Alas! They are like dead bodies who do not feel the heat of the fire. Had they been alive they would have felt the pain and torture of burning their bodies. Therefore, oh people of insight! Learn a lesson and be thankful to the Lord of the worlds who has bestowed upon you the blessing of His Guidance." -Qurrateh al-Ayoon, Faiz, p-466.

The God-Almighty said in the Holy Quran:

"Lo Those who devour the wealth of orphans wrongfully, they do but swallow fire into their bellies and they will be exposed to burning flame." -the Holy Quran (4:10)

A human being in this world either accumulates enlightenment and insight or cruelty and darkness for the Next World. If he remained blind and without enlightenment in this world tomorrow he will be raised up in the Next World with the same condition.

The Holy Quran said:

"Whoso is blind here will be blind in the Hereafter, and yet further from the road."
-the Holy Quran (17:72)

The most eminent scholar Allameh Tabatabai (R.A.) had stated the following interesting story:

"Once upon a time there used to live a pious ascetic and saintly personality known as Sheikh Abud in Najaf Ashraf. He was a committed way farer upon the road of gnosticism, continuously worshiping and reciting invocation (dhikr). Sometimes he would visit the grave yard located in the Wadi-us-Salam, spending long hours walking, sitting, pondering, and looking carefully at the old and new graves. One day, while returning from such routine visits he was encountered by a group of curious people, who after offering salutations asked him: 'Sheikh Abud! What is new of Wadi-us-Salam?' 'There is nothing new'. Replied Sheikh Abud.

But the group insisted to hear some news from the Wadi-us-salam. Then the Sheikh Abud said:

"I encountered the most strange thing over there; in spite of careful looking through the new and old graves, I could not discover any traces of snakes, scorpions,

and the food stuff consumed by them. I therefore, asked one of the grave: in narrations it has been described that the human beings inside the graves are tortured by the snakes, scorpions, and other noxious creatures, but I do not see these creatures within these graves."

"The grave replied to me: 'Yes! It is true that snakes and scorpions do not exist among us, instead, you are the one who bring them with you from the world for your own fortune."

The internal and spiritual life of a human being is an actual and real life; a human being in his essence travels a real path which either leads him towards prosperity and perfection or terminates into cruelty and total annihilation. For continuation of this action he receives help and strength from his beliefs, morals and deeds.

God-Almighty in the Holy Quran said:

"Whoso desireth power (should knows that) all power belongth to God. Unto Him good words ascend, and the pious deeds doth He exalt." -the Holy Quran (35:10)

The ultimate status of human self is the outcome of his efforts and endeavors which depends upon his beliefs, morals, characteristics, liking, and deeds; the final result of which, whether good or bad, will be declared in the Next World.

What to Be?

The scientific higher learning had confirmed that the human sprit consists of a physical occurrence and a spiritual eternal dimension. That is, the Celestial Spirit is the same earlier physical form, which after passing gradually through various stages of perfection has now reached to the level of human soul meaning potential human being. This movement towards perfection never stops rather continues till the end of human life. At the beginning he is a celestial abstract superior than the matter, but at the same time he is not a full or complete abstract because, for his existence, he is related to a physical body.

The soul consists of two dimensional existence: The material dimension which is related to body and performs material acts, and because of this consideration the stages of movements towards perfection have been attached to it; the other dimension is an abstract superior than the matter capable of performing nonmaterial acts. One side of his existence is physical and animal while the other side is human and celestial. While he is not more than a single existence, possesses animal passions and desires and accordingly performs animalistic acts, but at the same times also possesses human desires and virtues and performs human obligations.

It was because of this wonderful creation that God-Almighty in Holy Quran said:

"So blessed be God -the best of creators" -the Holy Quran (23:14)

This wonderful creation at the very beginning is not complete, rather nourishes himself gradually towards his ultimate perfection. Beliefs, thoughts, virtues, and desires derived, from his actions and deeds build his real identity, thus gradually completing his perfection. Virtues and characteristics are not the sort of things which could be added to his existence from outside accidentally rather they are the real builders of his existence's identity from within.

Here it is interesting to note that beliefs, thoughts, and characteristics not only exert influence upon human existence but, also are effective in his deciding what to be come? That is, righteous beliefs and thinking together with good morals and virtues as a result of righteous actions gradually ascend a human being towards the path of perfection ultimately his becoming a perfect human being and thus, attaining God's Nearness.

Similarly ignorance, false ideologies, immoral deeds, and hard heartedness as a result of evil deeds pull human soul towards weakness and isolation, and after gradually leading him towards various animalistic stages eventually throws him inside the deep valleys of intense darkness. Because of his firmness, influence of animalistic characteristics and accumulation of ignorances and cruelties he turns into an animal form in his esoteric essence.

Yes, his essence indeed turns into an animal thus, acquiring an animalistic personality. He no longer remains a human being but is an animal or even worst than an animal because, he is an animal who has acquired his animalism after passing through the superior stage of humanism. Although, outwardly he lives a human life but, in essence has turned into an animal without being aware of this internal change. The animalism of animals is not due to their special faces or features, rather it is because of their animalistic selves and absolute obedience to their animalistic instincts and desires without any limitations and considerations.

A wolf is regarded as a wolf not because of his apparent wolfy face but, it is because of his brutal nature and his absolute obedience to this instinct without any limitations that he is regarded as a wolf. Therefore, if some one is completely subdued by animal brutality in a manner that his senses of seeing and thinking become out of order, then such a person in essence turns into a real wolf-a wolf far brutal as compared to common wild wolfs. Because, now his faculties of wisdom and thinking are being employed and are at the service of his brutal animalistic characteristics.

It is because of this reason that there are situations, where human being are charged with brutal crimes for which the wild wolf could not be charged. Are such human being not wolves? Yes! They are indeed true wolves, even though they do not understand and the others regard them as humans. But, on the Day of Resurrection, when the curtains shall be rolled up, their inner essence will be exposed. Obviously Paradise is not a place for wolves, because they can not become companions for saints and righteous servants of God. Such a wolf who has been demoted to lower animal status from the superior human status, deserves to be confined, punished, and tortured inside the dark and horrible environment of Hell.

Therefore, a human being in this world is an undetermined existence who builds himself his future personality. Either he becomes human thus, surpassing in excellence even with the most intimate God's angels, or descends whereby his inner essence turns into an animal. This is something whose authencity have been proved by higher scientific learning as well as confirmed and certified by Divine Prophets. Also, the Holy Prophet (S) and the Infallible Imams (A) of his Holy Progeny (Ahlul Bayt) have informed about that.

Holy Prophet (S) had said:

"On the Day of Resurrection the people will reappear in faces that the faces of monkeys and pigs are far better than theirs." -Qurrath al-Ayoon, p-479.

The Commander of the Faithful Imam' Ali (A) about the corrupt scholar, has said:

"Although, his outward appearance is like a human being but his heart is like an animal heart. He does not recognize the path of guidance so that he could follow it, and does not know the path of deviation so that he could avoid it. Such a person is indeed a dead one living among the alive." -Nahjul Balagha, sermon 87.

Imam al-Sadiq (A) had said:

"The arrogant people on the day of Resurrection will be transformed into tiny ants to be trampled by the people till accounts of all the people are settled."

-Bihar al-Anwar, vol. 7, p-201.

The God-Almighty in the Holy Quran said:

"And when the wild beasts are herded together." -the Holy Quran (81:5)

Some of the commentators of the Holy Quran have interpreted the phrase "wild animals" in the above verse for human beings who will reappear with animal faces on the Day of Resurrection, because, unlike human beings the animals are not required to be judged for their deeds, hence their appearance does not make any sense.

God-Almighty in Holy Quran said:

"A day when the trumplet is blown and ye come in multitudes." -the Holy Quran (78:18)

According to some of the commentators the above verse has been interpreted that on the Day of Judgment, human beings will be separated from each other and will appear in different groups in accordance with their esoteric faces. There is an interesting narration from the Holy prophet (S) regarding the interpretation of the above verse:

Ma'z bin Jabal said: "I asked the Holy Prophet (S) about the interpretation of the above verse. He replied: 'Oh! Ma'z you had asked about a very important subject while shedding tears from his eyes the Holy Prophet (S) said: My ummah will reappear in ten different groups on the Day of Judgment as follows:

"Some of them will reappear as monkeys while some of them will look like pigs; some of them will reappear while walking up side down,. some will reappear as blind and wandering,. some of them will reappear as deaf and dumb understanding absolutely nothing; some will reappear with chewing their tongues while blood and pus will be coming out of their mouths making the people around them uncomfortable; some of them will reappear with their hands and feet cut off; some will reappear as being hanged upon branches of fire; and while some of them will reappear with dress of molten lead pressed to their bodies."

Then he explained these ten categories as follows:

"Those who will reappear as monkeys are the tale bearers or spies;, those who will reappear as pigs are the ones who accepted bribes and had illegal income those who will be walking up side down are the ones who practiced usury, those who are blind are the judges and officers who oppressed the people, those who are dumb and deaf are the ones who were egotistic and ambitious; those who will reappear with their hands and feet cut off are the ones who pained and troubled their neighbors; those who are hanged upon the branches of fire were the people who indulged in slandering and backbiting against the masses for the pleasure of kings and rulers; those whose odors is worst than dead bodies are the ones who indulged themselves in worldly desires and passions without paying Divine Share from their wealth, and those who are dressed with molten lead dress are the arrogant ones who took pride in themselves." -Tafsir Majma al-Bayan, vol. 10, p-423, Ruh al-Bayan, vol. 10, p-299 and Nur al-Thaqalain, vol. 5, p-493

In the light of above, the ethical and moral matters cannot be treated as minor and insignificant rather are the most important crucial and determinant matters which build the esoteric and spiritual life of a human being and even influence his "what to become"? Thus, moral education not only teaches how to live, but also deals with "what to become" for human beings.

The Heart in Quran

The phrase heart carries special importance and has been used extensively in the Holy Quran and narrations. But what is meant with this phrase is not the pine-shaped physical heart located in the left side of the chest which support the animal life system by continuously pumping fresh blood into various parts of the body. Because, the Holy Quran relates things to heart which are not comparable with this pine-shaped heart. e.g.:

Reasoning and Comprehension

The Holy Quran said:

> "Have they not traveled in the land and have they hearts wherewith to feel and ears wherewith to hear."
> -the Holy Quran (22:46)

Un-comprehending and Reasoning

The Holy Quran said:

> "Having hearts wherewith they understand not, and having eyes

wherewith they see not."
-the Holy Quran (7:179)

And said:

"And their hearts are sealed, so that they apprehend not."
-the Holy Quran (9:87)

Faith

The Holy Quran said:

"These are they into whose hearts He has impressed faith and strengthened them with a spirit from Him."
-the Holy Quran (58:22)

Blasphemy and Disbelief

The Holy Quran said:

"And as for those who believe not in the Hereafter there hearts refuse to know, for they are proud."
-the Holy Quran (16:22)

And said:

"Such are they whose hearts and ears and eyes God hath sealed. And such are the heedless."
-the Holy Quran (16:108)

Dissension

The God-Almighty said in the Holy Quran.

> "The Hypocrites fear lest a surah should be revealed concerning them, pro-claiming what is in their hearts."
> -the Holy Quran (9: 64)

To Receive Guidance

The God-Almighty said:

> "And whosoever believeth in God, He guideth his heart. And God is knower of all things." -the Holy Quran (4:11) And God said:
> "Most surely there is a reminder in this for him who has a heart or he gives ear and is a witness." -the Holy Quran (50: 37)

Negligence

The God-Almighty said:

> "And obey not him whose heart we have made heedless of Our Remembrance, who followeth his own lust." -the Holy Quran (18:28)

Certainty and Tranquility

The God-Almighty has said:

> "Verily in the remembrance of God do hearts find rest."
> -the Holy Quran (13:28)

And said:

"He it is who sent down peace of reassurance into the hearts of the believers that they might add faith unto their faith." -the Holy Quran (48:4)

Anxiety and Conflict

The God-Almighty has said:

"They alone ask leave of thee who believe not in God and the Last Day, and whose hearts feel doubt, so in their doubt they waver." -the Holy Quran (9:45)

Blessing and Kindness

The God-Almighty has said:

"And places compassion and mercy in the hearts of those who followed him." -the Holy Quran (57:27)

And said:

"He it is who supporteth thee with His Help and with the believers. And (as for the believers) hath attuned their hearts." -the Holy Quran (8: 62-63)

Hot-temper and Cruelty

The God-Almighty said:

"If thou hadst been stern and fierce of heart they would have dispersed from round about thee." - the Holy Quran (3:159)

Therefore, heart in the Holy Quran has been assigned the most important privileged position, and various psychic tasks have been related to it, namely: faith, blasphemy, hypocrisy, reasoning, understanding, not understanding, acceptance of truth, unacceptance of truth, guidance, deviation, sin, intention, purification, corruption, benevolence, aggravation, love, invocation, negligence, fear, anger, doubt, conflict, mercy, cruelty, regret, assurance, arrogance, jealousy, rebellion, offense, and other similar acts. Since the pine shaped piece of flesh called heart could not be the origin of these effects, instead these effects are the consequences of human self and spirit. Therefore, it could be said: What is meant with heart is the same "Celestial Jewel" which controls the degree of humanness within a human being :

The heart possesses such exalted position in the Holy Quran that it is mentioned when the topic of revelation i.e. communication between God and men is discussed. God-Almighty said to Holy Prophet (S):

> **"Which is the true spirit hath brought down, upon the heart, that thou mayest be (one) of the warners."**
> **-the Holy Quran (26:193-194)**

And said:

> *"Say (O Muhammad, to mankind) who is enemy to Gabriel! For he it is who hath revealed (this scripture) to thy heart by God's leave."*
> *-the Holy Quran (2:97)*

The heart's position is so eminent that it sees the revealing angel and hears his voice. The God-Almighty has said:

> *"And He revealed unto His slave (Prophet Muhammad) that which he re-vealed. The Heart lied not (in seeing the angel) what it saw."*
> *-the Holy Quran (53:10-11)*

Soundness and Sickness of Heart

Our living depends upon spirit and heart because, they are the ones who manage the bodies. All the parts of the body obey their command and all deeds and action initiate from the heart. Therefore, the salvation and cruelty of a person depends upon his hearts condition. It has been inferred from the Holy Quran and narrations that like the human bodies which are healthy and sick at different times, his heart's condition may also follow the same cycle (i.e. some times it is healthy while at other times it is sick).

God-Almighty in Holy Quran said:

> *"The day when wealth and sons avail not (any man). Save him who bringeth unto God a whole heart "* -the Holy Quran (26: 88-89)

And said:

> *"Lo! therein verily is a reminder for him who hath a heart"* -the Holy Quran (50:37)

And said:

> *"And the Garden is brought nign for those who kept from evil, no longer distant. (And it is said): that is that which ye were promised, (it is) for every pertinent and heedful one, who feareth the Beneficent in secret and cometh with a contrite heart."* -the Holy Quran (50: 21-33)

Therefore, the above verses make it explicit that health of a person is related to his heart's condition and his eternal salvation depends upon his return to God-Almighty with a pure and humble heart. On the other side the Holy Quran introduces some examples of hearts which are sick as follows:

> *"In their hearts is a disease, and God increaseth their disease."*

-the Holy Quran (2:10)

And said:

> "But as for those in whose hearts is disease, it only addeth wickedness to their wickedness."
> -the Holy Quran (9:125)

And said:

> "And when the hypocrites, and those in whose hearts is a disease were saying: God and His Messenger promised us naught but delusion."
> -the Holy Quran (33:12)

And said:

> "And thou seest those in whose heart is a disease race towards them, saying: We fear lest a change offortune befall us."
> -the Holy Quran (5: 52)

In these verses the blasphemy, hypocrisy, and friendship with the pagans have been introduced as heart's sicknesses. Similar verses and hundreds of authentic traditions narrated by Holy Prophet (S) and infallible Imams (A) of his Holy Progeny had stated that human heart and soul are susceptible to sickness like human bodies.

God-Almighty the Creator of heart and soul, the Holy Prophet (S), and Infallible Imams (A) who are the specialists of human beings and their hearts had informed us about the sickness of some of the hearts. Why should we ignore this reality? The real human specialists after identifying the symptoms namely: blasphemy, dissension, unacceptance of truth, arrogance, revenge, anger, criticizing, slander, treason, self-conceit, fear, malevolence, defamation, illspeaking, backbiting, harshness, oppression, felony, misery, avarice, fault-finding, lying, ambitiousness, hypocrisy, deceit, suspicion, cruelty, self-weakness and many other indecent characteristics, have introduced them as the sickness of heart and soul. Therefore, those who leave this world with such contaminated hearts will not be returning to God with a pure and sound heart to be worthy of the verse:

"The day when wealth and sons avail not (any man). Save him who bringeth unto God a whole heart." -the Holy Quran (26: 88-89)

The sicknesses of heart and self could not be considered as small or insignificant rather they are much more dangerous and incurable as compared to bodily diseases. In case of bodily diseases the physical order of the body looses its equilibrium thus, causing pain, discomfort, and inflicting damage upon a specific part of the body. But this is rather limited and in any case these effects cannot go on beyond the physical life span of the inflicted person. However, the sickness of heart and self are accompanied with continuous anguish, torture, and eternal punishment; the pain and punishment which penetrate until the very depths of heart engulfing the soul with eternal flames.

The heart which remained completely ignorant of God's existence without witnessing His signs by spending a life of disbelief, deviation, and sins in reality is blind and dark, which will be raised on the Day of Judgment with similar condition, and will have no other choice except to be condemned into Hell to live a painful eternal life full of anguish and torture. The God-Almighty in Holy Quran said:

"But he who turneth away from remembrance" of Me, his will be a narrow life, and I shall bring him blind to the assembly on the Day of Resurrection. He will say: 'My Lord! wherefore hast thou gathered me (hither) blind, when I was wont to see?' He will say: 'so (it must be) our revelations come unto thee but thou

didst forget them. In like manner thou art forgotten this Day."
-the Holy Quran (20:124-126)

And said:

"Have they not traveled in the land, and have they hearts where with to feel and ears wherewith to hear ? For indeed it is not the eyes that grow blind, but it is the hearts, which are within the bosoms, that grow blind."
-the Holy Quran (22:46)

And said:

"Whoso is blind in here will be blind in the Hereafter, and yet further from the road."
-the Holy Quran (17:22)

And said:

"And he whom God guideth, he is led aright, while, as for him whom He sendeth astray, for them thou wilt find no protecting friends beside Him, and We shall assemble them on the Day of Resurrection on their faces, blind, dumb, and deaf "
-the Holy Quran (17:97)

May be you will find the above, something strange and may ask: How the esoteric eyes will become blind on the Day of Judgment? Do we have eyes and ears other than these apparent bodily eyes and ears? The reply is: Yes! The Creator of human beings and Divine human doctors had informed that human heart and also soul, have their own eyes, ears, and tongue but of their own kind.

Human self is a mysterious existence possessing a special life in his inner essence. Self has his own world in which there is light as well as darkness, there is purity and cleanliness as well as indignation and contamination, and there is seeing and hearing as well as blindness and deafness. But the light and darkness of that special world is not similar to the light and darkness of this world, rather the belief in God-Almighty, Day of Judgment, Prophethood, and the Holy Quran is the illumination for self's world.

The God-Almighty has said:

"Then those who believe in him (Muhammad) honor him, help him, and fol-low the light which is sent down with him: They are the successful."
-the Holy Quran (7:157)

And said:

"Now hath come unto you light from God and a plain scripture."
-the Holy Quran (5:15)

And said:

"Is he whose bosom God hath expanded for the surrender (unto Him), so that he followeth a light from His Lord (as he who disbelieveth)? Then woe unto those whose hearts are hardened against remembrance of God. Such are in plain error."
-the Holy Quran (39: 22)

God-Almighty has informed that Islam, Quran, faith, and Divine obligations are all illumination and their obedience makes the heart en-lightened; although, in reality this happens in this same world but its final result is declared in the Next World. Also, He had informed us that blasphemy, hypocrisy, sinning, non-acceptance of truth all are darkness and make the heart dark and contaminated, which would certainly become manifested in the Next World. The Divine Prophets were dispatched by God-Almighty with the mission of leading human beings out of darkness of blasphemy towards the environment of illumination and belief.

The God-Almighty has said:

> "We have revealed unto thee (Muhammad) that thereby thou mayst bring forth mankind from darkness unto light."
> -the Holy Quran (14:1)

The believers, by means of illumination of faith, self-purification, good moral conducts, God's-Remembrance, and righteous deeds make their heart and souls illuminated; witness the sublime realities through their esoteric eyes and ears; and ascend toward God's Nearness through various stages of perfection. Such souls when leaving this world will turn in to absolute illumination, joy, cheerfulness, beauty, and in the Next World will be utilizing the same illumination accumulated by them in this material world. The God-Almighty has said:

> "On the day when thou (Muhammad) wilt see the believers, men and women, their light shining forth before them and on their right hands (and will hear it said unto them): Glad news for you this day: Gardens underneath which rivers flow, wherein ye are immortal. That is the supreme triumph."
> -the Holy Quran (57:12)

Yes! The illumination for the eternal world must be arranged in this world, and it is because of this reason that the pagans and hypocrites do not have illumination in the Next World. The God-Almighty has said:

> "On the Day when the hypocritical men and the hypocritical women will say unto those who believe, look on us that we may borrow from your light! It will be said: Go back and seek for light!"
> -the Holy Quran (57:13)

Heart in Traditions

The pioneers of religion and real human specialists have left many interesting narrations about the heart. Following are some of the examples: In some of the narrations the hearts have been classified into three categories:

Imam al-Baqir (A) said:

"There are three kinds of hearts:

a: First type: Reversed heart which lacks feelings for any sort of righteous deeds. Suchheart is the heart of a unbeliever.

b. Second Type: The heart which contains a black spot in which a war is being waged between the truth and falsehood, and whichever becomes victorious will take over the heart's control.

c. Third type: The conquered heart in which there is a lighted lamp which is never going to be turned off. Such a heart is the heart of a believer." -Bihar al-Anwar,vol. 70, p-51.

Imam al-Sadiq (A) has quoted from his learned father:

"There is nothing worst than sinning for the heart. When the heart is encountered with sin, it struggles against the sin until sin becomes victorious thus, making the heart as a reversed heart."

-Bihar al-Anwar, vol. 70, p-54.

Imam al-Sajjad (A) has said:

"A man possesses four eyes, with two apparent eyes he sees the affairs relev-ant to his world, and with two esoteric eyes sees the affairs related to the Next World. Therefore, whenever God-Almighty desired the good for a believer, He opens his heart's eyes to enable him to witness the hidden world and its mysteries. But when He does not desire his welfare, leaves the heart with his esoteric eyes closed."

-Bihar al-Anwar, vol. 70, p-53.

Imam al-Sadiq (A) has said:

"The heart possesses two ears, the spirit of belief slowly invites him towards righteous deeds, while the Satan slowly invites him towards evil deeds. There-fore, whoever becomes victorious in this struggle takes over heart's control."

-Bihar al-Anwar vol. 70, p-53.

Imam al-Sadiq (A) quotes from the Holy Prophet (S)

"The darkness of the heart is the worst kind of darkness."
-Bihar al-Anwar, vol. 70, p-51.

Imam al-Baqir (A) said:

"Initially there is a white spot and light within the heart of a human being and as a result of his committing sin, a block spot appears. If the person repents the black spot gets wiped out, but if he persisted in sinning, the blackness gradually increases ultimately covering the entire white spot, When this happens the owner of such heart will never return towards goodness and become manifestation of the Quranic verse:

'Nay, but that which they have earned is rust upon their hearts.'"
-al-Kafi, vol, 2, p-273.

The Commander of the Faithful Imam" Ali (A) has said:

"Every one who lacks self restraint and piety will have a dead heart; whoever have a dead heart will enter inside the Hell."
-Nahjul Balagha, saying 324

He further emphasized this matter in his last will addressing to his son:

"Oh my son! The poverty is one of the most horrible calamity,. But still severe than poverty is the bodily sickness; and the sickness of soul is harsher than the bodily sickness. Plenty of wealth is one of the God's blessing, but sound health is better than that, and the piety of heart is even superior than sound health."
-Bihar al-Anwar, vol. 70, p-51.

There is a narration quoted from Anas bin Malik from the Holy Prophet (S) who said:

"The prophet David (A) asked God; 'Oh God! All the emperors possess treasure then where is Your treasure ? God-Almighty replied: 'I possess a treasure which is greater than the sky; vaster than the Heaven's firmaments; smells better than the perfumes ofParadise, and is beautiful than the Celestial Kingdom. Its earth is enlightenment; its sky is belief, its sun is enthusiasm; its moon is love,. its stars are inspiration and attention towards Me; its clouds are reason,. its rain is blessing, its fruits are obedience; and its yield is wisdom. My Treasure has four doors, the first one is the door of knowledge, the second one is the door of reason, the third one is the door of patience, and the fourth one is the door of contentment. Know that My Treasure is -the heart of a believer'".

-Bihar al-Anwar, vol. 70, p-59.

The Divine Heart Specialists have described many interesting topics in these traditions. They have divided the hearts into following three categories:

The Heart of an Unbeliever

These Divine Specialists have described that the heart of an infidel is a reversed or over-turned heart which does not contain any goodness in it. Such heart' is deviated from its primordial nature; does not look towards the Upper-Heavens and keeps itself amused and preoccupied into worldly affairs, therefore, it does not witness the existence of God-Almighty and I. Eternal-World. It lacks the proper imagination for good-ness and righteous deeds, because, the righteous deeds reach the perfection stage and Gods-Nearness only in cases when they are performed with the intention of attaining His pleasure. But since an infidel has reversed his heart, he does not see God-Almighty any more, and therefore, does not have any other aim except this world in all his affairs.

Such an heart in his primordial nature was blessed with esoteric eyes which now have been blinded because, he cannot witness the most explicit shinning realities i.e. the Creator of the Universe. He is blind and will be raised as blind in the Next World too. In this world he is attached to worldly affairs, and will be raised in the Next World possessed with the same attachment, but since the Eternal-World lacks these worldly amusements, he will burn with the fire of separation. In such heart the light of faith has been extinguished and therefore, it is totally filled with absolute darkness.

The Heart of a Believer

Just opposite to the heart of an unbeliever is the heart of a perfect righteous believers; whose doors are open towards the Upper-Heaven and Unseen-World; is illuminated with the light of faith which will never be turned off; and through its two esoteric eyes witnesses the mysteries of the Hidden-

World. Such a heart continuously strives for achieving absolute t perfection, beauty and salvation and seeks God's Pleasure and Blessing. Since he wants God-Almighty therefore, continuously strives to move in His Direction by means of good moral conduct and righteous deeds. Such heart is wider than the Celestial Sky and Divine Thrown, beautiful than the Paradise, is the Divine Treasure and center of mani-festation of Heavenly Light; his earth is enlightenment, his sky is faith; his sun is enthusiasm for God's countenance; his moon is God's love; where the wisdom rules and absorbs the rain of Divine Blessings for producing the fruits of worship and obedience; is filled with absolute light, joy, cheerfulness, purity, and will be raised in the next world in the similar state.

The Heart of a Believer-Occasionally Contaminated

The heart of a believer which occasionally gets contaminated with sin is not dark and confined rather is illuminated with the light of faith and remained open for receiving guidance and Divine Blessings. But as a result of sinning it has developed a black spot and Satan has succeeded to make an entry into it. Although, the esoteric eyes are not quite yet blinded but because of sinning have caught a disease which might render them blind. Both angels as well as Satan have access within such heart. The angels enter through the doors of faith and invite him towards goodness while the Satan influences through the black spot inviting him towards evil.

In such a heart both Satan and angel are engaged in a continuous confrontation. Angle wants to take over the control of entire heart forcing Satan out through good deeds on the other side Satan through seduction and sins makes the darker heart further darkest and strives to take over the control of entire heart by forcing out the angel and permanently closing the gateway of belief forever. These two are permanently engaged in a continuous war until one of them become victorious over his opponent, and what is the magnitude of victory achieved. The esoteric life and eternal destination of human being depends upon this struggle. It is here that the struggle with the self becomes of crucial importance, which will be discussed later on in the book.

Hard-heartedness

In his initial primordial nature the heart is bestowed upon with special virtues such as purity, enlightenment, kindness, and blessing. He is sensitive towards other people's difficulties and feels uncomfortable while seeing others in pain even animals. He desires that others should live a pleasant and comfortable life and takes pleasure in doing favors towards them. In accordance with his pure nature is inclined and pays attention towards God-Almighty; takes pleasure in performing worship, prayer, supplication, and other righteous deeds, while immediately feels ashamed and offer repentance if commits sins.

In case the heart accepted invitation of his pure primordial nature and acted accordingly, he becomes purest, kindest, sincerest, and enlightened, because of the effects of worship and prayers his enthusiasm and love for these things increases day by day. But if he neglects and acts against his inner natural feelings and sentiments, they gradually get subdued and eventually become completely silenced and eventually annihilated.

If after seeing the horrible tragic scenes involving others does not show any reaction, gradually becomes used to such things to the extent that further repetition of such encounters will produce least reaction. Also, it is possible that one may reach to a point where seeing the poverty, hunger, and wretchedness involving others not only produce any disturbance with in his conscience on the contrary while seeing the painful scenes of imprisonment, torture, and murders feels happy and pleased. [16]

If someone commits a sin for the first time, he feels guilty and ashamed about it, but having committed a sin for the first time, to repeat it for the

---

[16] The video tapes commercially produced by the Serb criminals showing the most horrible brute crime scenes of mass killings, torture, and raping in recent ethnic cleansing in Bosnia-Herzegovina under the very nose of the United Nations, in the heart-land of civilized Europe, and their welcome by the sadists in the Western countries proves the au-thenticity of this statement [Tr].

second and third time relatively becomes easier for him, and in case of his persistence in sinning reaches to a point, where not only he does not feel any sense of guilt and shame, on the contrary considers himself victorious and feels happy.

The heart of such persons has become dark and reversed and in the words of the Holy Quran and narrations has acquired hard-heartedness. Satan has occupied these hearts forcing the God's Angels out, and the doors of salvation have been closed permanently leaving no hope for repentance and return towards God-Almighty.

The God-Almighty said in the Holy Quran:

"If only, when our disaster came on them, they had been humble! But their hearts were hardened and the devil made all that they used to do seem fair unto them!"
-the Holy Quran (6:43)

And said:

"Then woe unto those whose hearts are hardened against remembrance of God. Such are in plain error."
-the Holy Quran (39:22)

Imam al-Baqir (A) said:
"There is a white spot inside the heart of each believer. Once he commits a sin or repeats it, a black spot appears inside the heart. In case of persistence of sins, the black spot, increases, gradually in size filling the entire heart with blackness. When this happens the owner of such heart never returns towards goodness, and this, is what God meant in the verse:
"Nay, but that which they have earned is rust upon their hearts."
-Bihar al-Anwar, vol. 73, p-361.

The Commander of the Faithful Imam' Ali (A) said:
"The tears of eye never get dried but for the sake of hardheartedness,. the heart never acquires hard-heartedness but for the sake of excess of sins."

-Bihar al-Anwar, vol. 73, p-354.

The Holy Prophet (S) said:

"The following four things are the indicators of human cruelty:

1) Dryness of eyes (ii) Hard-heartedness (iii) Excessive greed for earning a living (iv) And persistence of sins.

-Bihar al-Anwar, vol. 73, p-349.

It was because of this reason that the Infallible Imams (A) of prophet's progeny in their supplications took shelter in God-Almighty against hard-heartedness.

Imam al-Sajjad (A) said:

"Oh God! I do complain to you against hard-heartedness —the heart which by means of whims and passions is in the state of continuous revolution and has become contaminated. And I do complain to you against the dryness of eye which does not cry and is not afraid of you, and instead takes pleasure in looking towards whatever makes it pleased."

—Bihar al-Anwar, vol. 94, p-143.

Therefore, a human being who desires his own prosperity and soundness of heart must prevent himself from committing any sin however small it might seems; should gradually motivate his self for performing righteous deeds namely: worship, prayer, communications with God, sincerity, kindness and help towards others, defense of oppressed and deprived, benevolence, and cooperation for achieving social welfare and social justice, so that it performs them as a matter of habit. His inner pur-ity and illumination continues striving for perfection and purification fill his heart becomes a special center of God's favorite angels.

Heart's Physicians

It has already been explained earlier that like human bodies, hearts could also be healthy and sick, and the eternal prosperity or salvation of a person depends upon his returning to the Next World with a pure and sound heart. It is therefore, important for us to be knowledgeable about the health and sickness of the heart; must identify the symptoms of the disease; and should understand the causes and factors in order to implement all the health care hygienic measures to prevent its spread.

Do we possess self-sufficiency in this matter or do we need the prophets? There is absolutely no doubt that we lack sufficient knowledge about the special creation of human-self and the secrets and mysteries which have been incorporated by the Creator in this Celestial existence. In fact we are ignorant about our psychological and esoteric life; do not well recognize the factors and causes responsible for the self's sickness; cannot properly diagnose the symptoms of the disease; and are not well aware about various kinds of diseases, preventive measures required against their spread, and the available methods of their treatment. There-fore, the presence of Divine Prophets is really required in order to provide guidance and lead us in solving the above mentioned problems.

The prophets are the real physicians and specialists of the souls, who through Divine Blessing and revelations understands very well about the pain as well as the treatment of self. They have been educated and trained in various disciplines dealing with human beings and their souls in the school of revelation, and are thoroughly knowledgeable about the secret and mysteries of this special celestial existence. They understand the straight path of guidance and ascend towards the God-Almighty as well as the causes and factors of deviations, and therefore, are in a position to help lead the human beings in following the straight path and can prevent their deviations.

Yes! the prophets are God's physicians who have rendered most valuable services for humanity throughout the history, which are relatively more valuable than the services rendered by physicians of the human bodies. The prophets were able to discover the mysterious abstract (i.e. Celestial Spirit) for themselves, and by introducing this "Celestial Jewel" to human beings succeeded in reviving their human personality. They were the ones who introduced and enlightened human beings with learning, spirituality, and moral ethics by showing them the path of journey leading towards God's Nearness.

They are the ones who made the humanity familiar with the unseen world and strived for self-purification, self-nourishment and self-refinement of human beings. If there are marks of meaningness, sentiments, love, moral ethics, and other virtues found among human beings it is all due to the blessing of painstaking continuous efforts and endeavors of all God's physicians and specially the Last Divine Messenger Prophet Muhammad (S). If the Divine Prophets would not have been dispatched for human-guidance, certainly the conditions of human beings would have been something different. Yes! The prophets are real distinguished personalities of the humanity, and because of this distinction have been called as physicians of self in the traditions.

The Commander of the Faithful Imam 'Ali (A) said about the Holy Prophet (S).

"Muhammad (S) was a traveling physician who continuously endeavored for the treatment of souls. He had prepared ready-made ointments and arranged other tools of surgery for the treatment of wounds and disinfecting the diseases at suitable occasions. He cured the heart's blindness, ear's deafness, tongue's dumbness, and prescribed medicine for all those who were living in the state of confusion and wandering because, they did not utilized the light of wisdom for abstraction of realities and thus, were forced to live like grazing animals."

-Nahjul Balagha, sermon,108.

The Holy Quran has been described as a health-giving medicine for the diseased hearts.

God-Almighty has said:

> *"There hath come unto you an exhortation from your Lord. A balm for that which is in the breasts."*
> *-the Holy Quran (10-57)*

And said:

> *"And We reveal of the Quran that which is a healing and a mercy for believers."*
> *-the Holy Quran (17:82)*

The Commander of the Faithful Imam 'Ali (A) said about the Holy Quran:

"Learn the Holy Quran because, it is the best of learning; pay attentions towards its verses because they are like the springs rain; its recital revives the heart; and utilize the Quranic illumination for the healing of your hearts."

-Nahjul al-Balagha, sermon-110.

At some other place he said:

"Know that anyone who possesses the Holy Quran would not require any thing else, and whoever is deprived of it will never be free from want. By means of the Holy Quran heal the sickness of your hearts and strengthen yourself through it while confronting hardships. Because, it contains the cure for the most severe diseases namely: blasphemy, hypocrisy, and deviations."

-Nahjul al-Balagha, sermon-176.

Yes! the Prophet of Islam is the best physician of the souls. He recognized well our pain and its treatment; brought the Holy Quran and presented it to us which the best program of healing for our internal pains. Apart from that various kind of psychic disease and their treatments have been explained for us through the Holy Prophet (S) and Infallible Imams (A) of his Holy progeny Ahlul Bayt which have been pre-served for us in the form of traditions.

Therefore, if we are interested in the happiness and soundness of our self, we must practice the hygienic measures for the psychic and physical health of our self. We must identify these diseases within our souls through Quranic verses and guidelines issued by the Holy Prophet (S) and Infallible Imams (A) and must seriously strive for their treatments. Any negligence shown in this important and crucial task would result in serious damage inflicted upon ourselves, which will become manifested in the Next World.

Refinement and Perfection of Self

It was already discussed that the self-building and self-nourishment are the most important crucial tasks, because, the happiness and prosperity of both worlds depends upon them. All of the God's Prophets were dispatched for accomplishment of this aim. Self-building must be undertaken into two stages:

- The first stage of self-refinement consists of cleansing of heart from indecent moral conduct and avoiding sins. This act is called refining and evacuation.
- The second stage of self-nourishment and perfection consists of acquiring higher learning for abstraction of absolute truth, attaining moral excellence in conduct, and undertaking of righteous deeds. This act is called nourishment and perfection.

Both the above mentioned stages are necessary for achieving self-building, because, unless and until the heart's ground is not thoroughly cleansed from evilness, it would not be available for acquiring higher learning, attaining moral excellence, and performance of righteous deeds. A heart which is contaminated with Satan's presence, how could become a center for the manifestation of Divine Light? How can God's intimate angels enter into such a heart? On the other hand if faith, enlightenment, moral excellence, and righteous deeds do not exist, through, which means the human self will attain nourishment and perfection?

Therefore, for self building both these stages must be attempted simultaneously. On one side the heart must be thoroughly cleansed and purified from all sort of impurities and falsies, and on the other side it should be encouraged and motivated for performance of righteous and virtuous deeds. Satan must be forced out and God's Intimate Angel should be welcomed. Any sort of foreign material other than God's should be thrown out from it, and God's Blessing and Illumination must be absorbed. These two stages are complimentary to each other.

It is not possible to purify the heart and let postpone the performance of righteous deeds for a later opportunity, and likewise we can not ignore the heart's internal impurities and evilness before undertaking the performance of righteous deeds. Therefore, it is necessary that both of these stages must be coordinated, and should be undertaken simultaneously. Avoiding sins and shameful moral deeds invites human being towards goodness, and similarly performance of righteous and virtuous deeds result in his acquittal of sins and obscene deeds. But in order to continue detailed discussion for the both stages it would be better to divide them into separate chapter. Firstly the stage of self-refinement will be discussed.

Self-refinement

At this stage the following three acts should be performed:

1. Refinement of self from all sort of false beliefs, evil thoughts, and superstitions.
2. Refinement of self from vices and moral indecencies.
3. Quitting all kind of sins and transgressions.

False beliefs and superstitions are ignorance and deviations that result in self's darkness and deviation from following the straight path of perfection and God's Nearness. Because, the believers in false beliefs never recognize the straight path of human perfection and wander aimlessly and confused in the darkest valleys of deviations and vices never reaching to their undefined final destination. How come the heart which is full of intense darkness can witness the ever shining sacred Divine illumination?

Also, moral indecencies strengthen the animalistic habits gradually silencing the light within the celestial human soul. Such a deviated person will never succeed in accomplishing the most exalted human objective of reaching the nearness of the supreme source of beauty and absolute perfection, i.e. God-Almighty.

Similarly, sinning and transgressions makes the human self dark and contaminated, thus, causing him further to deviate from the exalted path of human perfection and God's Nearness. Naturally, such a person will never reach to its ultimate cherished goal. Therefore, self-refinement determines our final destination and should be considered as an extremely important matter. We must, therefore, first identify the moral indecencies and sins and then must take remedial actions for cleansing and purifying our self from these impurities.

Fortunately, in the first part we do not have any problem because the physicians of the self or God's assigned human specialists -Prophet's and Infallible Imams have thoroughly defined moral indecencies, and even have given the prescription for their treatment; have counted various kinds of sins and taught us how to relinquish them. We all recognize moral indecencies and understand their ugliness. We know that hypocrisy, arrogance, jealously, revenge, anger, slander, treason, egotism, malevolence, backbiting accusation, ill-speaking, wrath, oppression, fear, stinginess, greed, fault-finding, lying, love of the world, ambitiousness, deceit, cheating, suspicion, cruelty, snobbery, self-weakness, and other such habits are bad and undesirable.

Apart from the fact that by features we understand and realize their ugliness, hundreds of Quranic verses and traditions also confirms their ugliness and indecencies. Our traditions in this field are extremely vast, rich and comprehensive that there does not exist the least shortage. Also, all forbidden acts and sins and their relevant punishments have been explained explicitly and comprehensively in the Holy Quran and traditions, and we do know about all of them. Therefore, as for as the identification of minor and major sins are concerned, we do not have any problem at all. But at the same time it must be frankly admitted that we all are captive of Satan and imperious self (*nafse-ammarah*), and unfortunately do not find the grace for purification of self from sins and moral indecencies. This is our real problem for which a solution must be found.

In my opinion these are two important factors relevant to the above problem:

First: We don't understand our moral diseases and do not have the courage to admit this sickness within ourselves.

Secondly: We regards them a minor thing and are negligent about the severe painful and catastrophic consequences arising thereof, and because of this reason are not concerned for their treatment. These are the two factors responsible for our negligence towards self-refinement. Therefore, these should be discussed in detail and the method of treatment should be discovered.

Negligence from the Disease

We probably understand the moral sicknesses and do appreciate heir ugliness but only in others, and not within ourselves. If we encounter impoliteness and moral indecencies in others we are quick to observe them immediately. While it is quite possible that the same moral indecency or may be worst than that might exist within ourselves, but we do not pay the east attention and ignore it completely. For example, we may regard transgression of others rights as something bad and might hate the transgressor, but at the same time it is possible that we ourselves might be transgressor, and may not realize it at all.

We do not consider our own act as a transgression, and on the contrary it is quite possible, that we might present it something as a glorious or virtuous act before ourselves, thus, by this means making it justified. Similar might be the case with other moral shameful deeds, and in this manner we never think about our own improvement. Because, if a sick person does not consider himself sick naturally he will never worry about his treatment. Since, we do not consider ourselves as sick, we are not concerned about our treatments either, and this happens to be our biggest problem. Therefore, if we care about our happiness and prosperity we must think for the remedy of this problem and by all possible means must endeavor to identity for internal psychological diseases.

Diagnosis of Self-sickness

Here it would be appropriate to describe the ways and means which could be useful for identifying the self-sickness.

Strengthening of Reason

The most exalted, celestial distinction of human beings, and the most perfect parameter of his existence distinguishing him over all other creatures, which in the terminology of the Holy Quran and traditions has been called by different names such as: spirit, self, heart, and intelligence, all are manifestations of one single reality, but because of different considerations have been given different names. But the fountainhead and origin of all thinking, rationalization, and intelligence have been named as reason.[17]

---

[17] "For God's-worship there is nothings superior than the reason. A believer is not wise until and unless he possesses the following ten characteristics:

1. The people should expect goodness from him.
2. They should feel immune from his wickedness.
3. He must evaluate the good deeds of others as too much even if they are small.
4. Should regard his good deeds as insignificant even if they re too much.
5. Should never be tired from acquiring knowledge through out his life.
6. Should never be annoyed while people approach him demanding fulfillment of their wants.
7. Should prefer seclusion and obscurity more than outwardly fame and popularity.
8. Poverty in his sight should be more dearer than the richness.
9. He must rely upon on only one single power in the world.
10. The tenth characteristic which is more important than all is -that while seeing others he must say: 'He is more better and pious than me.'

Because, the people belong to two categories: Either they are better or re worst than him.

"While encountering the better ones he must show humility and be courteous so that he could be associated with him. Regarding the latter who outwardly does not appear good, he must say: 'May his inner self is better than my own inner self or may be he will become ashamed from his devotion and may return towards God-Almighty through repentance and thus, might attain a prosperous end.

"If some one pays need to these dimensions he has indeed discovered his dignity and exaltedness and will be successful over his contemporaries."

In the books of tradition the reason (*aql*) has been treated with special distinction, and special chapters have been assigned for its detailed explanation. Reason in traditions have been titled as the most noble existence which is the source of all obligations, rewards, and punishments.

For example: Imam al-Baqir (A) has said:

"When God Almighty created the reason, it was blessed with the power of speech. Then it was ordered by Him to come and it obeyed; then it was commanded by him to return and again it obeyed. Than God-Almighty said:

"By the oath of My Honor and Glory ! I have not created any existence which is superior and dearer than you. You will not be perfected in anyone except the one who is dearer to me. Be aware! That obedience and transgression of My Commands depends upon you, and you will receive the rewards and punishment accordingly."

-al-Kafi, vol. 1, p-10.

Also the Holy Quran said:

> "**Thus, God expoundeth unto you His revelations so that ye may understand.**"
> *-the Holy Quran (2:202)*

> "**Have they not traveled in the land, and have they hearts wherewith to feel and ears wherewith to hear.**"
> *-the Holy-Quran (22:46)*

And said:

> "**Lo! The worst of beasts in God's Sight are the deaf, the dumb, who have no sense.**"
> *-the Holy Quran (8: 22)*

Those who possess ears, tongue, and reason, but do not utilize them in

---

-Nasayeh, Ayatullah Mishkini, p-301.

discovering the realities are introduced by the God-Almighty in the Holy Quran in the category of beasts and even worst than them, be cause they have not used their minds. God-Almighty said:

> "..He hath set uncleanness upon those who have no sense."
> -the Holy Quran (10:100)

Whatever goodness is possessed by a human being it is due to his reason; he recognizes God-Almighty by means of reason and worships him; accepts the Day of Resurrection and makes him readied for it; accepts the prophets and obeys them; understand the good moral conduct and trains him accordingly; identity the vices and evil and therefore, avoids them. It is because of this reason that the reason has been praised in the Holy Quran and traditions e.g. Imam al-Sadiq (A) replying to a beggar said:

"It is because of the existence of reason that God-Almighty gets worshipped, and one makes his entry into Paradise."

-al-Kafi, vol. 1, p-11.

He also said:

"Whoever is wise and intelligent possesses religion, and whoever has religion will enter into the Paradise."

-al-Kafi, vol. 1, p-11.

Imam al-Kazim (A) said to Hasham:

"God-Almighty has blessed the human beings with two proofs:

One is apparent and the other one is hidden. The apparent proofs are Prophets and Imams, and the hidden proof is the reason and intelligence within our existence."

-al Kafi, vol. 1, p-16.

Imam al-Sadiq (A) said:

"The most perfect human beings from the point of view of reason are those who are the best in moral conduct."

-al-Kafi, vol. 1, p-23.

"The reason is the guide of a believer."

-al-Kafi, vol. 1, p-25.

Imam al-Rida [18](A) said:

"The reason is the friend of everyone and the ignorance is his enemy."
-al-Kafi, vol. 1, p-11.

The Commander of the Faithful Imam' Ali (A) has said:
"Egotism of a person is the indication of his wisdom's weakness."
-al-Kafi, vol. 1, p-27.

Imam al-Kazim said to Hasham:

"Whoever desires to become contented without possessing health, a tranquil heart free from jealousy and soundness in religion must cry before God-Almighty and should ask for perfection of his reason. Therefore, whoever be-comes wise will be contented with modest means of livelihood, and thus, will be-come free from wants, and whoever is not contented with modest means of livelihood will never become free from wants."
-al-Kafi, vol. 1, p-18.

Imam al Kazim (A) [19] said:

---

[18] Imam Ali ibn Musa al-Rida (A): was born in Medina on Thursday, 11th Dhu'l-qi'dah 148 A.H. He lived in a period hen the Abbasids were faced with increasing difficulties because of Shi'ite revolts. After al-Mam'un the seventh Abbasid caliph and a contemporary of Imam al-Rida (A) murdered his brother Amin and assumed office, he thought he would solve the problems by naming Imam as his own successor hoping thus, to insure him in worldly affairs and turn the devotion of his followers away from him. After encouragement, urging and finally threats,
Imam accepted on condition that he be excused from dismissals, appointments, and other involvement in matters of state.
Making the most of this circumstance, the Imam extended guidance to the people, imparting priceless elucidation of Islamic culture and spiritual truths, which have survived in numbers roughly equal to those reaching us from the Commander of the Faithful Imam Ali (A), and in greater number than those of any other Imam.
Finally after al-Ma'mun realized his mistake, for Shi'ism began to spread even more rapidly he is said to have poisoned him; he died at the age of 55 in Mashhad Khurasan on Tuesday, 17th Safar 203 A.H.. He is buried in Mashhad Iran.

[19] Imam Musa al-Kazim (A): The son of sixth Imam J'afar al-Sadiq was born in Abwa' (between Mecca and Medina) on Sunday 7th Safar

"A wise person avoids even extra worldly-affairs what to say about sins, while quitting extra worldly-affairs is optional and avoiding of sins is mandatory."
-al-Kafi, vol. l, p-17.

And said:

"A wise person will never tell a lie, even if his self is tempted to do so."
-al-Kafi, vol. 1, p-19.

And said:

"Whoever lacks compassion does not have religion; whoever lacks wisdom does not have compassion; the most valuable person is the one who does not con-sider the entire world worthy of his self Know that: your bodies could not be traded with anything except Paradise. Therefore, be careful never to trade yourselves for a price other than Paradise."

-al-Kafi, vol. 1, p-19.

From the above tradition the preciousness of the reason, its important role in acquiring higher learning and sciences, accepting faith, worshipping God, recognizing and utilizing good morals, and quitting sins and other vices, could be understood well. Here, it should be emphasized that simply the existence of reason is not sufficient as for as the accomplishment of the above objectives are concerned, rather it is the commissioning and efficient utilization of the faculty of reason within human body which produce the cherished results. Within human body the presence of reason could be compared to like a righteous judge or expert, but he could only issue the correct judgment if, the required safe and peaceful environment

---

128 A.H. He was contemporary with four Abbasid Caliphs as al-Mansur, Hadi, Mahdi, and Harun. Because of the sever oppression, the necessity of taqiyya grew more stringent, and since he was under close surveillance, he admitted only a few elect Shi'ites. Finally he was martyred - poisoned by owner of the second Abbasid Caliph al-Mansur on 25th Rajab 183 A.H. He is buried in Kazimayn in Iraq.

Despite of most stringent need for caution and taqiyya, he enjoyed in promulgating the religious sciences and made many prophetic sayings available to the Shi'ites, to the extent that he left more teaching on Jurisprudence than any other Imam with the exceptions of Imam al-Baqir (A) and al-Sadiq (A) [Tr].

has been provided in which the verdict issued by him will be accepted. Or in other words we may compare reason with an intelligent, competent, sincere and resourceful governor of a region, but he could succeed only if his governance is officially certified and backed up by the ruling administration. The reason could be like a wise, trusted, and sincere adviser but only if it is being allowed to advice and if the attention is paid to its words.

If the reason becomes the ruling authority within a human body and could control the whims and passions of the self-it will govern it in an excellent manner; will achieve an equilibrium between the supply and demands; will arrange everything in a proper order, so that they may achieve perfection by ascending towards God-Almighty. But are the whims and passions of the self going to surrender themselves so easily and accept the governance of reason?

No! They won't, on the contrary they will engaged themselves into sabotage and other destructive work against it till the reason is forced out of the field of confrontation. There is no choice except that the reason should be strengthened, because, the stronger it is the better it recognizes the internal enemies and will be able to subdue and control them easily. Therefore, it is our utmost duty to endeavor and struggle for strengthening the faculty of reason.

Thinking before Action

In order to strengthen the reason we must seriously decide that before undertaking each action its over all worldly and eternal results and ultimate consequences must be thoroughly reviewed. This should be practiced till gradually it becomes a habit. It is because of this consideration that Islam encourages us to think about the ultimate consequences of our actions. e.g.: Commander of the Faithful Imam 'Ali (A) said:

"*By means of pondering deeply, make your heart aware and knowledgeable.*"
-al-Kafi, vol. 2, p-54.

Also said:

"*Pondering invites a person towards good works and actions.*"

-al-Kafi, vol. 2, p-55.

And said:

"Thinking about the ultimate consequences before action makes you safe against feeling sorry later on."

-Bihar al-Anwar, vol. 71, p-338 A man approached the Holy Prophet (S) and asked him:

"Oh Messenger of God! Please advise me. The Holy Prophet (S) replied:

"Will you follow my recommendation?" 'Yes! I will', Replied the man. This question and answer was repeated three times. Then the Holy Prophet (S) said: "My recommendation is that whenever you wanted to decide to undertake an action, then firstly you must ponder well about its ultimate consequences. In case you found it good then go ahead and do it, but in case you realized that it is not good, then don't do it."

-Bihar al-Anwar, vol. 71, p-339.

Also, he said:

"People were ruined because of being hasty. If they would have pondered about their actions none of them would have been ruined."

-Bihar al-Anwar, vol. 71, p-340.

And said:

"Delay and thinking about the consequences are blessings from God-Almighty while haste is from Shaitan."

-Bihar al-Anwar, vol. 71, p-340.

The following has been quoted from a tradition by the Infallible Imams (A).

"Pondering is like a mirror which shows your goodness and evilness "

-Bihar al-Anwar, vol. 71, p-325.

The animals in their actions follow the passions of their instincts and do not have the power of thinking and reasoning, but since a human being possesses reason, he must ponder and review the ultimate consequences before undertaking any action. Nevertheless, a man also possesses the same desires and animalistic passions, therefore, immediately reacts, gets stimulated, and absorbed as soon as he is faced with a desirable animal object of opposite sex from his own species. In this situation animal passions do not allow him to resort to thinking, because, once reason enters the scene it will prevent the action taken in accordance with animalistic passions.

Therefore, if we become habitual of practicing thinking and rationalizing before undertaking each action, then in that case, we will be opening a gateway for the reason so that it could be present at the scene. Once it enters at the scene, it immediately diagnoses our interest and benefits by subduing the animalistic passions, and will guide us towards the straight path of human perfection if it is strengthened and becomes ruler of the country (i.e. human body). It could diagnose the internal enemies and psychic diseases within his inner self, and accordingly may take the preventive measures and necessary treatments for their cure. It is because of these considerations that thinking pondering, and reasoning have been assigned special emphasis in Quranic verses and traditions.

Being Pessimistic towards the Self

If a human being takes a correct and in-depth review of his innerself and investigate his psychic characteristics, most probably he would be able to discover his psychic diseases, because, after all, one is more knowledgeable about his ownself as compared to others. God-Almighty has said:

> "Oh! But man is telling witness against himself, although he tenders his excuses."
> -the Holy Quran (75:14-15)

But our problem is that while judging we cannot remain impartial, because, we are optimistic about our souls; consider ourselves, our characteristics, our actions, and our opinions as faultless. The imperious-self (*nafse-ammarah*) makes the animalistic passions so charming, attractive, and appealing before our eyes that the evil deeds committed by us appears as virtuous acts. The Holy Quran said:

> "Is he, the evil of whose deeds is made fair-seeming unto him so

that he deemeth it good, (other than Satan's dupe)" God verily sendeth whom He will astray and guideth whom He will."
   -the Holy Quran (35:8)

It is because of this reason that we do not realize our defects and faults so that we could take remedial measures. Therefore, the solution of the problem consists that we must continuously be pessimistic and suspicious about the self; should presume or even must be assured that we possess vices, plenty of diseases, and with this reality should investigate the self. The Commander of the Faithful Imam' Ali (A) has said:

"A believer is continuously pessimistic about his self, always criticizes, and demands better deeds from him."

-Nahjul Balagha, sermon 176.

In praising the characteristics of the pious, he said:

"Their souls before them are always blamed' and criticized and they are always afraid of their deeds. While one of them is being praised, he is afraid of such praise and says: 'I am more aware about my own self; and God-Almighty is more knowledgeable as compared to me."

-Nahjul al-Balagha, sermon 193.

One of the biggest obstacle which never permits us to discover our psychic diseases and to seek treatment is our being optimistic and having a favorable opinion about our souls. Therefore, if this obstacle could be removed and the self is reviewed honestly, it would be possible to diagnose the disease and seek its treatment accordingly.

Consulting Spiritual Physicians

In order to diagnose our hidden internal faults and defects we may seek the assistance of a learned scholar of ethics who after having perfected his self has achieved a praiseworthy moral conduct. We must explain in detail the characteristics and internal behavior to him, and should request him to remind us about our psychic faults and moral indecencies.

A spiritual physician who Is a psychiatrist as well as a scholar of ethics, whose belief and action coincides, and is a true manifestation of higher moral excellence is extremely useful and influential for achieving self-perfection and undertaking a spiritual journey towards God-Almighty. If, one could succeed in finding such a person one must be thankful to God-Almighty for this blessing.

Unfortunately, such persons are not available easily and are in short-age. Also, this point needs to be emphasized that the correct diagnosis of the self's disease is extremely difficult. Therefore, it is patient's duty to describe in detail his deeds and internal characteristics without reservation before such a spiritual physician to enable him to diagnose his sickness correctly. If the patience did not cooperate and concealed the realities about him, then in that case, he will not obtain the desired results.

Consulting a Wise Friend

A good friend who is wise, intelligent, and well wisher is a great blessing of God-Almighty, and could be helpful in our efforts for achieving self-refinement and identification of moral indecencies, subjected to his being competent to identify our good and bad characteristics. Also, he should be a confident and well wisher. Because, if he could not diagnose the good and bad characteristics not only he can not help us, but on the contrary he may regard our weaknesses as virtues and visa versa. In case, if he is not a trusted well wisher, it is quite possible that for the continuation of friendship and not to hurt our sentiments, might conceal our faults and defects, and even for flattering and appeasement will mislead us by branding our moral indecencies as our virtues.

If, luckily we succeeded in finding such an ideal friend then we must demand him to feel free in frankly pointing out to us all our defects and faults observed by him. We must appreciate his reminders, should utilize them for improvement of the self, should make him understand that his criticism is sincerely appreciated and that not only we are not unhappy of his reminder on the contrary are grateful and pleased.

On the other hand, the person who has been trusted for this task is obliged to prove his honesty and sincerity through his practical actions. He must review the characteristics of his friend honestly without any reservations, and should let him know about his observations in a friendly and well-wishing manner in strict confidence. Also, pointing out defects and faults in the presence of others should be strictly prohibited. His aim should be to present out the facts and exaggeration should be strictly avoided, because, a believer is supposed to be like a mirror for another believer reflecting the later's beauty and ugliness the way they are without making any addition or subtraction.

Of course, such a friend who for the sake of reform reminds a person about his faults and defects are in shortages, but if one luckily y finds such an ideal friend, he indeed has received one of the greatest blessing. He must appreciate it, should be pleased for his comments, must thanks him, and must realize that a friend who criticizes for the sake of his improvement is one of the best and most valuable friend.

God forbids! If instead, a person feels offended with his positive criticism and for the sake of self defense starts thinking about taking revenge against him. If, someone reminded you that there are some poisonous scorpions upon your dress. Will you then feel offended with such a reminder and will take revenge or will you be pleased and thanks him? Yes! The undesirable characteristics are like scorpions and even worst than them because they sting and continuously strive their entries inside the soul. Some one who helps us to against them has indeed done the greatest services for us .

Imam al-Sadiq (A) said:

"The one who points out my faults to me is my best brother."

-Tohof al-Aqool, p-385.

Learning from Other's Faults

Most probably a human being is unaware of his own defects but sees them in others clearly and feels their ugliness very well. According to a famous proverb:

"They see a tiny piece of straw in the eyes of others and makes it big like a mountain, but can not see the mountain of their own eyes."

Therefore, one of the method for identifying our psychic defects is to detect these faults within other people. Once, a human being sees a defect of others, instead of paying attention towards it or criticizing, he should investigate his own inner-self for being contaminated with the

same faults, and in case he finds it, should try for its remedial. In this manner he could learn a lesson from the faults of other people, in continuation of his efforts for achieving self-refinement. The Holy Prophet (S) said:

"Fortunate is the one who learns a lesson from the faults of others."
-Bihar al-Anwar, vol. 71, p-324.

Learning from Criticism

Generally friends decline to point out the defects of a human being but opposite to that his enemies are quite eager to criticize. Of course, they are not sincere in their criticism and are motivated with their feelings of jealousy, enmity, and revengefulness but any way one might utilize their criticism to his best advantage.

When being criticized by his enemies a man has two options:

Firstly: He may take a defending position by taking the excuse that since the criticism is uttered by his enemies who are not his well wishers, therefore, he will defend himself by every possible means, thus, silencing their voices. Such a person had not only corrected his defects but on the contrary he might contaminate himself by committing further mistakes.

Secondly: He might pay good attention to his enemy's criticism, then with the aim of truth finding may refer to his own-self by reviewing him honestly. If, he found out that the enemy was right and his own-self was at fault, he should resort immediately to his own reform. In case, if it is feasible, he should even thank his enemy whose criticism be-came a means of his self-refinement-an enemy who is far better than those protecting friends who did not point out his defects, and with their flattering and appeasement kept him in the darkness of ignorance.

But if after referring to his self and reviewing, if he finds out that the defect does not exist within his self, then must thanks God-Almighty and be careful in guarding his self, lest it become contaminated with this defect later on. In this manner he could be benefited from the criticism of his enemies. Of course, this method of encounter will not be an obstacle as for as his utilization of other logical and legal means for dissipating the treacherous enemy plans are concerned.

Symptoms of Heart's Sickness

One of the best method for diagnosing a disease is to recognize its symptoms. The bodily sickness in generally identified by means of two indications i.e. either by feeling pain or by means of weakness of a particular part of the body in dischargement of its assigned function. Every part of the body is supposed to perform a special function, which in case of being fit performs it very well.

Therefore, if a part of the body is not performing its assigned function well it means that the part is sick. For example, the human eye in sound health under particular conditions sees the object, and therefore, if in spite of having suitable conditions does not see well, indicates that it is sick. Similarly, other organs of the body like ears, tongue, hands, feet, heart, liver, kidney, and others, each one of them is supposed to perform a particular function, which is performed by them in their being fit, and their failure to perform their relevant functions indicate their sickness.

Similar is the case with human self or heart which in accordance to his primordial nature is assigned to perform a special function. He has arrived from the Celestial Kingdom with knowledge, blessing, power, mercy, justice, love, enlightenment, illumination, and other moral virtues. By nature he is curious to discover the reasons and realities and desires God. Belief, attention, love, attachment, and worship towards God-Almighty all are symptoms of soundness of self and heart. Likewise, attachment shown towards knowledge and wisdom, benevolence and service for the God's Creatures for the sake of God-Almighty, sacrifice, generosity, seeking justice, and other moral virtues also are indicative of soundness of the self.

If, a person discovers such characteristics within him, it means that he possesses a sound heart, but on the contrary if he realized that he does not pay attention towards God; does not enjoy prayer, supplication, and worshiping ; does not like God; is ambitious for power, wealth, wife, and children; prefers sexual and carnal pleasures over God's consent; does not have any other goal in life except to safeguard his own interests; does not enjoy sacrifice, generosity, kindness, and service towards others human beings, and does not feel upset while seeing other people inflicted with calamities. Such a person must know that he is certainly sick, and if he is interested in his prosperity must resort to his reform and treatment as soon as possible.

Decision for Treatment

After the psychic sickness is diagnosed correctly, once we become sure that we are sick then its treatment must be started immediately, and the most important thing which matters at this stage -is to be able to take the firm decision. If, we really want and seriously decide that we must refine ourselves from the moral indecencies -it could be done. But if we treat. it something as insignificant, and do not decide, then in that case getting cured and achieving sound health would become impossible. It is at this stage that Satan and imperious-self enter into action and by means of playing dirty tricks prevent us from taking the right decision. But we must be careful and should not become victim of their treacherous deceit.

It is possible that he may justify the self's ugliness by pointing out: Don't you want to live with the people? Others do possess the same characteristics, look at Mr. so and so, they all possess the some characteristics even greater than yours. Do you alone want to be good?

"If you don't want to be insulted then better join the crowd."

But we must take a decisive and firm stand against their treacherous deceits and must say: The argument that the others are also contaminated has nothing do with me; there being contaminated does not give mean excuse or justification; in any case this defect and sickness exist within me; if I die in this condition; will be inflicted with eternal doom, and therefore, must endeavor for treatment and attaining self-refinement.

Sometimes it is possible that the Satan will enter the field with time killing and delaying tricks, thus, preventing us from taking the right decision at the right time. He might tell us:

True! This defeat exists within you and must be reminded .But it is not late. Why hurry up? Take it easy and let the other important works first be completed and then with complete ease you may engage yourself in self-refinement. Right now! You are too young. This is the time for fun and enjoyment. Wait till you become old. Then you may repent. God does accept repentance any way. Then you may get yourself busy in self-perfection.

We must, therefore, be intelligent enough to understand that these are Satanic tricks. Who knows that we will be alive till our old age? Perhaps, the death might arrive before old age and we might leave this world contaminated with the psychic diseases. In that case what will be our destiny? Any way even if we lived till that time but will the Satan and imperious self quit their treacherous filthy tricks and leave us free to pay attention towards the self-refinement? Even at that time by means of some other tricks they will prevent us from taking the right decision. Therefore, why not right now, we should take the action to subdue the rebellious imperious-self.

Sometimes, it is possible that imperious-self would tell us: You have become addicted to sinning and quitting this addiction is impossible for you. You are a prisoner of the whims and passions of your self. How could you free yourself from this imprisonment? Your self has become totally darkened by means of sins, and therefore, you do not have any chance for return. But we must better understand that the above argument is nothing but another treacherous trick of imperious-self.

In response we must tell him: quitting habit is not only impossible but on the contrary is quite possible. Of course, it is difficult but any how I must take action and must endeavor for self-refinement. If, quitting sins and bad characteristics would really have been impossible then in that case all these moral instructions, about their quitting, from the Prophet and Infallible Imams (A) would not have been issued. The path of repentance is never closed and is always open and therefore, we must decide and must get involved in achieving self-refinement.

Also, it is possible that the imperious-self may reflect their psychic diseases and moral indecencies as insignificant and unimportant by saying: you are committed for the performance of mandatory obligations as well as also perform such and such recommended obligations. Certainly you will receive the pardon of Merciful and Beneficent God and will be sent to Paradise. The moral indecencies which you possess are not so important to be concerned, and anyhow they will be compensated with your performance of recommended obligations (*Mustahabbat*).

Here, too it is important to be careful and to understand that such justifications are nothing but deludings of Satan and imperious-self. We must tell them: righteous deeds are accepted only from pious people, and achieving piety without self-refinement is impossible. If, the self is not cleansed thoroughly from evilness it could never be a place for goodness. Unless Satan is forced out the angels will never enter. If, by means of committing sins and other carnal desires the heart becomes contaminated and dark, it will remain without illumination and radiance in the Next World.

Serious attention should always be paid about the dangerous consequences of the psychic diseases which have already been summarized earlier. Apart from that, by referring to literature of moral ethics and traditions, the dangerous effects and eternal punishments of each psychic disease must be studied thoroughly; through these means the treacherous Satanic plans must be resisted by taking a definite and firm decision for starting a program of self-refinement. If we succeed passing through the decision stage we will become closer to the stage of action.

Control and Domination of Self

Human-self is the origin and source of all actions, deeds, sayings, virtues, and vices. If he is reformed one's success in both worlds is assured, but if becomes contaminated, will turn into a source of vices and will bring a catastrophe for this as well as the Next World. If, he started walking on the righteous path, might even surpass the God's most favorite angels; but if showed indifference towards the precious "Jewel-of-Hu-manity" (*Gowhare-Insaniyat*), and selected the animalistic way of life would become even lower then them, falling into the darkest valleys of ignorance.

The ways and means for following either one of these two paths have been incorporated within human existence. He has reason and wisdom, and in accordance with his primordial nature is inclined towards higher moral human characteristics, but at the same time he is also a biological animal possessing animalistic passions, desires, and energies. But it is not so that all of these animalistic characteristics are evil and damaging responsible for his eventual doom; on the contrary, their existence is necessary for the continuation of his human life; if utilized properly they even might be helpful in his journey towards attaining self-perfection and ascent towards God-Almighty.

But the problem is that animalistic passions and desires do not limit or stop themselves at certain predetermined level, and do not least care about the interests of others. Neither they offer any explanation for human requirements nor care about other desires, and do not follow any other goal except to achieve a saturation point. The sexual passions strive to achieve their own absolute climax and pursue this single goal without pursuing any other objective.

Other animalistic passion such as; pleasure of edible and drinks; ambitions for position, power, and fame; attachment to wealth, property, and other luxuries; power of revenge and wrath; and all other characteristics which arise from them do not stop themselves at a certain desired limit, rather each one of them demands its own absolute domination. It is because of this reason that the human-self becomes a battlefield where various passions wage war against each other continuously. This battlefield is never silent until one of them gains victory thus, taking the self into its absolute imprisonment.

But among them, reason possesses the most important position and power. By utilizing the religious guidelines might exert control over the passions and desires of self, thus, preventing their tendencies towards excessiveness or dissipation, may take control of the power center, maintain an equilibrium between the desire and passions and in this manner might rescue self's country from anarchy, disturbances and extremism, by guiding him towards the straight path of humanity and ascension towards God-Almighty.

However, taking over center of power by the reason is not an easy task, because, it is opposed by a most powerful deceitful enemy called the imperious-self, who is not alone and is supported by many of his friends and partisans. The God-Almighty has said:

"The (human) soul is certainly prone to evil, unless my Lord do bestow His Mercy."
-the Holy Quran (12:53) The Commander of the Faithful Imam' Ali (A) said:

"The reason and lust are opposite to each other; knowledge supports reason while the lust is supported by the passions and inordinate desires,. self is a battlefield where a war is waged between the reason and lust; whoever becomes victorious in this fight takes control of the self"
-Gharar al-Hukm, vol. 1, p-96.

And, he said:

"Evil and mischief are hidden inside every self; in case the master of self takes over his control, they remain hidden, but when opposite happens, they make themselves manifested."
-Gharar al-Hukm, vol. 1, p-105.

Therefore, reason is a good ruler but requires support and cooperation. If, we support reason in this confrontation by attacking the forces of passions and lusts, and handover the ruling of the body to reason then we indeed had accomplished a great victory. This is what have been de sired by all the religious pioneers, Divine Messengers, guides, leaders,

and seekers of truth through out the ages, and it was to accomplish this objective that they had issued plenty of instructions to mankind. e.g.:

The Commander of the Faithful Imam ' Ali (A) had said:

"Be careful! Passions do not take over control of your hearts; because in the beginning they will take you as their possessions, and will ruin you eventually."

-Gharar al-Hukm, p-16.

And said:

"Whoever does not take possession of his passions and desires will not be the master of his reason either."

-Gharar al-Hukm, vol. 2, p-702.

And said:

"The domination of passions is the -worst kind of catastrophe, and triumph over them is -one of the most precious possessions."

-Gharar al-Hukm, vol. 2, p-507.

Imam al-Sadiq (A) said:

"Whoever at the time of seduction, fear, lust, wrath, and consent, is in control of his self;. God-Almighty will make the Hell' s fire forbidden for his body."

-Wasail al-Shi'a, vol. 6, p-123.

The Commander of the Faithful Imam ' Ali (A) said:

"Take control of your self and do not allow him to indulge in sins, so that it is easier to guide him towards worships."

-Gharar al-Hukm, vol. 2, p-5-8.

Therefore, domination over the self and controlling his whims and passions is a matter of utmost importance and prerequisite for achieving self-refinement. Human self is like a mulish horse; if by means of hard training he becomes disciplined, you have the control of his straps in your hands, and is mounted upon his back, then in that case you may be benefited from his commissioning. But if he is not disciplined and wants to run away freely here and there without any control, then there is absolutely no doubt that you will have a crash. Of course, to discipline the rebellious self is an extremely difficult task; although, in the beginning he will offer resistance against you, but if you persisted patiently, he will be subdued eventually.

The Commander of the Faithful Imam' Ali (A) said:

"If self showed stubbornness and did not surrender against you, then deal harshly till be becomes tame. Act deceitfully against him until becomes obedient."

-Gharar al-Hukm, vol. 1, p-319.

And said:

"Lusts and passions of self are most fatal diseases, and the best medicines are patience and perseverance against them."

-Gharar al-Hukm, vol. 1, p-72.

Self-Struggle

Self is our biggest and most staunch enemy who is permanently and con-tinuously at war with reason; by listening to Satanic whispers he attacks the reason together with his soldiers to get it isolated and ultimately silenced, so that he becomes the sole-contender in the battle-field. His single goal is to force out God's favorite angels from the heart's kingdom and helping Satan to take over his absolute control. Naturally, defeating such a treacherous enemy is not on easy task, but requires determination, resistance, perseverance, and even crusade -a crusade not only for once or twice, for a few days and few years but continuous one till the last breath of life, which is a hard, difficult, and serious struggle.

In order to defeat the self and to control passions we must fight hard by strictly following the commands of Prophet (S) and Infallible Imams (A); with the help of reason must march forward preventing transgressions and encroachment of the self, and destroying the roots of his forces, so that reason could take over the power, and by taking inspirations from religious law could guide us upon the path of human perfection leading towards God's-Nearness.

We must know while confronting self, compromise and piece settlement is not possible, and what is required is a devastating blow making him crippled permanently from plotting any further conspiracies. In order to achieve happiness and salvation there is no other alternative except to follow this course, and because, of this reason struggle against the self has been called in traditions as -"Greater-Crusade" (*Jihad-e-Akbar*). Here we would quote few examples from the Commander of the Faithful Imam' Ali (A):

"Take over the possession of yourself—through continuous struggle."
-Ghararal-Hukm,
vol. l, p-131.

And said:

"Fight and dominate over self's whims and passions. Because otherwise if they succeeded in making you their prisoner -they will treat you in a most humiliating manner destroying you eventually. -Gharar al-Hukm, vol. 1, p-138.

And said:

"Be aware! That Paradise is purchased through self-struggle. Therefore, who is engaged in self -struggle will be victorious. Paradise (or self) is the greatest reward for some one who really appreciates their worth." -Gharar al-Hukm, vol. 1, p-165.

And said:

"By means of fighting against the self; incite him towards God's worshiping. Fight him the way one must fight with his worst enemy, and dominate over him like the domination of victor over his opponent. The most powerful person is the one who is victorious over his self" -Gharar al-Hukm, vol. 1, p-371.

And said:

"A wise man keeps himself engaged in struggle against his self, thus, reforming and preventing him from indulging into passions and amusements, and in this manner subdues him ultimately taking over his possession. Such a wise per-son is so must preoccupied in his self-refinement that he is totally detached with the world, whatever it contains and its dwellers." -Gharar al-Hukm, vol. 1, p-237.

Struggle against the self is the most crucial warfare which ultimately determines our destiny -a warfare upon which depends our 'how to live' in this world and the Hereafter. If, we do not dominate the self through struggle and take over the ruling authority in our own hands, he will take over the control of our possessions by pulling us in every direction at his will. If, we failed to make him our prisoner, he will certainly take us into his imprisonment as his slaves; if we could not succeed in inciting him for doing good moral virtuous deeds, he will force us to indulge into most shameful evil deeds. Therefore, it must be said that the struggle against the self is one of the most important and difficult duty which has been assigned upon the shoulders of the wayfarers journeying towards God, and whatever energy is spent by them in this struggle deserves merit and is energy well spent.

Greater Struggle (Jihad-e-Akbar)

The struggle against the self is so important that the Prophet (S) has described it as the "Greater-Struggle" *(Jihad-e-Akbar)*; It is so crucial that it has been described, even greater than the armed conflict. The Command-er of the Faithful Imam 'Ali (A). had narrated:

"That the Prophet (S) dispatched his soldiers to battle front to fight against the enemy. When the soldiers returned triumphant, the Prophet said: ' Congratulations! For those who have successfully completed the "Minor-Struggle" (Jihad-e-Asghar), but they have yet to engage themselves into Greater-Struggle (Jihad-e-Akbar)'. He was asked: 'Oh Prophet of God! What is the Greater-Struggle?"

'Struggle against the self.' Replied the Prophet (S)."

-Wasail al-Shia, vol. 2, p-124.

The Commander of the Faithful Imam 'Ali (A) said:

"The best crusade is the, struggle of some one, who fights' against his self located between his two sides."

-Ghararal-Hukm, vol. 11, p-124.

In his death will the Prophet (S) said to Imam 'Ali (A):

"Oh Ali! The best struggle is the struggle of some one who made his night in-to morning without thinking to oppress a single individual." -Wasail al-Shi'a, vol. 11, p-123.

In these traditions the importance of struggle against the self have been described as "Greater-Struggle" or Supreme Crusade -the crusade which is even superior than the crusade for the sake of God-Almighty *(Jihad fi*

Sabil illah). Considering the exalted position of crusade for the sake of God, which is considered as one of the most superior worshiping -the importance and worth of self-struggle becomes explicitly clear. In order to further explain its superiority in detail we may point out the following three reasons:

First Reason

Each act of worship even armed struggle required self-struggle from the following two considerations.

1. Firstly: The performance of each act of worship with perfection and in accordance with certain requirements itself requires self-struggle.

For example:

Is the performance of daily prayer [20] with presence of mind as well as meeting all other conditions, so that it indeed becomes -a believers heavenly journey preventing him from fortifications and forbidden deeds -possible without efforts and self-struggle?

Is fasting with perfection satisfying all its requirements so that it becomes -a shield against Hell's fire -possible without self-struggle? Is it possible for a valiant, crusader eager for martyrdom, to appear on the battle field to fight bravely with the enemies of Islam without self-struggle? And similar is applicable to all other worships.

1. Secondly: Every act of worship is accepted by God-Almighty and becomes a means of attaining His Nearness, subjected to its being per-formed solely for the sake of His Pleasure, being purified from ,all traces of polytheism, self-deceit and other selfish passions, and

---

[20] Daily prayer: the Prophet (S) has called the prayer: the ladder of a believer carrying him higher towards the heavens. Also, God-Almighty said in the Holy Quran:

"For prayer restrains from shameful and unjust deeds." -the Holy Quran (29: 45) [Tr].

performance of such acts without self-struggle are not possible. Even the armed struggle and martyrdom are worthy of merit and become means of attaining God's Nearness -only if they are performed purely for the sake of God's Pleasure and declaration of slogan of Monotheism (*Towheed*).

But, if this superior worship was performed with the intention of achieving fame and glory: taking revenge from the enemy, for the sake of lasting the name in history, for showing off and deceit, for achieving wealth and position, running away from facing life's difficulties, and other desires of the self - then in that case they lack any spiritual distinction and do not become means of attaining God's Nearness. Therefore, self-struggle is superior then all worships and virtuous deeds, even armed struggle undertaken for the sake of God-Almighty, because, it is a pre-requisite for their genuine dischargement with perfection. It is because of these considerations that this has been called as the -Greater-Struggle (*Jihad-e-Akbar*).

Second Reason

Armed struggle becomes compulsory only under certain special times and circumstances, further it is not incumbent upon everyone (*Wajib-e-aini*), rather is a collective obligation (*Wajib-e-kifai*), and some people are free from this obligation. During certain periods armed struggle is not required at all, or is required to the extent of collective obligation, e.g. if required number of people had assumed this obligation, then the others are excused. Apart from this it is not incumbent upon women, elderly men, handicapped, and sick people. But on the contrary, struggle against the self is incumbent upon everyone as an individual obligation (*Wajib-e-aini*) during all times, circumstances, and situations, must be continued till the very last moments of life, and no body under any condition except the impeccable (*Masoomin*) (A) will ever be free this requirement.

Third Reason

The struggle with self is harder than all the worships even the armed struggle in which a combatant risks his life by accepting martyrdom. Be-cause, absolute surrender before God-Almighty, self-struggle against self's whims and passions for the entire life, and journeying towards the straight path of perfection is much more difficult than the fighting of a valiant warrior with the enemy in the battle field for a moment and ultimately achieving martyrdom. In fact, self-struggle is so hard that except with continuous resistance, tolerance of pains and anguishes, and without God's Assistance it is not possible. It is because of this reason that we recite five times every day in daily prayers the sentence:

"Show us the straight path" [21]

To follow up the straight path of perfection is so difficult that the Prophet of Islam (S) said to God-Almighty:

"Oh God! Don't leave me at the disposal of myself even for the fraction of a second."

Struggle and Divine Assistance

True, that self-struggle is extremely difficult, requires resistance, perseverance, and intelligence, but any how it is possible and is something absolutely necessary for human happiness. Therefore, if one decides seriously to begin it, he will certainly receive Divine Assistance and will succeed in his efforts.

---

[21] *"If a man could have a superior and more vital aim than the "guidance", certainly that would have been included in the Surah Praise -a Surah which is the Opening Chapter of the Holy Quran and forms an important part of the prayer, and it would have been recited as a prayer for acceptance from God. It is by way of His direction or guidance that the intellect and experience set their course in the correct, advantageous, and suitable position widening the path of a wayfarer. Otherwise, without it, the intellect and experience would turn into alight in the hands of a thief, or a piece of sharp blade in the hand of a mad man."* -Profundities of Prayer, Sayyid Ali Khamenei, p-33 [Tr]

As God-Almighty has promised in the Quran:

"And those who strive in our cause -we will certainly guide them to our paths. For verily God is with those who do right."

-the Holy Quran (29:69)

Imam al-Sadiq (A) said:

"How good is a servant of God who struggles against the self and his passions for the sake of God's Pleasure. Whoever becomes victorious over the self's whims and passions has already achieved God's-Pleasure. Whoever offers resistance, and with humility in front of God, allows the reason to control imperious-self would receive the greatest blessing."

"There exists between the servants of God and Him nothing darker and horrible barrier than the imperious-self and his passions, and in order to destroy their roots forever, the realization to seek God, humility, hunger, thirst during the day (i. e. fasting), and night awakening (i.e. engaging in night prayers and having humming communications with God-Almighty). Such a person if dies in this course has left the world as a martyr, and if remains alive would ultimately attain the exalted position of God's Nearness. God-Almighty has promised in the Holy Quran that those who strive in His cause will certainly be guided to-wards His path and verily, God is with those who do right."

"When you encounter another struggler endeavoring in self-refinement better than your own efforts, then reprimand your self severely, and , remind him to be more careful and determined. In accordance with Divine do's and don'ts make a bridle for the self and like a master, training his inexperienced and wanton slave, encourage your self towards virtuous deeds. The Prophet (S) offered so much prayer that his feet become swelled, in response to people' s complaint, replied: should not I be thankful to God-Almighty ?"

"By these serious endeavors in worship the prophet (S) wanted to teach a lesson to his community. Therefore, one should never be negligent from endeavors, worship, and ascestism. Know that! if you could witness the sweetness of worshiping and other blessings and if your heart becomes illuminated with Divine Light -you will not be ready to discontinue if for an hour, even if they cut off your body into several pieces. Therefore, the negligence from worshiping shall never be possible except being deprived from advantages of competing for achieving immunity

against sins and attaining God's -Blessings."
-Bihar al-Anwar, vol. 70, p-69.

Self struggle is exactly like the armed struggle. Each blow inflicted upon the enemy, and every stronghold captured by means of soldiers make the enemy weaker in the same proportion, thus, making the, forces psychologically stronger and better prepared for subsequent assaults and later victories. It is in accordance of this Divine Tradition that we are told in the Holy Quran:

> *"Oh ye who believe! If you help God's cause, He will make your foothold firm."*
> *-the Holy Quran (47:7)*

The same is true with self-struggle. Each blow inflicted upon imperious-self and his whims and passions being opposed, makes him weaker in the same proportion and, thus, making us stronger and better prepared for subsequent assaults and later victories. But opposite to that any amount of irresolution shown and surrender to self's whims and passions make us weaker and making him stronger and better equipped for later assaults. If we could take the first giant step towards self-refine-ment, then with Divine Assistance will be able to achieve absolute domination over the self, but if we ran away from the battle field against the passions and self's soldiers, then they will become more stronger and ultimately take over our absolute control.

Man -His own Physician

It is true that Prophets and Infallible Imams (A) are the teachers and physicians of human souls, but the responsibility for treatment, refinement, and purification of their souls have been assigned upon their own shoulders. Although, the Prophets and Infallible Imams (A) have lectured and explained to human beings in details about their psychic dis-eases and symptoms, issued relevant prescriptions for their treatments, so that they could become familiar with their pains and treatments, and could assume the responsibility of their own self reforms.

Because, nobody could diagnose the disease and take the necessary action for its treatment, better than the man himself. Man listens about the psychic disease and their treatments either from the tongue of a preacher, or learns through reading a book, but the one who must discover the disease with in his own-self, and should use a particular medicine for its treatment -is no body except man himself. A man could feel about his own pains, and is knowledgeable about the hidden mysteries within, far better than anyone else. Therefore, if he himself is not careful in con-trolling his own-self, then of course, the preaching and warning issued by others would not produce any useful outcome.

Islam believes that reforms must begin from the inner existence of human beings, they must be prepared for undertaking self-refinement, should pay attention to psychological hygiene, and should be assigned the responsibility to guard their own souls. This in itself could be con-sidered as one of the important principle of Islamic training. The God-Almighty, said in the Holy Quran:

"Oh, but man is telling witness against himself, although he tender his excuses."
    -the Holy Quran (75:14-15)

Imam al-Sadiq (A) said:
"You have been appointed physicians of your own self pains, prescriptions, and symptoms of sound health all have been explained for you; now let us see, how are you going to act for the treatment of your self?"
-al-Kafi, vol. 2, p-454.

And said:
"Whoever does not have a preacher within his own-self, preaching by others, will not be of any use for him."
-Bihar al-Anwar, vol. 70, p-70.

Imam al-Sajjad (A) said:

"Oh son of Adam! So for as you have a preacher inside your self -you are bound to do good deeds."
-Bihar al-Anwar, vol. 70, p-64.

The Commander of the Faithful Imam 'Ali (A) said:
"The most helpless person is the one— who is helpless in reforming his self."
-Gharar al-Hukm, vol. 1, p-196.

And said:
"It is desirable that a man should assume the responsibility of supervision over his own-self He should continuously watch out his heart and control his tongue."
-Gharar al-Hukm, vol. 2, p-862.

Part 2
The Stages of Self-refinement

Prevention

Observance of psychological hygiene and prevention of sins and obscene moral deeds are the best and easiest stages of self-refinement. At these stages the self is not yet quite contaminated with sins, still possesses his natural purity and enlightenment, and is better prepared for perform-ance of good deeds and acquiring of good morals. He has not yet blackened and darkened, Satan has not yet made his entry inside him, and has not accustomed to evil deeds. Because, of these factors he is bet-ter prepared for quitting sinful deeds.

Teenagers and young people, if, decide for purifying their souls and quitting sinful and moral absence deeds, it is relatively easier for them, because, they still are at the preventing stage which is easier than quit-ting a chronic habit. Therefore, the youth, teens, and even childhood years are the best period for self-refinement. Likewise, so far as a man has not tasted the pleasure of a particular sin, he is in a better position not to commit it. Therefore, children, youths, and those people who not yet been contaminated with certain sinful deeds must appreciate this stage as something very important, guard themselves not to commit sin at all, and should maintain their state of purity and cleanness, because prevention is always better than cure.

They should better understand this important point that if they sinned and acquired obscene moral characteristics within their existence, than in that case they would have opened the gate for Satan's entry within their hearts, and onward, quitting a sin for them would become extremely difficult as compared to earlier. Satan and imperious-self, therefore, always try to present sinning for once and twice, something as minor and insignificant, so that by this mean they could increase their influence and make the self addicted to sinning.

Therefore, a man who is seriously concerned about his salvation and welfare must seriously resists self's whims and passions and should not allow his self to commit a sin even for once. The Commander of the Faithful, Imam ' Ali (A) said:

"Don't let your self allow to make an evil commitment or indulgence into evil deeds."

-Gharar al-Hukm, vol. 2, p-801.

And said:

"Dominate the passions of your self, before he becomes stronger, because, once he becomes stronger, he will take-over your control pulling you in every direction as he pleases, and in that situation you will not be able to offer resistance against him."

-Gharar al-Hukm, p-511.

And said:

"Habit is like an enemy who prefers his hegemony over you."

-Gharar al-Hukm, p-33.

And said:

"Addiction becomes second nature for a man."

And said:

-Gharar al-Hukm, p-26.

"Dominate your self's passions like an enemy dominates his enemy; wage a war against him like an enemy attacks his enemy; may be, through these means you might be able to dominate him."

-Gharar al-Hukm, p-509.

And said:

"Not to commit sin is better than repentance, because, many a times, an hour of carnal pleasures results in perpetual anxiety and distress. Death is a mean for discovering the scandalous nature of this world, which does not leave any pleas-ure left for an intelligent and aware person."

-al-Kafi, vol. 2, p-451.

Imam al-Sadiq (A) said:

"Before the soul departs from your body, do not allow your self to perform harmful deeds,. endeavor for achieving self's freedom the way you make efforts for earning your living. Because, the same self will be mortgaged against the deeds (on the Day of Judgement)."

-al-Kafi, vol. 2, p-455.

God-Almighty has said in the Holy Quran.

"But as for him who feared to stand before his Lord and restrained his soul from lust. Lo! the Garden will be his home."

-the Holy Quran (79:40-41)

Any how, the path of prevention is the best as well as the easiest path, and therefore, as much as a man endeavors seriously in this path is worthy of merit. How blessed is a young man, who subdues his imperious-self, does not allow him to indulge in sinful deeds, and with a purified and refined self follows the straight path of human exaltation ascending towards God's Nearness, till the very end of his life.

Sudden Renunciation

If the self has already crossed the preservation stage by becoming con-taminated with sins and moral vices, the alternative is to resort to cleans-ing, which consists of several methods. One of the best method of cleans-ing is the internal revolution and a complete sudden renunciation. A per-son who has become contaminated with sins and other moral vices may decide once to return towards God-Almighty through repentance -wash-ing and purifying the heart from all sorts of sins and vices. With a single bold definite decision, one force out devils from the heart by shutting the doors for their entry forever, thus, making the heart's dwelling readied for the descend of God's favorite angels and Divine illumination.

Having inflicted a devastating severe blow the imperious-self and Satan should be subdued thoroughly, and the power to rule over the self must be taken into hands firmly and forever. There were many such lucky individuals who were blessed with Divine Favor of attaining self-refinement by means of internal revolution within their inner existence, and remained faithful to their commitment till the last breath of their lives.

This internal spiritual revolution or awakening (or being reborn) oc-curs in the lives of peoples sometimes hearing a short sentence of a preacher and scholar of moral ethics, hints given by a Divine Guide, hap-pening of an unusual shattering tragedy, participation in a gathering of prayer and supplication, and listening to verses, traditions, and ponder-ing for a few minutes. Sometimes, a minor incident like a sparking illu-minates the heart's dwelling. There were individuals who were blessed to receive Divine-Grace to attain self-refinement through internal spiritu-al revolution in their lives, and thus, joined the ranks of wayfarers jour-neying towards God-Almighty. Following are few examples:

Bashar Hafi, was one of the most famous pious and religious personal-ities of his period. In his biography it has been written: Earlier he was an aristocrat who was continuously busy in world amusements and sexual pleasures round the clock; his house was the center of carnal pleasures, drinking, dancing, and loud music. But later on repented and joined the ranks of most distinguished ascetic and pious persons. Following is the story of his repentance:

"One day, a maid came out side the door of his house for emptying the garbage can; coincidentally at the same time Imam al-Kazim (A) was passing by through the alley near his house and the sound of loud music reached to his ears. He asked the maid:

'Does the owner of this house is a free man or servant (of God)?' 'Of course! He is a free man as well as a master.' Replied the maid.

'You are right, because if he was a servant -must have been afraid of his master and should not have been so bold in committing sins '. Replied the Imam.

"The maid returned back to the house. Her master, who was busy in drinking asked the maid:

'What is the reason of your delay?'

"The maid narrated for her master the encounter outside with an unidentified person and the details of questions and answers exchanged between them. 'What he said ultimately?' Asked the master. His last words were: 'You are right! Your master is a free man, because if he would have considered himself God's servant, then he would have been afraid of his Master and would not have shown such boldness in com-mitting sins ,. Replied the maid.

"This short sentence of Imam al-Kazim (A) like a sharp arrow pierced Bashar's heart and like a fresh illuminated and metamorphosed his inner existence. He left his drinking and came out, bare footed running fast in order to reach the un-identified person. Ultimately reaching near him, he said:

"'Oh my master! I beg God's as well as your pardon. Yes! I was and still am God's servant but had forgotten my servitude; because, of that acted so boldly in committing sins, but right now I have discovered my servitude, and want to repent for my past sins and omissions. Will God-Almighty accept my repentance ? I '"Yes! God-Almighty, will accept your repentance, will for give your past sins, and you must quit sinning for ever. I Replied the Imam.

"Bashar repented and become one of the most famous pious and saintly personality of his time, and in order to show his thank for this blessing used to walk bare-footed till the end of his life."

-Muntah al-Amal, vol. 2, p-126.

Abu Basir narrated:

"One of the agent of a tyrant king used to live in my neighborhood, who used to acquire his living through illegal means and had turned his home into a center of carnal pleasures, dancing, drinking, and music. Naturally, living next door to him was annoying and painful for me, but there was no alternative except to bear, because my repeated advises have not produced any improvement in his behavior. Finally, one day, when I pressed him hard to change his life style, he replied:

"'I am a prisoner of Satan, because of my addiction to eating, drinking, and sinning, I cannot quite them. I am sick but can do nothing for treatment. You are a good neighbor for me, but I am a bad neighbor for you. I am helpless and have become a prisoner of self's whims and passions, and don't know how to get myself out of this situation. When, you visit Imam al-Sadiq (A) in the near future, please plead may case with him, may be he will suggest a solution for my rescue.

Abu Basir continued: "I was deeply influenced with his words, and remained patient for a while till an opportunity aroused for me to go to Madina for seeing Imam al-Sadiq (A). When I saw Imam (A) I narrated the story of my neighbor for him. The Imam replied: 'When you returned back to Madina, your neighbor will come to see you, then you must tell him that Jafar bin Muhammad had said:

'Do not commit sins, so that I could guarantee Paradise for you.' Abu Basir said:

"When I returned back to Kufa after completing the pilgrimage, people came to see me including my next door neighbor. After exchanging formalities of greetings and inquiring about my trip when he wanted to leave, I gave him a hint that I have to discuss something in private. When other people left my house, I said to him that I narrated his story to Imam (A), and he replied:

'Upon your return to Kufa, that man will come to see you. Tell him that Jafar bin Muhammad said:

'Quit sinning so that I could guarantee Paradise for you:'

"This short message of Imam (A) so much touched his heart that he started crying and said to me: 'Do you swear by God that Imam said these words for me ?

"I swore by God and assured him that these are the exact words of Imam for him. He replied: 'These words are enough for me. , "He said these words and left my house. For several days I did not hear any news about him.

One day, he send a message for me to visit him at his home. I accepted his invitation and went to his house, he opened the door and hiding behind the door said: 'Oh Abu Basir! Every thing which I ac-quired through forbidden means have returned to their owners,. Right now, I possess absolutely nothing even a pair of clothing to cover myself and that is why I am standing behind the door. I have quitted all sins and have truly implemented the Imam's message in my life.

"Abu Basir said:

'I was indeed happy to learn about his repentance and changed condi-tion, and wondered about the impact of Imam' s short message upon him. I returned back to my home and arranged some clothing and some quantity of food and brought it for him. After a while he again called me and when I went to see him, found him sick. He remained in this condi-tion for quite some time, and during this period I frequently visited him to take care of his needs, but unfortunately treatment did not produce any improvement and his condition continued to deteriorate day by day till one day I found him in precarious condition hovering between life and death, while I was sitting on his side, and he was taking his last breaths, he suddenly opened his eyes and said:

'Oh Abu Basir! Imam al-Sadiq (A) had fulfilled his promise. He said these words and left for his eternal abode.

"After sometimes I had the opportunity for going to Hijaz for Hajj Pil-grimage, and also to see Imam al-Sadiq (A). When I was about to enter in his presence and my one foot was inside the hall while another one still in the yard, the Imam said: 'Oh Abu Basir! I have fulfilled the promise for your neighbor and the Paradise which I had guaranteed for him, was bestowed upon him. ' "

-Muntaha al-Amal, vol. 2, p-86.

There were and still are such individuals, who with single definite bold decision and act of bravery, subdued the imperious-self and took over the command of their affairs in their own hands, and with the oc-currence of a spiritual internal revolution polished and refined their hearts from all sort of impurities and vices. Therefore, the above stories indicate that following the above path is possible for all of us.

The Commander of the Faithful, Imam' Ali (A) said:

"For quitting habits subdue the self: by struggling against his whims and passions; may be you will succeed in making him your prisoner."

-Gharar al-Hukm, p-508.

And said:

"Best of the worships are achieving domination over habits."

-Gharar al-Hukm, p-176.

Imam al-Baqir (A) said:

"One the Day of Resurrection all eyes shall be crying except the following three kinds:

First: The eyes of some one who spent his nights awake in worshiping for the pleasure of God-Almighty.

Second: The eyes of some one who shed tears, because, of fear from God-Almighty.

Third: The eyes of some one who prevented them from looking forbidden things for the pleasure of God-Almighty."

-al-Kafi, vol. 2, p-80.

Imam al-Sadiq (A) said:

"God-Almighty said to Prophet Moses (A) through revelation that nothing is more effective in attaining my nearness as avoidance of forbidden things. 'The Paradise of Eden' will be bestowed upon them, and no one else would be allowed to enter therein"

-al-Kafi, vol. 2, p-80.

Of course, it must be admitted that self-domination and total avoid-ance of sin is not an easy task, but still with foresight, self-awareness, decisiveness, and pondering it might not be so difficult, considering the fact that one will be supported and strengthened with Divine Assistance as promised in the Holy Quran:

"As for those who strive in Our (cause) -We will certainly guide them to our paths. For verily God is with those who do right."

-the Holy Quran (29:69)

Gradual Renunciation

If we discovered that our inner existence does not have the courage and boldness required for quitting all sins at once, we may decide for gradual renunciation in stages. This procedure consists of beginning with quit-ting few sins at a time as a test of our will power, and the struggle should be continued till we become victorious over the self cutting the roots of those sins forever. Later on, the same procedure should be re-peated regarding some other sins and should be continued till the final victory is achieved.

Care should be taken that the sins quitted earlier should not be re-peated at all. Obviously, renunciation of each sin makes the imperious-self and Satan weaker in the same proportion; the place of each devil, forced out shall be immediately replaced by the entry of God's angel, and similarly the amount of darkness removed from the heart's surface shall be replaced with whiteness and illumination in the same proportion.

The abstinence from sins should be continued, in this manner, till self-perfection and final victory in controlling the self's desires is achieved. It is possible that while practicing abstinence of few sins at a time, we might reach to the limit, where we feel to have the necessary will power and determination to quit all sins at a time like sudden at once renunci-ation, in which case this golden opportunity should be utilized taking the decision to refrain from all sins.

By forcing out the Satan, the imperious-self should be subdued by al-locating the heart's dwelling for God-Almighty and his favorite angels. If we struggle and endeavor to achieve the above cherished goal, we will certainly be victorious. Self-struggle is exactly like waging a war against an enemy. A worrier must continuously watch over his enemy's move-ment, evaluate his own strength compared with enemy's resources, must strive for strengthening his forces, and by utilization of suitable oppor-tunities must attack his enemy inflicting devastating blows, thus, anni-hilating his soldiers completely or forcing them out of self's kingdom.

Part 3
Things which are Helpful for Self-refinement

Meditation

One of the most important obstacle for achieving the self-refinement is -negligence. If round the clock we are submerged in worldly affairs, running away from remembrance of death, are not prepared for thinking about dying even for a moment, and if incidentally this thought enters in our minds, we try to deviate from it immediately. If, we are negligent about the dangerous consequences of moral vices, are not concerned about the indictment for sins and eternal punishment, and the belief in the Day of Resurrection has not penetrated the profundities of our soul beyond a superficial mental concept; then with such negligence, how could we,-take the decision for self-cleansing and refinement, and con-trol and restrain him against his desires?

Negligence, in itself, is one of the most severe psychological disease and is the origin of many other diseases. The treatment of this disease is pondering, foresight, and strengthening the forces of belief. It is necessary that a human being should continuously keep a strict vigil upon his self, should never forget death, should ponder about serious con-sequences of self's diseases, indictment for sins and horrible punishment of Hell, and should always keep in mind about the accounting of his deeds on the Day of Judgment. In that case he is ready for self-refine-ment and should take a definite decision for purifying his heart from sins and other moral obscene deeds.

Imam' Ali (A) said:

"Whoever makes his heart's kingdom habitated with continuous pondering -his affairs would become good in outward appearance as well as inwardly."
-Gharar al-Hukm, p-690.

Reward and Punishment

In order to be victorious in attaining self-refinement and abstinence from sins, we may use the reward and punishment method. In the beginning we must address the self: I have decide to abstain from sins, if you do not-cooperate in this matter and committed sins, I am going to punish you with such and such punishment. That is, if you committed back-bit-ing, I will take a fast for one day, or will speak only the minimum re-quired for one week, will donate such amount for charity, will not drink water for one day, will deprive you from one diet, and will remain under the sun during summer, so that you should not forget about the temper-ature of Hell 's Fire.

After that we must watch over the self strictly so that he does not commit back-biting, and in case he commits it, we must take a bold stand against it without being lenient, and must execute the promised punish-ment against him. Once, the imperious-self realized that we are serious in refraining from sins and will strictly execute the punishment without least compassion, he will surrender himself before our genuine demands.

If, we implemented this program without any negligence, we may close the paths of Satan's entries, and achieve absolute domination over the self, with the condition that we must take a definite decision and must punish the rebellious-self without showing least compassion. It is strange that regarding minor violations of civil laws, the violators are in-dicted and punished, but unfortunately for self-cleansing and refinement this method is not practiced, in spite of the fact that our prosperity and eternal salvation depends upon it. Many of the God's deserving servants by utilization of the same method were able to attain self-refinement, self-cleaning, and self-domination.

The Commander of the Faithful, Imam' Ali (A) said:

"Hunger is the most effective tool for achieving self-domination and breaking habits."

-Gharar al-Hukm, p-773.

And said:

"Whoever practices self-asceticism is bound to earn benefits."

-Gharar al-Hukm, p-647.

One of the Prophet's companion said:

"Once on a hot summer day the Prophet Muhammad (S) was sitting under the shade of a tree,. suddenly a man appeared who after c taking, off his clothes laid down with bare back upon the hot sand and started rolling over it, alternatively making his back and stomach to bear the hot sand, occasionally covering his face with it, said: 'Oh my imperious-self! You better taste the heat of this hot sand particles, and know it that the heat of Hell's fire is for severe and painful than this.

"The holy Prophet (S) witnessed the above scene with interest, and having wore his clothes when the man wanted to return, the Holy Prophet asked the man to come near him, and said: 'I saw you doing some thing strange which is not done by any other person. What was the motive behind this act. ?"

"The man replied: 'Oh Prophet of God: The fear of God forced me to perform this act. By performing this act I said to my self. Taste the temperature of this hot sand and know that the heat of Hell's fire is much more severe and painful than the temperature of this hot sand."

"The Holy Prophet (S) said: Yes! you feared the God-Almighty the way one should. be really be fearful of Him, and he with this act has glorified you over the angels of His Thrown. 'Then he said to his companions: 'Come and stand closer to this man and ask him to pray for you." The companions assembled around the man and requested him to pray for them. The man raised his hand for prayer and said:

"O God! Guide our affairs. make piety provision of our journey, and bestow upon us Paradise in the Hereafter."

-Mohajateh al-Baiza, vol. 7, p-208.

The Commander of the Faithful Imam 'Ali {A.S.) said:

"Arise against the self and chastisement prevent: him from becoming addicted to various habits."

-Gharar al-Hukm, p-350.

Dignity of Human Essence and Strengthening Human Virtues

Earlier, it was pointed out that human self is a precious jewel which has come into existence from the world of life, knowledge, perfection, beauty, blessing, benevolence, and by nature is the origin of these things. Therefore, if he paid attention towards his exalted position and virtues within his existence, he will then realize that commitment of sins and other moral obscene deeds are below his dignity, and naturally will be disgusted with them. When he understood that, he is a human being has descended from the Upper Heavens to be God's Vicegerent upon earth, animalistic desires and passions will become worthless in his sight, and desire for achieving moral excellence shall be revived in his existence.

The Commander of the Faithful Imam 'Ali {A} has said:

"Whoever appreciated the greatness of his self, will regard passions as insignificant and worthless."

-Nahjul Balagha, saying 449.

Imam al-Sajjad was asked:

"Who is the worthiest person? 'The one who does not consider this world worthy of his own existence.' Replied the Imam."

-Tohf al-Aqool, p-285.

Therefore paying attention about the exaltedness of human soul, discovering the worth of his existence, and his lofty position, might be helpful in attaining self-refinement and abstinence from sins. If we address our self, we must say:

You belong to the heavenly kingdom of knowledge, life, perfection, virtues, benevolence and blessings; you are the God's Vicegerent upon the earth; you are human and have been created for eternal life of Next World and God's Nearness; you are superior than animals and following animalistic passions is not worthy of your existence. In this manner attaining self-refinement and abstinence of sins will become easier for us. Also, for self-refinement, each vice must be uprooted gradually by strengthening opposite characteristics, thus, replacing vices with virtues, which turn into habits or second nature.

For example, if we are jealous with respect to a certain individual, becomes sad and annoyed seeing his blessings and happiness, and by means of slander, insult, annoyance, obstruction, and indifference try to satisfy our own internal psychic disorder -must try to show praise, re-spect, goodwill, and cooperation towards him. When we behave in this manner exactly opposite to the feelings of jealously, slowly, this vice be-comes weaker day by day, and eventually is replaced by benevolence.

If, we are sick with the disease of stinginess, must imposed upon the self to bear the necessary expenditure for our genuine requirements, so that the undesirable habit of miserliness gradually become uprooted, and eventually become accustomed to spending money and beneficence.

If, we show miserliness regarding payment of religious dues, we must take stand against the self and without paying least attention to self's whims and passions, must remit our religious financial obligations. If, we show hesitation for spending money for ourselves and our family, then the genuine expenditure should be imposed upon the self so that it becomes accustomed to it gradually. If, because of miserliness we cannot participate in charitable affairs, we must take action by all possible means at our disposal; a portion of our financial assets should be spent in God's Way for supporting the destitute people so that gradually we become accustomed to it.

Of course in the beginning this task might appear as difficult but with perseverance and resistance it would become easier. over all in order to achieve self-refinement and to refrain from immoral deeds the following two tasks should be performed:

Firstly: We should not offer positive response to the demands of im-moral and obscene deeds, so that gradually their roots are dried off completely.

Secondly: The virtuous characteristic opposite to that particular vice should be strengthened; and in accordance with this virtuous characteristic, task must be imposed! upon the self so that gradually he becomes used to it, acquiring them as his habit and temperament, ! thus, cutting
    the roots of wicked deeds forever. The Commander of the Faithful Imam'

Ali (A) said:

"Force your self to perform good moral deeds, because the wickedness has been incorporated in your inner essence."

-Gharar al-Hukm, vol. 1, p-130.

And said:

"Make yourself used to performance of good deeds and for tolerance of pay-ment of severe reparation, so that he becomes noble, your Hereafter becomes fruitful, and your admirers become more."

-Gharar al-Hukm, p-492.

"Selfish passions and desires are fatal diseases, and the best medicines are se-lection of patience and abstinence from them."

-Gharar al-Hukm, p-72.

Renunciation of Bad Company

Human being are susceptible to being influenced with many of the characteristics, etiquette, and behavior of other people with whom they have social association, and in reality become like them, especially their best friends and close social associates play an influential role in their lives. Friendship with corrupt and wicked individuals forces a person towards corruption and evil deeds, while association with righteous people with good morals invites a person towards salvation and goodness. One of the characteristics of a human being is that he makes himself like others. If, he mixes socially with corrupt and sinful people -he becomes familiar with sinning and other immoral deeds, not only he does not see the ugli-ness of his actions, on the contrary, regards these acts as manifestation of acts of goodness.

Opposite, to that if his social circle consists of righteous people with good morals, he become thoroughly familiar with good morals and good character and desires to become like them. Therefore, a good friend is one of the greatest blessing of God-Almighty and is considered as an important factor responsible for progress and prosperity of a human being. And opposite to that a bad friend is one of the greatest problem and an important factor responsible for his adversity and deviation.

Therefore. the choice of a friend should not be regarded something as insignificant and unimportant. rather should be treated with utmost importance. because. it determines our ultimate destiny. The Commander of the Faithful Imam ' Ali (A) said:

"A Muslim should never take a sinful and corrupt person as his friend -be-cause, a sinful friend presents vices as virtues, and desires that his friend should behave exactly like himself A bad friend neither helps a person in worldly affairs nor in the affairs belonging to the Next World, and socialization with him makes a person disgraced."

-al-Kafi, vol. 2, p-640.

Imam al-Sadiq (A) said:

"It is not appropriate for a Muslim to make friendship with a lewd, stupid, and mendacious person."

-al-Kafi, vol. 2, p-640.

The Holy Prophet (S) said:

"A person is bound to follow the religion of his friend and social companion."

-al-Kafi, vol. 2, p-642.

The Commander of the Faithful Imam ' Ali (A) said:

"Association with evil person should be avoided strictly, because on evil per-son is like a burning fire and whoever nears him will be burnt."

-Gharar al-Hukm, p-147.

And said:

"Association With Wicked person should be strictly avoided, because, evil will be associated with evil."

-Gharar al-Hukm, p-147.

Also said:

"Strictly avoid companionship with an evil friend, because, he will lead his fellow companion towards destruction and will damage his reputation."

-Gharar al-Hukm, p-142.

Therefore, if some one is really striving to attain self-refinement, and if has bad friends and evil companions -should quite their company at once, because, with their company refraining from sins is almost im-possible. Bad friends slow down one's determination for self-refinement by encouraging him to get indulge into sins and other immoral deeds. To commit a sin is like a habit, and its quitting shall be possible only, if the socialization with other addicted persons should be avoided.

Avoiding Potential Blunders

Self-refinement and refraining from sins forever is something is not an easy rather is a difficult task. A human being is always susceptible to stumble by sinning, because the imperious-self naturally invites him to-wards vices. Heart -which is the command center for rest of the body is in a state of continuous change or metamorphism, is influenced by ex-ternal events, issues orders in accordance with the situation it encoun-ters, the things it sees, and the words it hears.

At centers of worships and religious spiritual assemblies the heart nat-urally shows inclination towards performance of virtuous deeds, and op-posite to that at the centers of corruption and vices pulls towards evil deeds. Seeing scenes of spirituality motivates heart towards spiritual matters, while seeing erotic scene of carnal acts makes him seduced. In a corrupted assembly the hearts becomes inclined to perform similar vices while in a spiritual gathering the heart gets motivated towards God-Almighty. If, he gets associated with worldly people infatuated with ac-cumulation of wealth and properly, the hearts become inclined towards animalistic desires, and if associates with God's pious servants -becomes' motivated towards virtuous deeds.

Therefore, those who are sincerely interested in self-refinement and abstinence from sins must close their eyes and ears from seeing erotic scenes of carnal desires, should not participate in such parties; should not mix socially with such corrupted individuals, otherwise they them-selves are most likely to stumble. It is because of these considerations that Islam forbids a man from participating in religiously prohibited (*Haram*), parties such as gambling, drinking, and other sinful assemblies. Also, looking at the face (with lust), meeting in private, hand-shake, jok-ing and laughing with women who are unlawful (*Na-mahram*) have been forbidden.

One of the great wisdom hidden behind the recommended Islamic Veil (*hijab*) is related to same matter. Since Islam requires an ideal social environment where self-refinement and abstinence from sins could be made possible. Otherwise, controlling imperious-self shall become impossible, because, the corrupt environment naturally pushes human be-ings towards corruption, even thinking about sin invites a man to com-mit that sin ultimately.

The Commander of the Faithful Imam 'Ali (A) said:

"When eye sees an erotic scene -the heart becomes blind from seeing its ulti-mate consequences."

-Gharar al-Hukm, p-315.

And said:

"Simply thinking about sinful carnal deeds encourages you to commit them eventually."

-Gharar al-Hukm, p-518.

Egotism – the Root of all Evils

The scholars of ethics have defined egotism as the mother of corruption (*Ummul Fisad*), the root of all vices and sins, and in order to attain self-refinement one must seriously struggle against it. Here, in the beginning, its meanings shall be explained and then the evil influences of this characteristic and confrontation methods against them shall be discussed. Meanwhile, it must be understood that each living existence by nature is an egotist and shows keen interest about his essence, characteristics, actions, effects, and perfection. Therefore, egotism cannot be condemned something as absolutely undesirable, but requires further explanation.

Earlier it was pointed out that a human existence consists of two stages and possesses two selves or two mines, i.e. animal-self and human-self. The human-self consists of a Celestial Spirit, (blown by God-Almighty), descended from Heavenly Kingdom to become God's Vice-gerent upon earth. From this point of view it belongs to the category of knowledge, life, power, blessing, benevolence, perfection, goodness, and by nature aspires towards these ideals.

Therefore, if a person recognizes himself (the human-self) and discovers the values incorporated therein, considers them as honorable, strives to achieve the nearness of the Fountainhead of Absolute Perfection, which results in his revival of moral decencies, virtues, and goodness. Considering the above, this type of egotism could not be regarded as un-desirable, rather is something good and praiseworthy, because this characteristic is not egotism rather in reality it is God-seeking. This matter has already been explained earlier and a detailed discussion shall be presented later.

The second stage of human existence consists of his animal-self, and in this stage he is like an animal exactly, possessing animalistic desires and passions. Although, in order to remain alive in this world and to sustain a living, a human being is supposed to provide his animalistic means of living up to a moderate limit, and up to this extent there does not exist any prohibition and reproach. But the most important and determining factor is that whether the body should be ruled by the wisdom and celestial human spirit or by the imperious-self and his animal-self.

If wisdom and human-self rule, then the animal-self and his passions are adjusted, optimized, and all of them are mobilized for journeying on the path of exaltedness and perfection leading towards God's Nearness. In this case the human-self which is the same existence attached to God -assumes his authenticity, whereby revival of moral excellence in conduct and God's Nearness become the primary goal, and taking care of one's animalistic requirement will become a secondary aim. Therefore, egotism and love for self not only has not been condemned, on the contrary have been praised.

But if the imperious-self and animal-self took over control of bodily affairs, the wisdom and human-self are subdued and become isolated, in which case a man gradually takes distance from God and human values, falling ultimately into deep and dark valleys of ignorance. He forgets his human-self (i.e. humanism) and recognizes in his place his unconscious self (*Na-khud*) (i.e. animalism). And these are the meanings of egotism which is called as the mother of all evils and is therefore, undesirable.

An egotist sees only his own animal-self and nothing else. All his actions, efforts, talks, and character revolves around the axis of satisfying his animalistic passions and desires. He practically considers himself as an animal and does not recognize any goal in life except meeting his animalistic requirements. In order to accomplish these base animalistic objectives considers himself as independent or renegade and justifies all his actions. His animal-self is the only thing which he considers something sacred and honorable.

He demands every thing for his own sake, even truth and justice, which should back up his animalistic desires, and if they are not on his side, does not need such justice, rather gives himself the right to wage combat against them. He even interprets and comments religious commands and obligations as he pleases, assigning authenticity to his own opinions and thinking, whereby the religious laws and obligations are supposed to adopt themselves in accordance with his whims and passions.

Since an egotist is deprived of real human dignity, virtues and moral perfection; he keeps himself amused with whimsical, false, and futile affairs such as: seeking false publicity, ambitiousness, covetousness, snob-bishness, eating, drinking, sexual pleasures, and remains totally ignorant from God's Remembrance and self-perfection.

Because an egotist is infatuated and obedient to his imperious-self, he does not have any other aim except satisfying the demands of his passions in the best possible manner; in order to meet this animalistic objective is not ashamed of performing the most shameful deeds and consider them as justified and permissible. He wants to accomplish his animalistic goals, and in order to achieve them does not refrain from indulgence in lying, accusing, oppressing, and breech of commitments, deception, treachery, and any other acts of transgression.

Therefore, egotism is the mother of all evils which makes all acts of abjectness justified and permissible, or in other worlds, it can be said that all acts of transgressions in reality are the by-products of egotism which are manifested in different manners at different occasions-. For example, oppression and trampling over the rights of others could not be anything other than self-centeredness. Likewise, lying, backbiting, ill-speaking, fault-finding, jealousy, and revenge all are the vices of egotism which have been manifested in these manners. It is because of this reason that self-centeredness is called as the root of all transgressions.

Self-centeredness consists of various degrees and stages the highest of them leads to the state of self-adoration a self-worshiping. If this ugly characteristic is not confronted strongly, it gradually becomes so intense whereby the imperious-self becomes an object of worship, whose commands must be obeyed absolutely, and a person becomes submissive to his whims and passions to the extent of adoration. God-Almighty said about such a person in the Holy Quran:

> *"Seest thou such a one as taketh for his god His own passion (or impulse)?"*
> *-The Holy Quran 25:43.*

Is worship means any thing else except that a worshipper in front of his object of worship humbles and bows down, and should be sub-missive to his commands absolutely without raising least objection? Similar is the case with an egotist person because he regards his self as an object of worship and humbles and prostrates in front of him by obeying his commands without any question. Therefore, an egotistic cannot be considered as a Monotheist.

Worldliness -the Source of all Sins

In Islamic narrations and Heavenly verses the world has been defined as a place of amusement, and an object of arrogance which has been severely condemned; its attachment is not worthy of the lofty status of believers, and therefore, they should strictly refrain themselves from being attached to its adornments. Following are few examples:

The Holy Quran said:

> *"For the life of this world is but goods and chattels of deception"*
> *-the Holy Qur-an (3:185)*

And said:

> "What is the life of this world but play and amusement but best is the home in the Hereafter, for those who are righteous. Will ye not then understand ?
> -the Holy Quran (6:32)

And said:

> "Know that the life of this world is only play, and idle talk, and pageantry, and boasting among you and rivalry in respect of wealth and children: as the likeness of vegetation after rain, whereof the growth is pleasing to the husband-man, but afterward it drieth up and thou seest it turning yellow, then it becometh straw. And in the Hereafter there is grievous punishment."
> -the Holy Quran (57:20)

The Commander of the Faithful Imam' Ali (A) said:

"So now, certainly I frighten you from this world for it is sweet and green, surrounded by lusts, and liked for its immediate enjoyments. It excites wonder with small things, is ornamented with (false) hopes and decorated with deception. Its rejoicing do not last and its afflictions cannot be avoided. It is deceitful, harmful, changing, perishable, exhaustible, liable to destruction eating away and destructive."

-Nahjul Balagha, sermon -111.

And said:

"The world is a place for which destruction is ordained and for its inhabitants departure from here is destined. It is sweet and green. It hastens towards its seeker and attaches to the heart of the viewer. So depart from here with the best of provision available with you and do not ask herein more than what is enough and do not demand from it more than subsistence.

-Nahjul Balagha, sermon -45.

There are plenty of narrations [22] and verses in which the world has been reproached, and the people .are warned to refrain from being attached to its adornments. Especially, in the precious book of Nahjul-Balagha (the Path of Eloquence), the world and worldly have been re-proached severely, and it has been emphasized that the people should not be attached to this perishable transient world, and should pay more attention towards the Hereafter. In this book the people have been di-vided into two groups: the worldly and the one who is attached to the Hereafter. Each one of these groups follow their own special program. The God-Almighty has said in the Holy Quran:

> *"Whoso desireth the reward of the world, we bestow on him thereof and whoso desireth the reward of the Hereafter, we bestow on him thereof."*
> *-the Holy Quran (3:145)*

And said:

> *"Wealth and children are an ornament of life of the world. But the good deeds which endure are better in the Lord's sight for reward and better in respect of hope.*
> *-the Holy Quran (18:46)*

What is World?

Anyhow, Islam considers world something as undesirable and demands from its followers to practice asceticism. Here, it would be appropriate to throw some light about the Islamic concept of this world, and why it

---

[22] [1] The dryness of eyes is the result of hard-heartedness, hard-heartedness is caused due to excessive sinning; excessive sins are the result of consumption of food which is arranged through forbidden and unlawful income; earning through forbidden and unlawful means is due to forgetting death; forgetting death is due to lengthy desires; lengthy desirers are caused because of attachment to world; and world's attachment is the root of all evils [Tr].

has been reproached? Does the world consist of worldly existence such as: earth, sun, moon, stars, animals, plants, trees, mines, and human beings? Therefore, the life of this world can be defined as working, eating, drinking, sleeping, marrying and other related acts of living. Does Islam re-frain from these things? Do earth, sky, animals, vegetables, and trees are bad things that a human being should avoid them?

Does Islam prohibits earning a living, acquiring of knowledge, business and production, and sexual relationship? Absolutely this is not the case, because all of the above things have been created by God-Almighty, and in case they were bad, He would not have created them. God-Almighty regards them as His Beautiful Bounties which should be conquered by human beings and should be utilized for their advantages. The wealth and property not only is not reproached but on the contrary has been introduced as blessing in the Holy Quran as follows:

"If he leaves wealth, that he bequeath unto parents and near relatives in kindness."
   -the Holy Quran (2:180)

Earning a genuine living by lawful means not only has not been re-proached, rather has been regarded as one of the best kind of worship.

Following is an example:

The Holy Prophet (S) said:

"Worship consists of seventy acts and the best among them is the act of earning a genuine living through lawful means."

-al-Kafi, vol. 5, p-78.

Imam al-Baqir (A) has said:

"Whoever endeavors sincerely for earning a genuine living (through lawful means); becomes self-sufficient in taking care of his expenditures; maintains a reasonably comfortable standard of living for his family; shows benevolence to his neighbors -such a person will meet God-Almighty in the Hereafter, while his face will be shining like the full moon."

-al-Kafi, vol. 5, p-88.

Imam al-Sadiq (A) said:

"*Whoever strives for earning a living for his family is tantamount to a warrior engaged in Holy War for the sake of God.*"

-al-Kafi, vol. 5, p-88.

The Islamic traditions emphasize the importance of work, farming, agriculture, trade, and even marriage. The life styles of Prophet (S) and Infallible Imams (A) indicate that they too have worked for earning a living. Commander of the Faithful Imam' Ali (A) the leader of the pious also mode endeavors and worked hard for earning a living in his life. Therefore, what is really meant with this reproached world? In the opinion of some people it is not the world which is reproached rather it is the attachment to world which has been strictly condemned. e.g. the Holy Quran said:

> "*Beautified for mankind is love of the joys (that come) from women and off-spring, and stored up heaps of gold and silver, and horses branded (with their mark), cattle, and land. That is comfort of the life of the world, God-Almighty ! With Him is a more excellent abode.*"
> -*the Holy Quran (3:14)*

The Commander of the Faithful Imam' Ali (A) said:

"*Be careful not to attach your self from this (transient) world, because love of world is the root of all sins and origin of all catastrophes.*"

-Gharar al-Hukm, p-150.

Imam al-Sadiq (A) said:

"*Attachment to World is the basis of all sins and transgressions.*"

-Bihar al-Anwar, vol. 3, p-7.

From these types of traditions it could be inferred that what is condemned is the attachment to these worldly affairs and not the affairs in themselves. Here the question arises whether absolute attachment and love to worldly affairs is condemned and should not a man have any attachment to his wife, children, house, wealth, and food? How could such a thing be expected?

Because, the attachment to these affairs is a natural thing for a human being; God-Almighty has incorporated these attachment within his primordial nature, and that is the way human beings have .been created by Him. Is it possible for a man not to love his wife and children?

Is it possible not to love clothing, delicious foods, and other beautiful things of this world? If love of these things was prohibited, God would not have created human being with these tendencies. A human being in order to keep himself alive requires these things, and accordingly he has been created in such a manner that he should feel a natural inclination towards these affairs. The Commander of the Faithful Imam' Ali (A) said:

"The human beings are the children of this World and they should not be blamed for loving their mother."

-Nahjul Balagha, saying 33

The Islamic traditions recommend that one must love and show affection towards his wife and children. The Holy Prophet (S) and Infallible Imams (A) too had shown affection towards their wives and children. Some of them liked foods and showed interest in them. Therefore, sky, plants, trees, mines, animals, and similar other God's bounties are neither bad nor condemned. Similarly, wife, children, wealth and property, affection shown towards these things and life of this world, are not only not condemned, rather in some of the traditions, the world even has been praised. Following is the example:

In reply to a person who has condemned the world, the Commander of the Faithful Imam Ali (A) said:

"Verily this world is a house of truth for those who look into it deeply and carefully, an abode of peace and rest for those who understand its ways and moods, and it is the best working ground for those who want to procure rewards for Hereafter. It is a place of acquiring knowledge and wisdom for those who want to acquire them, a place of worship for friends of God and for angels.

It is the place where prophets receive revelations of the Lord. It is the place for virtuous people and saints to do good deeds and to be given rewards for the same, only in this world they could trade with God's favors and blessings and only while living here they could barter their good deeds, with His Blessings, and rewards."

-Nahjul Balagha, short saying 130.

Imam al-Baqir (A) said:
"The world is the best support for the Hereafter."
-Bihar al-Anwar, vol. 73, p-127.

Imam al-Sadiq (A) said:
"Anyone who does not like earning a living by lawful means to maintain his prestige, to pay his obligations and to take care of his relatives, then -such a person lacks any merit and goodness."
-al-Kafi, vol. 5, p-72.

Therefore, what is meant by the condemnation of world and its love and attachment which is the roots of all evils? From the over all collection of these verses and traditions it could be inferred that, what is condemned is the worldliness and becoming infatuated with it, and not the creatures of the world, its life, and genuine liking of worldly affairs in themselves.

Islam, demands people to recognize the world the way it is and then they should appraise its worth accordingly; they should also discover the exalted Divine Goal behind their own creation as well as the world, and should move in that direction. If they acted in this manner –they belong to the Hereafter, otherwise they belong to the worldly group.

World's Reality

In order to explain this matter in the beginning we would discuss the reality and nature of world from Islamic point of view and then a conclusion could be reached. Islam believes in the existence of two worlds: The first one is the same material world where we live and is called world. The other one is where we will be transferred after death and is called Hereafter and Next World.

Islam believes that the life of a person does not terminate at his demise; rather he will be transferred after death to an eternal abode known as the Next World. Islam regards the world as perishable, transient, and a temporary abode, while considers the Hereafter and Next World as a permanent and eternal abode.

Men has not came to this world in order to live for a short while and finally to die and be destroyed, rather he has come to achieve self perfection through acquiring knowledge, good deeds, and training –and to live happily forever in his eternal abode in the Next World. Therefore, the world is like a form land for cultivation of fruits for Hereafter, place for acquiring knowledge, and a place for making arrangements for provisions of a journey.

However, man for the sake of his survival and in order to live in this world has no other choice except to utilize Divine Bounties which have been created for his consumption. But utilization of these Divine Bounties should be regarded as a mean and not an end in itself.

The aim of creation of human beings and world was not just to have comfortable luxurious life and to take the maximum advantage of worldly pleasures, rather there was an exalted and superior goal behind it e.g. the nourishment of the "Jewel of Humanity" (*Jowhar-e-Insaniyat*) through attaining self-perfection and ascending towards God's Nearness. Following are few examples of Islamic narrations in this matter:

The Commander of the Faithful Imam' Ali (A) said:

"Certainly this world has not been made a place of permanent stay for you. But it has been created as a pathway in order that you may take from it the pro-vision of your (good) actions for the permanent house (in Paradise). Be ready for departure from here and keep close your mount for setting off."

-Nahjul al Balagha, sermon-123.

And said:

"Remember that this world is a thoroughfare, a road upon which people are passing night and day, and the Next World is the abode of permanent stay. While, passing along this road make provision for the next where you will reside forever. Do not go with a burden of sins and vices before the One, Who knows everything about you. Remove vicious ambitions from your mind before death removes you from your surroundings.

Remember, that you are being tried in this world, and are created to be given a permanent residence in the Next World. When a man dies people ask what he has left behind as a legacy, and angels want to know what he has sent forward (good deeds and good words). May God have mercy upon you, send something in advance to the place where you will have to follow; it may be a sort of a deposit with God to be repaid to you on your arrival. Do not leave all of your's behind, it will be a drag upon you."

-Nahjul Balagha, sermon-203.

He further said:

"Remember, that this world which you covet so ardently and attempt to acquire so earnestly, and which some times annoys you and some times pleases you so much, is neither your home nor a permanent destination. You have not been created for it, nor invited to it as your resting place. It shall neither remain with you forever nor will you remain in it eternally.

"If it has enticed you with its charms, it has also warned and cautioned you of real dangers lurking in its folds. Take account of the warnings it has given you and do not be seduced or deceived by its allurements. These warnings should desist you from being too greedy or too covetous to possess it. Try, to advance towards the place where you are invited for eternal bliss, and turn your face away from the vicious world."

-Nahjul Balagha, sermon-173.

Therefore, as we can see the reality or the nature of the world in these narrations has been described such as: passage, a house of vanity, and deception etc. The human beings have not been created for this rather for the Hereafter, they have came here to nourish their humanism through knowledge and deeds and to arrange provisions for their eternal journey.

The Next Worlders

Islam requires that people should discover the reality, essence, and nature of this world the way it actually is and, therefore, should adopt their deeds and behavior in accordance to their own perspective. Whoever, has discovered the nature of such a world will never become infatuated or would be loosing his heart for its sake. They will never be deceived by its power of wealth and other allurements.

While living in this very world, and utilizing all of its lawful pleasures and bounties, will never become slaves and prisoners of this vicious world. They will never forget God-Almighty and Hereafter even for a single moment and will endeavor continuously for accumulation of provisions for their eternal journey through performance of virtuous deeds.

While they live in this world but with their esoteric hearts eyes look towards the sublime realities of Upper Heavens. In all situations, at all times, and in all their deeds they do consider the existence of God-Almighty and Hereafter and, therefore, are able to take advantage of these opportunities for enrichment of their eternal life. They regard the world like a form land for cultivating fruits for the Hereafter -a place for conducting business and endeavor to collect provisions for their journey to eternal abode.

They commission all the resources of this transient world to the full advantage of their Hereafter, even their working, eating, drinking, marrying, and other worldly deeds are utilized for the Next World. Such people are not worldly and belong to the Next World. Ibn abi Yafur narrated from Imam al-Sadiq (A) as follows:

"I said to Imam al-Sadiq:

'We like the world.'

'What do you do with its wealth'? Asked the Imam.

"I replied. 'By means of this wealth, we get married, go for Hajj-pilgrimage, take care of genuine family expanses, help our poor brothers and give alms for the sake of God.'

'This is not world, rather it is Hereafter.' Replied the Imam."

-Bihar al-Anwar, vol. 73, p-106.

The Commander of the Faithful Imam' Ali (A) said:

"O creature of God! remember that God fearing and pious persons passed away from this world after having led a respectable and fruitful life , and they are going to be well rewarded in the Next World (when compared with worldly people, they had equal opportunities of gathering fruits of this world and utilize them to the best of their abilities, and at the same time kept away from all wicked and vicious way of life). They did not jeopardize their salvation like worldly minded persons. They led a more contended, more respectable and happier life, than those who lived wickedly.

They enjoyed the fruits of their labors, and had more gratifying, sober and healthy experience of the pleasures of life than the rich and wealthy had. They regaled and enjoined the joys, the facilities and the bliss of this world as much as tyrant and vicious people desired to enjoy.

Yet, while leaving this world, they carried with them all which will be of .use to them in the Next World. While living in this world they enjoyed the, happiness of relinquishing its evil ways. They made themselves sure that in the life to come they will be recipient of His Grace and Blessings, their requests will not be turned down, and the favors destined for them in the Heaven will not be lessened or reduced."

-Nahjul Balagha, letter no.27.

Therefore, working as an employee to earn a living, being involved in trade, business and agriculture, and acceptance of positions involving social responsibilities not only are not the least incompatible of one's being a pious or man of Hereafter, on the contrary these very acts could be utilized as means of achieving God's Pleasure, and accumulation of provisions for the eternal abode.

The Commander of the Faithful Imam 'Ali (A) with all those serious efforts and endeavors for earning a living was the most ascetic person, but simultaneously was the ruler over his people. In the darkness of night he cried at the alter of the worship saying:

"O world, O world! Get away from me. Why do you present yourself to me? Or are you eager for me? You may not get that opportunity to impress me. Deceive some other person. I have no concern with you. I have divorced you thrice, where after there is no restitution. Your life is short, your importance is little, and your liking is humble. Alas! The provision is little, the way is long, the journey is far, and the goal is hard to reach."

-Nahjul Balagha, saying 77.

Also he said:

"Get away from me O world! Your rein is on your own shoulders as I have released myself from your ditches, removed myself of your snares, and avoided walking into your slippery places."

-Nahjul Balagha, letter no.45.

The Commander of the Faithful Imam 'Ali (A) while accompanying his soldiers and marching towards the battle field showed a very old and worn out shoe to Ibne Abbas and said:

"If I cannot establish a regime of justice and truth and if I cannot eradicate tyranny and impiety, than the value of this Government and Caliphate is less to me than the cost of this pair of shoes."

-Nahjul Balagha, sermon-33.

Such were and still are the God's most sincere servants; although, they live in this very world but they look towards the higher horizons and are the people who belong to Hereafter. Like other people they too are engaged in making serious efforts and endeavors for earning a living and sometimes even accept the highest social positions namely: commander, governor and ruler. But they accept these responsibilities solely for the sake of seeking God's Pleasure and fulfillment of their duties.

Within the lawful limits they utilize the God's Bounties, but at the same time have divorced this vicious world for three times and cleaned their hearts from its allurements. They wage war in order to take hold of the ruling power, but only for the sake of defense of truth and implementation of social justice and not simply for the sake of enjoying being a ruler.

The Worldly Beings

But whoever could not identify the world the way it is; become carried away and amused with its adornments; considered it as the main goal of the creation and after that there is no accountability and Hereafter; became prisoner of wealth and property, wife and children, and position and power; took hold of worldly life firm; forgot about the existence of God and Hereafter; closed his eyes from spiritual values and made sole aim of his life satisfying animal passions and taking the maximum advantage from worldly pleasures, then such a person would be considered belonging to the worldly people. Even though he might be a poor, destitute, monastic person, and might refrain from acceptance of positions involving social responsibilities.

The God-Almighty said in Holy Quran.

"They know only some appearance of the life of this world, and are needless of the Hereafter."
 -the Holy Quran (30: 7)

And said:

"Such are those who buy the life of the world at the price of Hereafter."
 -the Holy Quran (2: 86)

And said:

"Take ye the pleasure in the life of the world rather in the Hereafter ? The comfort of the life of the life of the world is but little than in the Hereafter"
 -the Holy Quran (9: 38)

And said:

"Lo! Those who expect not the meeting with Us, but desire the life of this world and feel secure therein, and those who are neglectful of our revelations, there home will be fire because of what they used to earn."
 -the Holy Quran (10: 7-8)

Imam al-Sadiq (A) said:
 "The worst condition for the relationship between man and God-Almighty is the situation, when a person does not have any other aim, except satisfying the hunger of his stomach, and taking care of his sexual requirements."
 -Bihar al-Anwar, vol. 73, p-18.
 The Commander of the Faithful Imam 'Ali (A) said:
 "In a heart infatuated with world, presence of piety is forbidden."
 -Gharar al-Hukm, p-383.

Also he said:

"It is the worst kind of trade, whereby one considers the world worthy of his self; and purchases the world at the expanses of Hereafter."

-Nahjul Balagha, sermon-32.

If, the world has been condemned, it is because of the reason of its being a place of vanity and deceit which makes people its prisoners. It manifests itself sweet and attractive keeping people amused with its pleasure, thus, preventing them from God's remembrance and collection of provisions for their journey towards eternal abode.

The world has been reproached, and this act has been so explicitly publicized so that people become cautious not to be deceived by its deceitful manners, and should not allow themselves to become infatuated with its charms or becoming its prisoners forever. What has been condemned is the attachment to transient world; forgetting the real aim of the creation; becoming totally negligent about the eternal life and not the God's Bounties.

The Worldly and Next Worlders

Therefore, whoever works in this world for Hereafter is a man of Next World, and the one who works for this world will join the worldly group. The Commander of the Faithful Imam Ali (A) said:

"There are two kinds of workers in the world. One is a person who works in this world for this world and his work of this world keeps him unmindful of the Next World. He is afraid of destitution for those he will leave behind but feels himself safe about it. So, he spends his life after the good of others. The other is one who works in this world for what is to come Hereafter, and he secures his share of this world without effort. Thus, he gets both the benefits together and becomes the owner of both the houses together. In this way, he is prestigious before God-Almighty. If he asks him anything He does not deny him."

-Nahjul Balagha, saying 269.

Also, he said :

"This world is a place for transit, not a place to stay. The people herein are of two categories. One is the man who sold away his self (to his passions) and, thus,

ruined it, and the other is the man who purchased his self (by control against his passions) and freed it."

-Nahjul Balagha, saying 133.

The difference between worldly and Next Worlders does not consist in their being rich or poor; occupied in worldly affairs or being without job; being social or living a monastic life; holder of worldly positions or not; being a business man, a religious scholar, preacher and writer; consumer of worldly bounties or otherwise; rather, the real difference consists of ones being attached to the life of this world or the next one; paying attention towards God-Almighty or world; considering the goal of life simply satisfying the animalistic passions or perusal of superior goals of attaining self-perfection and nourishment of human virtues.

Every thing, which keeps a man occupied in itself preventing him from God is remembrance and perusal of affairs related to Hereafter is considered as world. Although, it could be acquiring education, teaching, writing, and being a preacher or Imam. Even living a monastic life, being an ascetic, and being continuously engaged in worship, if is done for the sake of other than God, will be considered as world.

Therefore, it becomes explicitly clear that all the worldly people do not possess the same position; similar is the case with the Next Worlders; some of the worldly people are completely attached to the world and are totally negligent from God and Hereafter -such people are called the servants of world or worldly. Opposite to that, there are pure sincere servants of God-Almighty who are totally committed to Him and Hereafter and do not have any other goal except seeking His Pleasure.

Among these two opposite groups there exist various ranks and posittions. The degree of worldliness of each one depends to the extent of his being attached to the world and is being away from God's Nearness in the same proportion. On the opposite side, as much as one is busy in God's Remembrance and Hereafter, will be considered abandoner of the world in the same proportion, or in other words it could be said, that being worldly or being Next Worlder are two relative acts.

Piety – the Most Important Factor for Purification

In the Islamic School, piety has been assigned the most important position and the pious believers are regarded as the most distinguished and respectable persons in an Islamic Society. The phrase piety in the Quranic verses and narrations, and especially in the glorious book of Nahjul-Balagha (The Path of Eloquence) has been repeated quite frequently. The Holy Quran considers piety as the sole criteria for appraising the value and worth of individuals and said:

> "Lo! the noblest of you, in the sight of God-Almighty is the best in conduct."
> -the Holy Quran (49: 13)

The piety has been introduced as the best provisions for the Hereafter, and greatest means for achieving salvation. the Holy Quran said:

> "For such of them as do right and word off (evil), there is great reward"
> -the Holy Quran (3: 172)

And said:

> "Then whosoever refrainth from evil and amendeth -there shall no fear come upon them neither shall they grieve."
> -the Holy Quran (7: 35)

And said:

> "And vie one with another for forgiveness from your Lord, and for a Paradise as wide as are the Heavens and the earth, prepared for those who ward off (evil)."
> -the Holy Quran (3:133)

And said:

> "Lo! Those who kept their duty dwell in gardens and delight, happy because of what their Lord hath given them."
> -the Holy Quran (52:17-18)

Also, in the Nahjul Balagha and other books of traditions, piety has been assigned the most distinguished position in all ethical matters, and is the greatest means for achieving prosperity and salvation. The Commander of the Faithful Imam' Ali (A) has said:

"Piety acquires the most prominent position in all ethical affairs."
-Nahjul Balagha, saying 41.

The Holy Prophet (S) said:

There is a characteristic that whoever acquires it will have the world and Hereafter in his control. He was asked: 'Oh Prophet of God! What is that characteristic?

"The Prophet (S) replied: 'Piety! Whoever desires to become the most dearest person should become pious, and then he recited the following verse:

And who so ever keepth his duty to God, He will appoint a way out for him.

And will provide for him from (a quarter) whence he hath no expectation." [23]

-Bihar al-Anwar, vol. 70, p-285.

The Commander of the Faithful Imam' Ali (A) has said:

"Know, O' creatures of God, that the God-fearing have Shared the joys of this transient world as well as the Next World, for they shared with the people of this world in their worldly matters while their people did not share with them in the matters of the Next World. They lived in this world in the best manner of living and ate the choicest food and consequently they enjoyed herein all that the people with ease of life enjoyed, and secured from it what the haughty and the vain secured.

Then, they departed from it after taking provision enough to take them to the end of their journey and after doing a profitable transaction. They tasted the pleasure of renouncing the world in this world, and they firmly believed that on the coming day in their next life they would be neighbors of God, where their call would not be repulsed nor would their share of pleasure be small."

-Nahjul Balagha, letter no.27.

The commander of the faithful Imam Ali (A) said:

"Don't give up piety because it is the source of all benevolence and goodness,. blessing except piety does not exist; and the blessing which is achieved by means of piety can never be obtained without it,. be it blessing of this world or the Hereafter."

-Bihar al-Anwar,

vol. 70, p-285.

Imam al-Sajjad:

"The value and worth of each deed depend upon piety; only pious people may achieve righteousness and prosperity. God-Almighty said: Verily righteousness and prosperity belong to pious people."

-Bihar al-Anwar, vol. 77, p-386.

In some of the traditions, piety has been introduced as the most important factor for self-perfection and purification as well as the most effective medicine for curing the psychic diseases. The Commander of the Faithful

---

[23] The Holy Quran (65:2-3)

Imam' Ali (A) said:

"Piety is the only cure for wickedness of your heart. It is the Divine Light to expel darkness of your heart. It is a remedy for your ailing mind. It is the only way of improvement for your corrupt soul. It purifies your conscience. It brings back sight to the eyes blinded by ignorance of truth."
-Nahjul Balagha, letter no.198.

Piety -Objective Behind the Divine Commands

In Islam the piety has been introduced as a genuine moral virtue and the real aim for explanation of (Divine) Commandments. Following are some of the examples God-Almighty said in Holy Quran:

> *"Oh mankind! Worship your Lord, who hath created you and those before you, so that you may ward off (evil)."*
> *-the Holy Quran (2:21)*

And said:

> *"O you believe! Fasting is prescribed for you, even as it was prescribed for those before you, that ye may ward off (evil)."*
> *-the Holy Quran (2:183)*

And said:

> *"Their flesh and their blood reach not God, but the devotion from you reacheth him."*
> *-the Holy Quran (22:37)*

And said:

> *"So make provisions for yourself (Hereafter); for the best provision is to ward off evil."*

-the Holy Quran (2:197)

Therefore, it could be seen that the aim behind explaining some of these commandments or worships is actually to encourage people to ac-quire piety by performing those particular acts of worships. Piety in Islam have been attached so much importance that it has been intro-duced as the sole criteria for the acceptance of other deeds, so much so that the deed without piety shall be worthless and will not be accepted:

The Holy Quran said:

> *"God accepteth only from those who ward off evil."*
> *-the Holy Quran (5:27)*

The Holy Prophet (S) said to Abu Dhar:

"Try your best to acquire piety, because, nothing accompanied by piety shall be regarded smaller, and how come a thing accepted by God-Almighty, could be regarded smaller ? Because, the Holy Qur'an said: God accepts only from pious ones."

-Bihar al-Anwar, vol. 77, p-89.

Imam al Sadiq (A) said:

"Do not let their crying deceive you, because, the piety exists only in heart."

-Bihar al-Anwar, vol. 70, p-286

God-Almighty said in Holy Quran:

> *"But if ye persevere and ward off (evil), then that of the steadfast heart of things."*
> *-the Holy Quran (3:186)*

Therefore, as could be seen that piety in Holy Quran and other Islamic traditions has been mentioned as a genuine moral, virtue, best provisions for the Hereafter, important medicine for curing the heart's disease, and greatest means for attaining spiritual purification and self-refinement. In emphasizing its importance, it is sufficient-to say that it has been mentioned as the real aim behind explanation of all Divine Commandments and Regulations. Now let us discuss its meanings in details.

Definition of Piety

Generally, piety is defined as a negative program i.e. refraining and avoidance from sins and other transgressions. It is interpreted that with being pious, participation in social affairs is very difficult rather impossible. Because, naturally, human-self is inclined towards sinning and in case of acceptance of social responsibilities, one will be forced to indulge into sins. Therefore, either one should acquire piety or must refrain from acceptance of social responsibility.

Or, one must accept social responsibilities and should renounce the piety, because, they are not compatible with each other and their combination is not possible. The inevitable result of such thinking is that –the more one lives an isolated and monastic live the better he will be prepared to acquire piety.

But piety in some Quranic verses, traditions, and in the Nahjul Balagha has been defined as a positive quality and not a negative virtue. Piety, not only means renunciation of sins, rather it consists of possess-ing an internal energy and power of self-restraint, which are achieved because of undertaking continuous rigorous self-discipline, whereby self acquires a super strength, which makes him obedient to God's Commandments. The self acquires such strength that he shows resistance and steadfastness against unlawful whims and passions. Also, the meanings of piety in the dictionary includes the similar aspect.

The phrase piety (*taqwa*) is derived from the Persian word (*waqaya*), which means protection and defense. Piety means self-restraint and self-control which is a positive quality bestowing an immunity upon the pious, and not a negative act or program. It means commitment of a human being to obey the religious commandments. Every act of abstaining from sinning is not called as piety but the power of self-restraint and self-control responsible behind this abstaining is called piety; which has been described as the best provisions of journey for the Hereafter, and naturally making provisions for a journey is a positive act and not a negative one. Here, it would be appropriate to quote few narrations from the Commander of the Faithful Imam 'Ali (A), in this matter, as follows:

"O creatures of the Lord! I advise you to be afraid of Him. I advise you to adopt piety, because, piety is the safest way to salvation and the best support for religion. Keep yourself attached to it and never forsake it. It shall lead you to places of safety, to positions of honor and pursuits bringing you peace and contentment."

-Nahjul Balagha, sermon 195.

And said:

"Piety will act as your shield and defense and in life and Hereafter as your guide to Heaven. Its ways are clear and simple. Those of you who espouse it will be benefited by it. And the one who has imposed it upon you will guard it and will guard you."

-Nahjul Balagha, sermon 191.

And said:

"Know O Creatures of God! That piety is strongly forfeited and a respectable Heaven, and sinful and vicious life is such a undependable refuge that it can neither protect nor guard those who take shelter there. Remember that fear of God can protect one against the evils of sins."

-Nahjul Balagha, sermon 157.

And said:

"Oh people! Piety prevents good people from indulging in sins and vices; it makes them God fearing, it persuades them to spend their nights in His Worship, and to pass their days in fasting."

-Nahjul Balagha, sermon 114.

And said:

"The same piety is shelter for you in this world, and will be a source of prosperity and salvation in the Hereafter."

-Gharar al-Hukm, p-222.

As could be seen that the piety in the above mentioned narrations has been introduced as a positive virtue, a powerful force introducing restrain and immunity and an important preventing factor. It should be compared to a bridle used for training a mulish horse for riding or restraining and controlling the whims and passions of a rebellious-self. It is like a formidable fortress and firm fortification which protect a human being from the devastating attacks of internal enemies i.e. the unlawful selfish whims and passions and Satanic whispers. It is like a shield [24] which protects a crusader in the battlefield from the piercing of poisonous arrows and other Satanic devastating blows.

Piety frees a person from the imprisonment of whims and passions and cuts off the chains of greed, prejudice, lust, and wrath wrapped around his neck. Piety is not a limitation, but on the contrary it bestows the mastership and being in control of one's own-self. It bestows upon a human being prestige, honor, nobility, power, dignity, and steadfastness. It protects the heart from Satanic assaults, thus, making it readied for the descent of God's angels, illuminating him with Divine-Light and bestowing upon him peace and tranquility. Piety for human being is like his home and clothing which protects him from natural calamities, cold and hot temperatures. The God-Almighty, in Holy Quran said:

"But the best raiment is the raiment of righteousness."
-the Holy Quran (7:26)

Therefore, piety is a virtue, excellence, provision for the Hereafter, and is not a negative quality .Of course, in the Holy Quran and in traditions piety has also been used in places of fear and avoidance of sins but these are the requirements of piety -and not piety itself.

---

[24] An impatient (or impious) person could be compared to a soldier in the battlefield, who is fighting virtually naked without armor. Such an ill-equipped soldier is most likely to be killed and disappear from the scene during the very first encounter, with the same analogy a patient (pious) person could be compared to a soldier, who is clad in a coat of mail from head to toe and is fully equipped with all the required armaments. Obviously, to defeat such a well equipped soldier by the enemy is relatively a difficult task.-Discourse of Patience, Ayatullah Khamenei, p-102 {Tr}.

Piety and Seclusion

Therefore, monasticism, and declining acceptance of social responsibilities not only cannot be considered as manifestations of piety, but on the contrary in some cases they are contradictory with righteousness. Islam does not believe in seclusion and monasticism, and in order to refrain from sins, it does not recommend its followers to decline acceptance of social responsibilities and living a secluded life, rather emphasizes them to accept social obligations, while at the same time by means of piety should practice self-restraint and self-control for avoiding sins and deviations.

Islam does not say: don't accept lawful positions of power rather says: do accept them but for the sake of God's Pleasure, serve the people, and don't be a slave of rank and position. Don't allow your position and authority as a mean of accomplishing your sole aim of satisfying selfish whims and passions and don't deviate from the straight path. Islam does not say: in order to acquire piety close your business activities and don't make efforts for earning a living, instead it says: Don't be a slave and prisoner of world. Islam does not say: quite this world and live a monastic life to worship God-Almighty is seclusion, rather it says:

Do live in this world and do your best for its development and progress but don't become worldly or becoming infatuated with its charms -instead, utilize it for attaining higher exalted spiritual stations, and ascension towards God's Nearness. This is what piety is supposed to be in Islamic school, which has been described as one of the most exalted human virtue or characteristic.

Piety and Insight

It may be interpreted from the Quranic verses and traditions that piety bestows upon and human being a sense of profound insight and intelligence enabling him to diagnose, and to follow up his genuine interests of this world and Hereafter. Following is an example:

> "Oh ye who believe! If you keep your duty to God, He will give you discrimination (between right and wrong)."
> -the Holy Quran (8:29)

That is, God-Almighty open his esoteric eyes bestowing upon him a special insight to enable him to diagnose his prosperity, adversity, benefits and losses. In other verse God-Almighty said:

> "Observe your duty to God. God is teaching you and God is knower of all things."
> -the Holy Quran (2:282)

Although, the Holy Quran has been descended from the Heavenly-Kingdom for the common people but especially the pious people receive guidance and advice. It is in this background that the Holy Quran said:

> "This is a declaration for mankind, a guidance and an admonition unto those who ward off evil."
> -the Holy Quran (3:138)

The Commander of faithful Imam Ali (A) has said:
"It is the only way of improvement for your corrupt soul, it purifies your conscience. It brings back sight to the eyes blinded by ignorance of truth."
-Nahjul Balagha, sermon 148.

Imam al-Sadiq (A) quoted a tradition from his father:
"For heart's corruption there is nothing more damaging than sinning, in which case the hearts struggles and offers resistance against sins until it becomes completely subdued by sins becoming an overturned heart."
-Bihar al-Anwar, vol. 70, p-54.

Therefore, it could be inferred from such verses and traditions that piety is responsible for enhancement of reason with insight and brightness as well as strengthening his power of comprehension. The faculty of reason, a precious Celestial Jewel, has been bestowed to enable him to correctly identify and diagnose his gains and losses, prosperity and adversely, welfare and wickedness, and last but not the least do's and don'ts. The Commander of the Faithful Imam Ali (A) has said:

"The reason within human body is like the messenger of God."

-Gharar al-Hukm, vol. 1, p-13.

Such an important mission has been assigned to reason, and it is quite competent to discharge this responsibility, only if, self's whims and passions accept its rule, ,do not oppose, sabotage, and create problems in its administration. Unfortunately, passions are bitter enemy of reason and do not allow it to perform his function in an excellent manner. The Commander of the Faithful Imam 'Ali (A) said:

"Whims and passions of self are the enemies of reason" -Gharar al-Hukm, p-13.

And said:

"Whoever does not have control over his passions will not be the master of his reason."

-Gharar al-Hukm, p-702.

And said:

"Self-conceit and egotism corrupts reason."

And said:

-Gharar al-Hukm p-26.

"An obstinate person does not have correct opinion."

-Gharar al-Hukm, p-31.

It is true that the ruling authority over human body has been assigned to reason (*Aql*) which is quite competent for this job, but self's whims and passions are the biggest obstacles in its path. If, one of the passions or all of them became out of control and revolted against it, than how could the reason will succeed in discharging its function well? Such a person does possess reason but lacks the sense of comprehension and correct diagnosis. He does possess a lamp but the whims, passions, lusts, and wrath like a dark thick cloud have covered it completely, thus, not making him appreciate his welfare and control his rebellious passions.

When could an egotistic person find an opportunity to identity his faults and take the corrective action? Likewise, how could he refrain himself from moral indecencies such as wrath, jealousy, greed, revenge, stubbornness, ambitions for wealth, passion, and power?

If one of them or more succeed in taking over self's control, they will prevent the reason to truly apprehend the realities, and in case it wants to take action against their wishes, they will oppose it by creating troubles and mobilizing their partisans for rebellion, making environment unfavorable for the rule of reason, and ultimately making it helpless to discharge its obligations properly. A person who is a prisoner of his whims and passions could not be benefited by lectures and preaching, rather it produces opposite reaction, thus, increasing his hard-heartedness.

Therefore, piety may be considered as one of the best and most effective factor of insight, enlightenment, and conscientiousness. In the end it must be clarified that when it said that piety is responsible in enhancing the sense of insight -it means the practical aspects of reason, ability to diagnose the duties, or in other words recognize the do's and don'ts. It has nothing to do as for as the theoretical aspects of wisdom are concerned; it is not so that an impious person would not be able to understand mathematical and scientific problems, however piety to a certain extent might be effective in enhancing the power of intelligence and comprehension in these matters.

Piety and Victory over the Difficulties

One of the most important effect of piety is the ability to dominate over the difficulties of day to day life. God-Almighty said in Holy Quran:

> "And whosoever keepeth his duty to God, He will appoint a way out for him, and will provide for him from (a quarter) whence he hath no expectation."
> -the Holy Quran (65:2-3)

And said:

"And whosoever keepeth his duty to God, He maketh his course easy for him."
-the Holy Quran (65:4)

The Commander of the Faithful and Imam' Ali said: "Do you know how piety. helps those who make It the basic : principles of their lives ? It wards off the calamities which have crowded round them and laid siege of them. It converts bitter disappointments of their affairs into pleasant achievements. It acts as a break water against the waves of disasters and destruction which want to dash against lives and ambitions."

-Nahjul Balagha, sermon 198.

Therefore, it can be inferred from the above mentioned verses and traditions that piety helps a person in solving his problems and overpowering the obstacles in his day to day life. Now let us see what influence does piety exert in these matters? The life's hardships can be divided into two categories:

The problems of first category consist of physical-bodily defects, incurable fatal diseases, unpredictable natural disasters, and similar other calamities whose solution and prevention is out of our control. The problems of second category consists of psychological, physical, family, and social problems, where our intentions and decisions could be influential in their solution and even prevention.

Of course, piety could play an important role in offering solutions for each one of the above mentioned problems. Although, in the farmer case, even though prevention may be difficult, and total avoidance might be practically impossible but still the technique of how to encounter these problems is in our control. A self-restraint and pious person who completely dominates over his passions regards this world and its problems as transient and short lived, while considers the Hereafter as real and permanent abode; rests his trusts upon the Supreme and Absolute Power of God-Almighty; treats the hardships and difficulties of this world as insignificant and temporary; does not become desperate and anxious, rather offers his absolute surrender to the Divine Will.

A pious person is familiar as well as confident about God-Almighty and Hereafter; calamities and hardships of day-to-day life do not disturb his state of ease and tranquility, because, hardships, calamities, and tragedies in essence are not painful, rather it is the anxiety and intolerance of self which makes a person uncomfortable, and piety could be helpful for him in such cases.

But most of the severe problems and catastrophes of the second category which make the human life bitter like burning Hell are the result of moral indecencies, self-whims and passions, and domination of Satanic desires. In majority of the cases the family problems are created because of failure on the part of husband, wife, or both of them, in controlling passions, thus, burning and frightening in the fire, which was ignited by their own hands. Similar is the case with other problems.

The moral vices such as jealously, revengefulness, stubbornness, prejudice, egotism, greed, lust, wrath, extravagance, arrogance, and other similar rascalities are responsible for causing problems and hardships for human beings, creating pains and anxiety, and turning the sweetness of life into bitterness. Such a person is a prisoner of his carnal desires and passions to the extent that he is even helpless to identify his disease and its treatment.

The best and most effective thing which could prevent such catastrophies is the same piety, self-restraint or self-control. In the life of a pious such painful horrible catastrophes do not exist at all; with tranquility of heart and enlightenment, he lives a peaceful life as well manages to collect sufficient provisions for Hereafter. The love of world is the roots of all evils but a pious person does not become infatuated with its allurements and charms. The Commander of the Faithful Imam' Ali (A) has said:

"Be careful of world's love because, it is the roots of all sins."
-Gharar al-Hukm, p-150.

Piety and Freedom

It is quite possible that someone may infer that piety deprives freedom and creates limitations making life difficult and unpleasant, but Islam rejects this belief and on the contrary consider piety as the source of freedom, comfort, dignity exaltedness, and regards an impious person simply as a prisoner or slave. The Commander of the Faithful Imam ' Ali

1. has said:

"Verily piety is a key to the doors of righteousness and virtue. It is a provision for the Next World. It is a source of freedom from slavery of evil desires and a wall of protection from every ill-luck and misfortune. It is a refuge for those who try to run away from vice and wickedness and through it a person can achieve his aim."
-Nahjul Balagha, sermon 230.
And said:
"There is no distinction higher than Islam, no honor more honorable than fear of God'; no asylum better than self-restraint."
-Nahjul Balagha, saying 371.

In the above traditions piety has been introduced as the key for solution of problems, bestower of freedom and dignity, rescuer from the waves of disasters and destruction, and as the most formidable shelter for human beings. Therefore, piety does not deprive and create limitations, rather it revives human personality and free a human being from the imprisonment of carnal desires, wraths, revengefulness, selfishness, self-conceit, prejudices, stubbornness, greed, mammonism, egotism, selfishness, ambitiousness, gluttony, and desire for fame and publicity.

It strengthens wisdom and human personality in order to dominate over the passions and rebellious self, adjust them in accordance to genuine requirements, provide leadership to guide them properly preventing extravagance and dissipation of forces. The Holy Quran considers the persons who become prisoners and slaves of their desires, endeavored to satisfy their passions, did not recognize any limits in order to satisfy their carnal desires as idolaters and self-worshipers. The Holy Quran said:

"Hast thou seen him who maketh his desire his god, and God sendeth him astray purposely, and sealeth up his hearing and his heart, and setteth on his sight a covering ? Then who will lead him after God (hath condemned him)? Will you rest them heed?"
   -*the Holy Qu'ran (45:23)*

Yes! The person who has surrendered himself absolutely to his whims and passions, in order to accomplish his passionate desires strives frantically and does not hesitate to indulge into most degrading acts, does not pay attention to the voice of wisdom and guidance of prophets, such a person is indeed is a slave and prisoner of his self. His passions have completely dominated and imprisoned his human personality and the precious jewel of wisdom, and in order to rescue them there is no other alternative except piety. Therefore, piety does not create limitations rather blesses human beings with freedom.

Piety and Treatment of Diseases

It was earlier prove that moral abjectnesses such as: jealousy, hatred, revenge, fault-finding, wrath, prejudice, greed, egotism, arrogance, fear , indecisiveness, temptation, and similar other things are psychological diseases. The hearts of such people are indeed sick. Also, it has been confirmed that between the man and his self not only there exists a firm connection rather they are united, and because of this connection and communication they exert an influence upon each and other.

Physical sicknesses make the self-disturbed and uncomfortable, and similarly opposite to that psychological diseases effect human body and nerves. In majority of cases the psychological diseases and nervous disorders are the result of moral abjectness. Even some of the bodily diseases like ulcer and swelling of intestine, indigestion, acidity, headache, and stomachache are more likely the result of moral abjectness such as; jealously, hatred, greed, egotism, and ambitiousness.

It is has been proved beyond doubt that excessive indulgence into sexual activities results in dangerous fatal bodily diseases such as AIDS etc. Therefore, as was mentioned earlier the sole curing medicine for such psychological diseases is piety. It could be said that piety plays the most effective role as far as the treatment of psychological and physical diseases, hygiene, and fitness of human beings are concerned. The Commander of the Faithful Imam ' Ali (A) has said:

"Certainly piety is the medicine /or your hearts, sight for the blindness of your spirits, the cure /or the ailments o/your bodies, the rectifier o/ the evils of your breasts, the purifier of the pollution of your minds, the light of the darkness of your eyes, the consolation for the fear of your heart, and the brightness for the gloom of your ignorance."

-Nahjul Balagha, sermon 198.

The Characteristics of Pious (Sermon of Hammam)

In order to appreciate the attributes of piety and to understand its profundities in detail, let us quote here the famous sermon of Hammam from the Nahjul-Balagha explaining the qualities of pious and God-fearing persons. In this sermon the Commander of the Faithful Imam' Ali (A) has explained what piety really means and what sort of human beings pious people are, describing the graphic details of their ways of living, thinking, praying, and dealing with other men.

Hammam was one of the companions of Imam' Ali (A), a very pious and God fearing man. He once asked Imam to explain at length the qualities of pious person. He wanted the explanation to be so graphic and so vivid that he could get the picture of a pious man in his mind's eyes. Imam knew that Hammam had a very tender heart and was disinclined to explain piety in the way that Hammam had requested and evading the subject he replied.

"Hammam! Fear God and do good deeds. Remember that God is always a companion of pious and good people!" But Hammam was not satisfied with this reply and wanted to say something more. He pressed so much and others joined him and seconded his request that Imam reluctantly delivered the following sermon. After praising the Lord and praying Him to bless the Holy Prophet (A) Imam thus, continued the sermon as follows:

"When God created mankind He was not in need of their obedience and prayers, neither was He nervous of their disobedience. Because, disobedience or in-subordination of men cannot harm Him, similar obedience of obedient people cannot do Him any good. He is beyond the reach of harm and benefit. After creating man He decided for hi the variety of food which his body could absorb and assimilate, and the places which were congenial for him to live and to propagate.

Among these human beings excellent are those who are pious and who fear God."

"They possess preeminence and excellence because they always speak truth-fully, rightly and to the point, their way of living is based upon moderation, and their mode of dealing with other men is founded on their good will, fellow feeling and courtesy towards them. They deny themselves the things prohibited by God. They concentrate their minds upon knowledge of things which will bring them eternal bliss. They bear hardships and sufferings as happily as they enjoy comforts and pleasures. If God had not fixed the span of life for each one of them, their souls in desire of attaining His Heaven and out of fear of falling into His displeasure, would not have stayed in their bodies for long."

"They have visualized mentally the glory of God in such a way that beyond him nothing in this world alarms, frightens or awes them. Everything other than His might appears to them as insignificant and humble. They believe in the Heaven and its blessings like a person who has been there and has actually seen everything of the Heaven with his own eyes. Similarly, their faith in the Hell and its torments is as strong as that of a person who had passed through its sufferings. They feel that the tortures of the Hell are around them and very near to them."

"The ways of worldly people make them sorry. They harm nobody. They do not indulge in excessive eating and pleasure seeking. Their wants are limited. Their wishes are few. They have accepted patiently sufferings and adversities in this mortal and transitory life for the sake of eternal bliss which by the grace of God proved for them a very profitable transaction. The vicious world desired their fellowship but they turned their faces away from it. It wanted to snare them, but they willingly accepted every trouble and discomfort to free them-selves from its clutches."

"Their nights they spend in carefully studying the Quran, because, of their weaknesses and short-comings, and try to find ways from this Holy book for improvements of their minds. In the study of the Quran when they came across a passage describing the Heaven they feel highly attracted towards it and develop such a keen desire to reach it; that the Heaven with all its blessings is visualized by their minds, while a passage about the Hell frightens them and makes them feel as if they are seeing and hearing the raging fire and the groans and lamentations of those who are suffering the tortures of the Hell."

"Nights they spend in praying before the Lord and requesting and beseeching Him to deliver them from the Hell. Days find them occupied with such works that clearly indicate their wisdom, depth of knowledge, virtuousness, and piety. Constant fasting, simple diet: avoidance of every aspect of luxury and regular hard work make them look lean and haggard, but they possess very sound and robust health. When people hear them discussing various problems of life they often take them to be whimsical fanatic or even half-witted. But it is not so, they are not satisfied with the quality and quantity of the work done by them in the cause of religion and humanity .The more they work the less they feel satisfied. Having set up a very high standard of efficiency for their work they fell nervous that indolence may not make it impossible for them to attain those heights."

"If anyone of them is praised for piety, virtuousness and the good deeds done by him, he does not like to be so complimented; he is afraid that such praise may not allure him towards vanity, self flattery, and self glorification. He says, I know my mind and my work more than others, and God knows much more than me. O Lord! Please do not hold me responsible for what they have said about me. You know very well that I did not instigate them for such praises. Please Lord! Grant me excellence far greater than what they complimented me for. And Lord! Please forgive those of my sins short-comings which they do not know."

"You will find every pious person possessing the following attributes. He is resolute though tender-hearted and kind. He is unwavering in his convictions and beliefs. He is thirsty for knowledge. He forgives those who harmed him, fully knowing that they have wronged him. Even when owning wealth his ways of life are based upon moderation. His prayers are models of humility and submissiveness to God. Even when starving he will maintain his self-respect. He will bear sufferings patiently."

"He will resort only to honest means of living. Leading others towards truth and justice, will give him pleasure. He disdains avarice and greed. Though he does good deeds all the time, yet he feels nervous of his short-comings. Every night, he thanks God for having passed one more day under His Grace and Mercy. Every morning finds him starting the day with the prayers of the Lord. Of nights he is cautious that he may not carelessly waste those hours in comfort and ease. He starts his days happy with the thought the Lord has given him another day to do his duty."

"If his mind wishes for something unholy and impious he refuses to obey its dictates. He desires to achieve eternal bliss. Worldly pleasures do not interest him. His wisdom is mixed with patience. His deeds reciprocate his words (he does what he says). Inordinate desires do not trouble him. He has few defects in him. He is courteous to others. He possesses a contended mind. He eats little, he does not harm anybody. He is easy to be pleased. He is strong in his faith. His passions are dead. His temper is controlled."

"People expect good out of him and consider themselves immune from his harm. Even if he is found among godless people his name will be written in the list of Godly persons. If he is in company of those who always remember God, naturally his name will not be included amongst those who forget Him. He forgives those who harm him. He helps those who have forsaken him and have refused to help him. He is kind to those who have been cruel to him. He does good to those who do evil to him. He never indulges in loose talks. He has no vice in him, and his good qualities are outstanding, noticeable, and prominent, when facing dangers and disasters he is calm and undisturbed. In sufferings and calamities he is patient and hopeful. In prosperity he is thankful to God. He would not harm his worst enemy. He will never commit a sin even for the sake of his best friend."

"Before anybody has to bear testimony to his fault he accepts and owns it. He never misappropriates anything entrusted to him. He never forgets what he has been told. He does not slander anybody. He does not harm his neighbors. When misfortunes befall any person he does not blame him, neither is he happy at the losses of others. He neither goes astray from the right path nor follows a wrong one. His silence does not indicate,. his moroseness nor his laughters are loud and boisterous. He bears persecution patiently and God punishes his oppressor. He is hard to himself and very lenient to others. He bears hardships in this life to attain eternal comfort and peace. He never wrongs a fellow being. If he avoids anybody it is to retain his piety and uprightness. If he forms contract with anybody it is on account of his kindness and clemency. He does not avoid anybody because of his pride and vanity, and he does not mix with others with ulterior motives of hypocrisy, pretense, and vile."

-Nahjul Balagha, sermon 193.

"The narrator says that Hammam was hearing the sermon very attentively when Imam reached the above passage, Hammam fainted and died it during the faint. Seeing this Imam said: "By God, I was hesitating to all this to Hammam because of this very reason. Effective advises on minds ready to receive them often bring almost similar result".

Supervision – the Most Important Factor for Self-restraint

One of the most important factors for self building and self-refinement is guarding, supervising, and paying attention towards the self. A wise person who is concerned about his well-being and prosperity would not remain ignorant about his own moral abjectness and psychological disease rather he would be continuously guarding and supervising his self and would be strictly controlling his habits, etiquettes, actions, deeds, and even thoughts. We would discuss this matter in details as follows:

Recordings of Deeds

The Qur'anic verses and traditions from the Holy Prophet (S) and his Ahlul Bayt (A) indicate that all actions, deeds, sayings, even breathings, intentions, and thoughts of human beings are recorded in his letter of deeds, will remain filed for the Day of Resurrection, and each person will be judged on that Day strictly in accordance to his performance. For example: God-Almighty said in Holy Quran:

"That day mankind will issue forth in scattered groups to be

shown their deeds. And whoso dath good an atom's weight will see it then. And whoso doth ill on atoms weight will see it then."
   -the Holy Quran (99: 6-8)

And said:

"And the book is placed, and thou seest the guilty fearful of that which is therein and they say: What kind of a book is this that leaveth not a small thing nor a great thing but hath counted it! And they find all that they did confronting them, and Lord wrongeth no one."
   -the Holy Quran (18: 49)

And said:

"On the Day when every soul will find itself confronted with all that hath done of good and all that it hath done of evil (every soul) will long that there might be a mighty space of distance between it and that evil."
   -the Holy Quran (3:30)

And said:

"He uttereth no word but there is with him on observer ready."
   -the Holy Quran (50:18)

Therefore, if we believe that all our movements, actions, deeds, sayings, and even thoughts are being registered, recorded, and saved then how could we remain naive about the consequences arising therein?

Accounting on the Judgment Day

A lot of Qur'anic verses and traditions confirm that human beings will be accounted for their deeds accurately on the Day of Resurrection. All their deeds whether small a big shall be checked and even the most insignificant action shall not be neglected. e.g. God-Almighty said in the Holy Quran:

> *"And we set a just balance for the Day of Resurrection so that no soul is wronged in aught. Though it be of the weight of a grain of mustard seed, We will bring it. And We suffice for reckoners."*
> *-the Holy Quran (21: 47)*

And said:

> *"And whether ye make known what is in your minds or hide it, God will bring you to account for it."*
> *-the Holy Quran (2:284)*

And said:

> *"The weighing on that day is the true (weighing). As for as those whose scale is heavy, they are the successful. And as for as those whose scale is light: Those are they who lose their souls because they disbelieved Our revelations."*
> *-the Holy Quran (7: 8-9)*

The Holy Quran describes the Day of Resurrection as the Day of Auditing and the God-Almighty as the one who audits promptly. According to lots of Qur'anic verses and traditions one of the most difficult stage, through which we all have to pass over on the Day of Resurrection–is the stage of auditing of deeds. During our entire span of life we perform various deeds which are forgotten by us after a while, but they are registered and recorded in our letter of deeds by God-Almighty, in a manner that not even the smallest or insignificant action is removed from the letter of deeds.

All of them are registered and recorded right here in this world and will remain with the human being forever, although he might be ignorant of them completely in this world, but after death when his esoteric eyes will be opened, he will see them all intact written in a single file.

Then he will realize that all the actions, deeds, beliefs, and thoughts written over there are indeed belong to him and henceforth shall never be separated from him. The God-Almighty said in Holy Quran:

> *"And every soul cometh, along with it a driver and a witness, (and unto the evil-doer it is said): Thou wast in heedlessness of this. Now We have removed from thee thy covering, and piercing is thy sight this day."*
> *-the Holy Quran (50: 21:22)*

The Holy Prophet (S) had said:

"On the Day of Judgment, each servant of God will not be able to move forward even a single step without being questioned about the following :

How he spent his life ? How he spent his youth ? Through what means he earned the money and how was it spent ? And about the friendship of us (Ahlul Bayt)."
-Bihar al-Anwar, vol. 7, p-258.

In another narration the Prophet (S) said:

"One of the Day of Judgment when a servant of God is being readied for accounting, for each day of his living in the world, twenty four treasure boxes (each one representing an hour) are brought in front of him. Then they open a treasure box which is full of light and joy, whereby seeing it the servant of God becomes so happy that if his happiness is distributed among all the dwellers of Hell, they will forget the pain and torture of Hell's fire -this treasure box represent the hour when he was busy in God's Worship."

"After that another treasure box is opened which is frightening, dark and full of odor, whereby upon seeing it he becomes so frightened and sad that if his grief is distributed among the dwellers of Paradise, all of the blessings of Paradise will become unpleasant for them -this treasure box represents the hour when he was

busy in sinning."

"Then another treasure box is opened before him which is completely empty and neither contains deeds producing joy nor deeds producing sadness -this treasure box represents the period when he was either sleeping or was busy performing allowable religious acts (Mubah) (which may or may not have been performed). But having seen this empty treasurer a servant of God feels sorry because he could have utilized this hour for doing righteous and good deeds. It is because of this reason that the Day of Judgment has been named by God-Almighty as the Day of Regret."

-the Bihar al-Anwar vol. 7 p-262.

On the Day of Judgment the accounts of our deeds will be audited swiftly and most accurately determining the final destinies accordingly; all the past deeds shall be scrutinized; human limbs and bodily members, prophets, angels, and even earth will offer their testimonies; it will be real tough scrutiny indeed, and will determine one's eternal destination. Because, of the anxiety of result the hearts palpitate and bodies tremble in fear -a fear so horrible and frightening that mothers will ignore the breast feeding of their babies and pregnant women will loose their conception by miscarriages.

All are anxious and worried to learn about their ultimate consequences. Is the result of their scrutiny would be God's pleasure, securing a draft for freedom, being honorable among God's prophets and saints, eternal living in Paradise in the company of God's most favorite and descent servants? Or, would it be wrath of God, humiliation and disgrace before other creatures and eternal living in the Hell?

Therefore, from the above narrations it could be concluded that scrutiny of people's deed is not same and differs; for some of them it would be extremely complicated and lengthy while for others it would be swift and easy. It would be done at various stops several times and at each station some of the questions would be asked. The most horrible and difficult station is the stop for oppressors, where the question are asked regarding trampling of human rights, oppressions and tyrannies.

Here the accounts must be settled completely and everybody should pay his debt to the creditors. Unfortunately, over there, no one possesses ready cash to pay for his debt and therefore, he has no choice except to pay from the account of his righteous deeds. If, he had some in his account, he may exchange them for clearing his debt. If, he does not possess righteous deeds in his account then in that case, the creditor's sins are transferred into the balance sheet of his deeds.

Any way, it is a horrible and tough day indeed, and may God helps all of us. Of course, the length and toughness of scrutiny is not same for all and differ in accordance to the magnitude of good and evil deeds, but for the pious and God's descent servants it would be extremely swift and easier. In replying to a question regarding the length of Day of Judgment the Holy Prophet (S) said:

"By God! For believers it would be so swift and easy -even easier than recital of an obligatory prayer."

-Majma al-Dawaid, vol. 1, p-337.

Self-scrutiny Before the Judgment Day

Someone who believes in Day of Judgment, scrutiny of deeds, rewards and punishment, knows that all the deeds are registered and recorded, and verdict would be issued either good and bad; than how could such a person would remain naive about his deeds, actions, moral etiquettes, and thoughts? Wouldn't he really care about what has been done by him during the days, months, years, and entire span of his life? And what provisions have been forwarded by him for the Hereafter?

One of the precondition of belief is that it demands from believers to scrutinize their accounts of deeds in this same world, must ponder profoundly about what they have done in the past, and what is being done right now? Acting in a manner like a wise businessman, who cheeks his accounts each day and each month, in order to determine his profits and losses. The Commander of the Faithful Imam' Ali (A) had said:

"Before being audited on the Judgment Day better self-scrutinize your deeds in this same world."

-Gharar al-Hukm, p-385.

Also said:

"Whoever scrutinizes the account of his self in this world would earn profit."

-Gharar al-Hukm, p-618.

Imam al-Naqi (A) [25] said:

"Whoever does not scrutinize his actions daily does not belong to us; then if, he found that he has performed some righteous deeds, he should request God-Almighty to increase His Grace, and in case if he has done an evil act, he should seek pardon from God-Almighty by offering repentance."

-Wasail al-Shi'a, vol. 11, p-377.

The Commander of the Faithful Imam 'Ali (A) has said:

"Whoever scrutinize the account of his self will earn a profit and whoever will be negligent will suffer a loss, whoever is fearful in this world will be safe in the Hereafter, whoever will pay heed to counseling will see the realities; whoever is able to see the realities would understand; and whoever understands would be-come wise and intelligent."

-Wasail al-Shi'a, vol. 11 p-379.

The Holy Prophet (S) said to Abu Dhar:

"Oh Abu Dhar! Before they scrutinize your account of deeds on the Judgment Day, do your own self-auditing in this world because today's review would be

---

[25] Imam al-Naqi (A): The Tenth Imam' Ali ibn Muhammad al-Naqi

(A) son of Imam Muhammad al-Taqi was born on Friday 2nd Rajab 212 A.H. in Suryah in the vicinity of Medina. He was only six years old when his father Imam al-Taqi was poisoned by Abbasid Caliph al-Mu'tasim. The Holy Imam devoted himself to the sacred mission of preaching in Medina and did, thus, earn the faith of people as well as their allegiance and recognition of his great knowledge and attributes. This reputation of

the Imam evoked the jealousy and malice of Abbasid Caliph al-Mut-awakkil against him.

Al-Mutawakkil imprisoned Imam under his strict vigilance for a number of years during which he was subjected to severe tortures. But even in this miserable imprisonment, the Imam kept devoting himself at all times to worship God-Almighty. The watchman of the prison used to comment that Imam al-Naqi seemed to be an angel in human grab. He was poisoned by Abbasid Caliph al-Mut'azz billah on 26 Jumada'th-thaniyah 254 AH. The Imam was only forty two years old at the time of his martyrdom. The period of his Imamat was thirty five years. He was buried in Samarra in Iraq.

lot more easier than tomorrow's auditing on the Judgment Day, try to attain self-purification in this world instead of his being cleaned on Judgment Day -The Day when the deeds will be presented to God-Almighty and even the smallest deeds will not be hidden from him. Then the Holy Prophet (S) continued:

"O Abu Dhar! One never acquires piety unless until he self-scrutinize his own deeds -a scrutiny much more severe than the auditing of accounts between two business associates. A man must ponder seriously as through what means has he acquired his means of living ? Were it earned through lawful means or through forbidden means ?

"O Abu Dhar! Whoever does not respect the Divine limitations for earning a living, God-Almighty too would not have slight hesitation in dispatching him inside the Hell's fire through either passage." -Wasail al-Shi'a, vol. 11, p-379.

Imam al-Sajjad (A) said:

"O son of Adam! You will be continuously accompanied by goodness and blessing so for as you possess a preacher in your heart, practice self-scrutiny for your deeds and fear God-Almighty."

"O son of Adam! verily you will die, will be raised on the Resurrection-Day, and your deeds will be judged in accordance with Divine-Justice. Therefore, get yourself readied for getting scrutinized for your deeds on the Judgment Day."

-Wasail al-Shi'a, vol. 1, p-378.

A man is like an investor in this world, his limited capital –life span -consists of these very hours, days, weeks, months, and years. This most precious capital i.e. one's life span, either willingly or unwillingly gets consumed and eventually one approaches death. The youth turns into old age, strength gives up to weakness and sound health changes into sickness. If, against this spending of capital one has performed righteous deeds and forwarded some provisions for Hereafter, then in that case he has not suffered a loss, because he had secured for himself a happy and prosperous future.

But if he wasted his precious capital consisting his life, youth, strength and physical fitness, and against all this spending no righteous deed was deposited for his Hereafter; instead, with moral abjectness, and indulgence into sins and transgressions, made his heart dark and contaminated, then he has inflicted upon himself -the most severe damage and loss, which could never be compensated. God-Almighty said in the Holy Quran:

> *"By the declining day; lo! Man is a state of loss, save those who believe and do good works, and exhort one another to truth, exhort one another to endurance"*
> -the Holy Quran (103:1-3)

The Commander of the Faithful Imam' Ali (A) said:
"A wise man is the one who is all anxious today about his tomorrow -the Resurrection Day, must strive for achieving freedom of self; Because, of the realities of death and Resurrection Day, he has no choice except to perform righteous deeds."
-Gharar al-Hukm, p-238.

Also said:
"Whoever scrutinizes his deeds will discover his faults and sins. Then, he will offer repentance for his sins and will strive for correcting his faults "
-Gharar al-Hukm, p-696.

How to Scrutinize?

Supervision and management of self is not an easy task and requires determination, maturity, sincerity, efforts, endeavors, and specific program. Will the imperious-self offer surrender so easily? Will he present himself for cross-examination and verdict? Will he agree to pay his dues so easily? The Commander of the Faithful Imam' Ali (A) said:
"Whoever has not programmed his self for performance of righteous deeds has indeed wasted him."
-Gharar al-Hukm, p-640.

And said:
"Whoever is not careful of self's frauds and cheating will be destroyed (by self)"
-Gharar al-Hukm, p-685.

And said:

"Whoever possesses self-awakening and self-enlightenment, God-Almighty will assign Divine angels for his guidance and protection."
-Gharar al-Hukm, p-679.
And said:
"Subdue your self through continuous struggle and resistance, and firmly take over his control."
-Gharar al-Hukm, p-131.

The self-accounting must be accomplished in three steps in order to acquire this habit gradually:

1. **Making Commitments (*Mosharateh*)**

The self-accounting should be started as follows:
As the early hour of the day before starting daily routine activities some time must be allocated for this purpose. For example, after offering morning prayer one may sit alone in an isolated place and should address to his self in the following manner:

Right now, I am alive but don't know how long it may last, may be for next one hour or may be little bit more. The time of life already spent has all been wasted, and the remaining time left might be counted as capital still at my disposal. For each hour spent out of this remaining life, I could arrange some provisions for the Hereafter. If right now the Israel -the angel of death would have arrived for receiving my soul I would have desired for living one more day or even one extra hour.

Oh helpless poor self! Just imagine that you are in such a condition and your desire for this living a little longer has been granted and you have been allowed to return to this world. Oh self! Be kind to me as well as to yourself and don't waste these precious hours for indulgence into nonsense amusements. Don't be negligent now, otherwise you will be ashamed tomorrow on the Judgment Day -the Day when being regretful will not be of any help. Oh self! For each hour spent during this life God-Almighty has created a treasure box in which good and evil deeds will be deposited, to be opened on the Judgment Day. Oh self! Try to fill this treasure with righteous deeds. Be careful not to fill this treasure with sins and transgressions.

Likewise, all the parts of the body should be addressed individually to comment themselves not to commit sins. For example, the tongue should be asked that lying, backbiting, tellbearing, fault finding, abusing, babbling, insulting, self-praising, disputing, and false testimony are moral abjectness and divinely forbidden, which destroy eternal life of human beings. Therefore, I will not allow it to indulge in these acts. Oh tongue! Be kind to me and yourself and don't commit immoral acts because everything said will be taped and deposited into the treasure box containing the deeds and I will be accountable on the Day of Judgment.

In this manner the tongue should be required to commit itself not to indulge into sinning. After that the righteous deeds which could be performed by it should be reminded and their performance should be made obligatory during each day. For example, it could be said to the tongue: you may recite such and such invocation (*dhikr*), such and such supplication, may fill up the treasure box of deeds with joy and illumination and may receive a good result in the Hereafter. Therefore, don't be negligent otherwise you will feel terribly sorry later on. Similarly, all other parts of the body should be required to commit themselves to perform only righteous deeds and to strictly guard them against sins and transgressions.

Imam al-Sadiq (A) narrated a tradition from his father as follows:

"When night approaches it makes an announcement which is heard by all the creation except human being and jins as follows:

Oh sons of Adams! I am a new creation and will testify about all the, deeds performed during my tenure. Utilize my existence to the best of your advantage, because, after the sunrise you will never see me again. After that you would not be able to increase your righteous deeds and offer repentance for your sins and transgressions. After the night departs each coming day repeats the same announcement."

-Wasail al-Shi'a, vol. 11, p-380.

It is quite possible that Satan and imperious-self may tell us: You cannot live a life with such program. Is it possible to live a life with such limitations and restrictions? How could you allocate a certain hour for auditing program every day? With these whispers the Satan and imperious-self want to deceive, thus, preventing us from taking the important decision. We must offer resistance against these Satanic plots and must neutralize them by telling them:

This program is absolutely feasible and does not have any contradiction with life's daily routine activities, and since it is necessary for attaining self-refinement and self-purification as well as for accomplish-ing the eternal salvation, I must undertake this program. It is not so difficult either, and once you have decided firmly it would become easier. Even if it is a little bit difficult in the beginning, would become easier gradually.

1. **Supervision and Control (*Moraqebat*)**

After passing through the stage of making commitments we enter into the stage of contact execution. At this stage all the self's actions should strictly be monitored all along the day to be sure that they are being performed in accordance to commitments made earlier. A human being should remain awake in all situations and should strictly guard his actions. He should remind himself continuously: that God-Almighty watches all our actions, and must remember the commitments made earlier. Even, a slight negligence might provide opportunity for Satan and imperious-self to make their entry and, thus, disrupting the entire program.

The Commander of the Faithful Imam' Ali (A) said:

"A wise man offers continuous resistance against the self, endeavors for self's correction, preventing him following passions and in this manner makes him subdued. A wise man with absolute domination over the self will dejected from the world and its allurements."

-Gharar al-Hukm, p-237

And said:

"Whoever possesses a guard to reprimand, with m his self;. God-Almighty, will appoint for him Divine Protectors."

-Gharar al-Hukm, p-698.

And said:

"Being optimistic and confident about self provides the best opportunities for Satan to deceive us."

-Gharar al-Hukm, p-54

A cautious and aware human being is continuously occupied in God is Remembrance and sees him in His presence. He does not perform any task hastily without profound thinking and appraising all the consequences. If he commits a sin or transgression, immediately reminds himself about God-Almighty and Judgment Day and refrains from its continuation. Does not forget his earlier commitments and in this manner keeps the self continuously subdued, preventing him from indulgence into evil and obscene deeds. This program is one of the best means for attaining self-refinement and purification.

In addition to that a cautious believer thinks continuously about obligatory and recommended deeds, fulfillment of duties, righteous deeds, and charity through out the day; try his best to offer daily prayer on preferred time with humility, devotion, and presence of mind, offering in a manner as though this would be the last prayer of his life; keeps himself occupied with remembrance of God-Almighty in all situations and involvement.

Does not spent his free time in nonsense amusements, instead utilize it to the maximum advantages of affairs related to Hereafter; knows the importance and preciousness of time and endeavors seriously for utilization of every available opportunity for achieving self-perfection; strives to perform recommended deeds (*Mustahabbat*) as much as his capacity permits. How good it is that a believer should try to become habitual of performing at least some of the recommended deeds. Remembrance of God-Almighty and recital of invocation (*dhikr*) is one such recommended deed which could be done easily in all circumstances.

Also, it is important that a believer with sincerity and pure intention of God's Nearness (*Qurbat*), should direct all his daily activities for worship, spiritual migration and ascend towards God is Countenance. Even, working, eating, drinking, sleeping, marrying, and all other lawful desired acts through sincerity and pure intention could be made as part of worshiping. Work and business if done with the intention of earning a lawful genuine living and serving the people would became an act of worship. Similarly, eating, drinking and resting if are preliminaries for living and being a devoted servant of God are considered as worship. That is the way God's pure servant used to live and they still live in this manner.

Accounting of Deeds

The third stage is the accounting of deeds performed every day. It is necessary that a person should fixed a certain hour to scrutinize his deeds and the most suitable time would be the hour when he has finished all his daily activities. At this time he should sit alone in a corner and should think what he has done during this stay. He should begin from the very first hour till the last hour of the day checking every minor activity accurately. If he finds that he has performed a righteous deeds and worship at that time he should thank God-Almighty for bestowing his Divine grace and should decide for its continuation. But if finds that he has committed a sin or transgression he must show his wrath against the self addressing him: Oh you wretched self! Look what have you done? You destroyed my letter of deed and made it totally dark. What will be your reply to God-Almighty on the Day of Judgment? What are you going to do with the painful punishment of Hell? God-Almighty bestowed upon you life, health, and resources in order to enable you to collect provisions for Hereafter, instead you blackened your letter of deeds with sins. Why don't you consider the probability of death approaching you at this very moment? In that case, what are you going to do? Oh shameless self! How come you are not ashamed from God-Almighty? Oh you liar and wretched hypocrite! You claim to be a believer in the existence of God-Almighty and Hereafter then how come your actions reflect contradictions with your belief?

Then, he should repent sincerely and should decide firmly never to indulge into sins and transgressions as well as to compensate for his past omissions. The Commander of the Faithful Imam 'Ali (A) said:

"Whoever would reprimand self for his faults and sins-would be able to restrain

himself from indulgence into sins."

-Gharar al Hukm, p-696.

If he realizes that the self is showing rebellious tendencies and is not ready for repentance and abstinence from sinning, then he must take a firm stand against the imperious-self through offering resistance. He may threaten the self that serious consequences will arise in case he continued to show disobedience. For example, if the self has consumed the forbidden (*haram*) an unlawful food, or has committed other sins then to punish him will donate some money for charity for God's pleasure, will do fasting few days, temporarily will refrain himself from eating delicious foods or cold water, or other food which is self's favorite, or will stay out side under the burning sun for a certain period.

Any way, one should not show weakness and negligence against the self or otherwise he will take the upper hand eventually throwing a human being into the darkest and deepest valleys of deviations and misfortune. But if you acted strongly offering stiff resistance against him, he will become subdued.

If he finds that at a particular hour he has neither performed any righteous deed nor has committed any sin even in that case he should show his anger and reprimand the self that how come this particular hour which was the precious capital of the life has been wasted for nothing? You could have performed righteous deeds in this period and could have deposited it in the accounts of your deeds for the Hereafter. Oh you wretched looser! Why have you wasted this valuable precious opportunity? You will certainly feel sorry for your this negligence on the Day of Judgment -a Day when regret will not be of any use. In this manner, acting like a strict business associate all the daily transactions of the self should be scrutinized strictly. Of course, it would be better if the result of this scrutiny could be recorded in a notebook.

Anyway, the matter of supervision and scrutiny for attaining self-purification and refinement is an important, useful thing that is absolutely necessary; whoever is serious, and who is serious and aspires for his salvation and prosperity, should pay special attention to it. Although, in the beginning it might appear as a difficult task but with firm determination and perseverance it would become easy and imperious-self would become subdued surrendering completely to your supervision and domination. The Holy Prophet (S) once asked his companions: *"Shouldn't I inform you about the most intelligent person among the intelligent and the most stupid one among the stupid ?*

"They replied: 'Oh Prophet of God please tell us.'

'The most intelligent person is the one who is audits his self's account and performs righteous deeds for his life after death, and the most stupid person is the one who is a prisoner of self's whims and passions and keeps himself amused with long term desires! Replied the Holy Prophet (S).

"He was asked: 'Oh Prophet of God! How the account of self should be audited ? ' The Prophet (S) replied:

'When the day has finished entering into night the!' communicate with your self as follows:

"Oh self! This day too is passed and will never return, God-Almighty is going to ask you about it as how did you spend it and what deeds were performed? Did you remember and praise him? Did you discharge your due obligations as regards to the rights of a brother believer? Did you remove the sorrow from his heart ? Did you take care about his children and family in his absence? Did you pay his due share to his offspring after his death ? Did you help a fellow Muslim ? What have you done during this day ?

"Therefore, remind it to your self one by one whatever you have done, and if you find that you have done some righteous deed then thanks God-Almighty for

bestowing His grace, but if you find that you have committed a sin then immediately offer repentance and decide firmly never to commit any sin again. Through recital of salutation. (Salawat)upon the Holy Prophet (S) and his Holy Progeny

1. purify your self from impurities andcontamination.

"Take the oath of allegiance for the friendship of the Commander of the Faith-ful Imam' Ali (A) and should imprecate his enemies: If one acted in this manner the God-Almighty would tell him: ' I am not going to have any controversy with you at the time of auditing your account of your deeds on the Day of Judgment, because, you were friend with my favorite saints and showed enmity towards their enemies."

-Bihar al-Anwar, vol. 70, p-69.

Imam al-Kazim (A) said:

"Whosoever does not scrutinize the account of the self does not belong to us; thus, if he has done some good deeds should request God-Almighty for increasing His Favor and if he has sinned should offer repentance."

-al Kafi, vol. 1, p-453.

The Holy Prophet (S) said to Abu Dhar:

"A wise person should distribute his hours as follows: One hour should be assigned for being occupied in Prayers, supplications, and hymns with God-Almighty. One hour should be allocated for auditing the account of self's deeds. And one hour should be reserved for pondering the Divine Blessings bestowed upon him."

-Bihar al-Anwar, vol. 70, p-64.

The Commander of the Faithful Imam 'Ali (A) said:

"Let the self be accountable for his deeds, should be demanded to discharge his due obligations by utilizing this transient world properly. You should collect provisions for the Hereafter and make yourself readied for that journey before being forced to be transferred."

-Gharar al-Hukm, p-385.

Also, said:

"How much is it necessary for a person to allocate a free time for himself to scrutinize the account of his deeds, and see what kind of good and useful, or bad and harmful deeds, have been performed by him during the past twenty four hours."

-Gharar al-Hukm, p-753.

Also said:

"Wage a continuous crusade against the self; like a strict business associate check precisely the account of his deeds, and like a creditor force him for payment of God's dues, because, the most prosperous person is the one who does his own

Supervision – the Most Important Factor for Self-restraint

self-scrutiny."

-Gharar al-Hukm, p-371.

"Do your own self-auditing for the account of deeds in this world before being forced to be audited on the Judgment Day, because over there, this would be done over fifty stops -each stops being one thousand years long." Then he recited the following verse:

"The day whose length is equivalent to fifty thousands years." [26]

-Bihar al-Anwar, vol. 70, p-64.

In the end this point should be emphasized that at the time of self-scrutiny a person should not be optimistic and trust his self because the deceitful imperious-self with hundreds of deceits and tricks manifests evils as good and visa versa; does not allow a person to identify his duties and their fulfillments; justifies refrainment from worshiping and encourages indulgence into sins and transgressions. He makes you for-get your sins or regard them as minor omissions and presenting minor acts of worships as great, thus, making you proud about it. He cleans the thoughts of death and Resurrection Day from the memory of your mind, encourages the hopes and long-term desires; and presents self-scrutiny something as difficult, impracticable, and even unnecessary. Therefore, because of these considerations a person should be pessimistic while auditing the account of his deeds, and should scrutinize strictly with precision without paying least attention to Satanic justifications and interpretations.

The Commander of the Faithful Imam 'Ali (A) has said:

"There are some people devoted to the remembrance (of God), who have adopted it, in place of worldly matters so that commerce or trade does not turn them away from it. They pass their life in it. They speak into the ears of neglectful persons warning against matters held unlawful by God, they order them to practice justice and themselves keep practicing it, and they refrain them from the unlawful and themselves refrain from it."

"It is as though they have finished the journey of this world towards the Next World and have beheld what lies beyond it. Consequently, they have become

---

[26] 2.The Holy Quran (70: 4) [Tr].

acquainted with all that befell them in the interstice during their long stay therein, and the Day of Judgment fulfills its promises for them. Therefore, they removed the curtain from these things for the people of the world, till it was as though they were seeing what people did not see and were hearing what people did not hear."

"If you picture them in your mind in their admirable positions and well-known sittings, when they have opened the records of their actions and are prepared to render an account of themselves in respect of the small as well as the big things they were ordered to do but they failed to do, or were ordered to refrain from but they indulged therein."

"They realized the weight of their burden (of bad acts) on their backs, and they felt too weak to bear them, then they wept bitterly and spoke to each other while still crying and bewailing to God in repentance and acknowledgment (of their shortcomings). You would find them to be emblems of guidance and lamps in darkness, angels would be surrounding them, peace would be descending upon them, the doors of the sky would be opened for them and positions of honor would be assigned to them in the place of which God had informed them. There-fore, He has appreciated their actions and praised their position."

-the Nahjul Balagha, sermon 222.

Repentance and Self-cleansing

Prevention and refrainment from sins is the best way for attaining self-refinement. A person who has never been contaminated by Sins and possesses his original purity and righteousness certainly is far superior than a sinner who has repented after committing a sin. The person who has not yet tasted the pleasure of sin and is not used to it may refrain himself from sinning much more easier as compared to the one who has been contaminated by sins and now wants to refrain from them. The Commander of the Faithful Imam' Ali (A) said:

"Refraining from sin is far easier than repenting after sinning."
-Bihar al-Anwar, vol. 73, p-364.

But if a person becomes contaminated after sinning, he should not be disappointed from God's blessings because, the path of spiritual migration, self refinement, and ascent towards God-Almighty remains forever open and is never closed. The Most Merciful and the Most Benevolent God-Almighty has kept the path of repentance always open for the sinners and have especially asked them to return towards Him after cleaning and purifying the self's tablet from the impurities and contamination of sins through the water of repentance. God-Almighty said in the Holy Quran:

"Say: O My slaves who have been prodigal to their own hurt. Despair not of the Mercy of God, who forgiveth all sins. Lo! He

is the forgiving the Merciful."
   -the Holy Quran (39:58)

And said:

"And when those who believe in our revelations come unto thee say: Peace be unto you! Your Lord hath prescribed for Himself Mercy, that, those whoso of you doth evil and repenteth afterward thereof and doeth right, (for him) Lo ! God is forgiving, Merciful."
   -the Holy Quran (6:54)

The Need for Repentance

I don't imagine that there exists a thing which is more essential for a sinner than the repentance. The one who believes in God, Prophet, Resurrection, Rewards and Punishment, Accounting of Deeds, Paradise, and Hell does not contradict the urgency and necessity of repentance. Then, how come are, we negligent from repentance, inspite of being knowledgeable about the self and the sins committed by him? Don't we believe in the existence of Resurrection, Accounting of Deeds and Hell's punishments? Or, Do we contradict the God's promise that He will fill the Hell with sinners? Through sinning the human self becomes dark, black, and contaminated, even there is possibility of loosing the human face and turning into a brute animal.

Then how could we still expect finding the path leading towards Gods-Almighty and sitting in the company of His favorite saints in Paradise with such contaminated, darkened, and polluted self? Because, of indulgence into sins the straight path of human exaltedness and ascension towards God-Almighty has been lost, and now we are wandering into the darkest valleys of ignorance and deviations. We have parted from God-Almighty and have become close to Satan. Inspite of all that we are still expecting to receive eternal salvation in the Next World and would be blessed with

Divine bounties in the Paradise! What a wishful and immature thinking indeed?

Therefore, for a sinner who is concerned about his prosperity and salvation there is no choice left except to repent and return towards God-Almighty. This is one of the great blessing of God-Almighty that the path of repentance has been left opened for his servants. A person who has been poisoned does not allow the least delay in his being taken to the hospital for treatment, because, he knows that any negligence would result in his quick demise. Similarly, sins for human-self are far more fatal than the most deadly poison for human body. If, a poison could threaten the worldly life of a person quickly, sinning would inflict an eternal doom upon the self and would result in the destruction of his eternal life.

If poisoning results in cutting off a person's connection with the transient world instantaneously, likewise sinning makes a person far removed from God-Almighty depriving him from the God's Countenance and Nearness. Therefore, repentance and return to God-Almighty for us is something more urgent and essential than any thing else, because, our eternal prosperity and salvation depends upon it. God-Almighty said in the Holy Quran:

> "And turn unto God-Almighty together, O believers in order that you may succeed."
> -the Holy Quran (24: 31)

And said:

> "Oh ye who believe! Turn unto God-Almighty in sincere repentance! It may be that your Lord will remit from your evil deeds and bring you into Gardens underneath which rivers flow."
> -the Holy Quran (66:8)

The Holy Prophet (S) said:
"There is a medicine for each pain and the medicine for sins is repentance."

-Wasail al-Shi'a, vol. 11,p-354.

Imam al-Sadiq (A) said:

"Delaying repentance is a sort of arrogance and deceit; continuation of delay results in confusion and astonishment; excuses in front of God-Almighty is total destruction and persistence in sinning is due to feeling secure against Divine punishment and except the people who are losers no one else feels secure against it."

-Bihar al-Anwar, vol. 73, p-365.

In the light of above it would better that we should take an in-depth look within our lives; should remember all our past sins and transgressions; should ponder about the ultimate consequences; should think about the accounting of our deeds and being ashamed before God-Almighty and being insulted in front of angels and mankind; we must momentary manifest before our sight the horrible torture of Hell and deprivation from the God's Countenance.

This should create a transformation and internal revolution in our lives encouraging us to repent immediately and should return towards God-Almighty. All the past sins and transgressions should be washed with the pure life-giving refreshing water of repentance. All the self's impurities and contamination must be set aside and forgotten; a firm decision should be made, to refrain from sins to strive for collection of provisions for Hereafter, and start marching upon the path of spiritual ascent towards God-Almighty.

But would Satan leave us alone so easily? Would he ever permit us to repent and return towards God-Almighty? The same Satan who reduced us to indulge into sinning would also prevent us from repentance; would manifest sinning something as minor offense and insignificant; would wipe them out thoroughly from" our mental memory in a manner as though they never happened at all; would completely set aside thoughts related to death, account of deeds and punishments from our mind, keeping us amused in worldly allurements. So that we never think about the repentance until death approaches suddenly and, thus, being forced to leave this world with a self, contaminated with sins. Woe upon us, our negligence, and misfortune! !

Acceptance of Repentance

If repentance is indeed offered correctly it would receive Divine acceptance certainly which is one of the most unique favor of the Most-Compassionate and Most-Merciful Lord. Because, He has not created his servants for Hell and its tortures, rather has created us for Paradise and its eternal prosperity. Divine Messengers were assigned to guide the mankind towards the path of salvation and to invite the sinners towards repentance and return to God-Almighty. The door of repentance and return always remains opened for everyone inviting them to enter into it.

Divine messengers and saints throughout the human history continuously motivated the mankind towards repentance. The Most Compassionate and the Most-Merciful Lord in plenty of Qur'anic verses invites the sinners to return to Him and had promised them to accept their repentance and His promises are not lies. The Holy Prophet (S) and Infallible Imams (A) through hundreds of traditions have invited the man-kind for repentance and return towards God-Almighty, thus, making them hopeful of Divine blessings. Following are few examples:

God-Almighty said in Holy Quran:

> *"And He it is who accepteth repentance from His bondsmen, and pardoneth the evil deeds and knoweth what ye do."*
> *-the Holy Quran (42:25)*

And said:

> *"And lo! Verily I am forgiving towards him who repenteth and believeth and doth good, and afterward walketh aright."*
> *-the Holy Quran (2:82)*

And said:

> *"And those who, when they do an evil thing or wrong themselves,*

remember God-Almighty and implies forgiveness for their sins –who forgiventh sins save God-Almighty only ? And will not knowingly repeat (the wrong) they did."
  -the Holy Quran (3:135)

Imam Baqir (A) said:

"After repenting a person becomes like some one who has never sinned, and the one who is continuing sinning while reciting the phrase of repentance upon his tongue is like someone who ridicules himself."
-al Kafi, vol. 2, p-435.

There are plenty .of verses and traditions dealing with this matter and therefore, one should not have any reservation regarding the acceptance of repentance. Not only God-Almighty accepts repentance from a sinner but also loves him for undertaking this bold initiative. God-Almighty said in the Holy Quran:

"Truly God-Almighty loveth, those who turn unto him, and loveth those who have a care of cleanness."
  -the Holy Quran (2:222)

Imam al-Baqir (A) said:

"The happiness of God-Almighty from seeing a sinner repenting is much more than the joy of a lone traveler who finds his missing animal together with the provisions of journey in a dark night."
-al-Kafi, vol. 2, p-436.

Imam Al-Sadiq (A) said:

"When a servant of God offers pure and firm repentance, God-Almighty loves him and deletes all of his past sins. The narrator asked; 'Oh son of Prophet! How are the sins deleted ?'

'The two angels responsible for writing of deeds forget about his sins, simultaneously, God-Almighty orders his bodily parts, limbs, and different places upon earth to cancel his sins from their register of deeds. Thus, he meets God-Almighty in a manner whereby nobody and nothing is a witness to his sins. ' Replied the

Imam."
-al-Kafi, vol. 2, p.-436.

What is Repentance?

Repentance could be defined as a feeling of being ashamed, sorry, and regretful for past sins. Some one who is indeed ashamed by heart for his past sins may truly be called as a repentant. The Holy Prophet (S) said:
"Feeling ashamed and being sorry (for past deeds) is repentance."
-Haqayaq, p-286.

It is true that God-Almighty accepts repentance and forgives the past sins, but simply recital of the sentence: "I ask God to forgive me" (*Astaghferullah*), being ashamed and regretful or even. crying for past sins may not be considered as sufficient for a pure and sincere repentance, but with the existence of the following three symptoms the repentance could be considered as true and realistic:

1. First: He must be disgusted by heart for his. past sins and his self should have a feeling of shame, regret, and sorrow.
2. Second: He must take a firm decision not to indulge into sinning in the future.
3. Third: If, because of indulgence into a particular sin, he has done something, which could be compensated then he must take a firm decision for its compensation. For example: If he owes dues of people, has usurped property or stolen money, must decide to return it to its owner in the first available opportunity. In case he is not in a position to pay at present, he should try to get the owners consent or satisfaction through whatever means at his disposal.

If he has committed backbiting against some one, should seek his pardon, if he has oppressed some one, should try to redress the aggrieved. If religious dues have not been paid he must arrange for their payment, and if the daily prayers and the fasting have been missed, he must perform them as makeup (qadha) obligations. If some one has undertaken all the above steps, then he may truly be called as a sincere repentant, who is indeed ashamed for his past deeds and such atonement certainly receives God's acceptance.

But if some one recites the sentence: "I seek God's forgiveness" upon his tongue, but by heart is not ashamed for his past sins, does not decide for avoidance of future sins and is not ready to compensate for those sins which could have been compensated -then such a person has not atoned and should not expect acceptance of his repentance, even though he might appear in a prayer assembly and, thus, being affected sentimentally might shed some tears or may cry loudly. A person recited the sentence: "I seek God's forgiveness" in the presence of the Commander of the Faithful Imam ' Ali (A). The Imam said:

"May your mother lament for you, do you know what is repentance ? The repentance can be defined with the following six parameters:

1. *Feeling ashamed and regretful for the past sins.*
2. *Taking firm decision for avoidance of sins forever.*
3. *Paying all the dues of the people so that when he meets God-Almighty on the Resurrection Day, he does not have any pending claim against him.*
4. *All the religious obligations (Wajibat) which have not been performed in the past should be discharged as makeup (Qadha) obligations.*
5. *Should feel so sad about his past sins that all the bodily flesh formed as a result of eating forbidden (Haram) should be melted in a manner that skin should touch the bare bones until the new flesh is reformed again.*
6. *The inconvenience and hardship of worshiping should be imposed upon the body as a compensation for the pleasures it fasted because of past sins. Only after performing all the above, you may recite the sentence I seek forgiveness from God."*

-Wasail al-Shi'a, vol. 11, p.361.

Satan is so deceitful that sometimes he even deceives a person regarding repentance. It is possible that a sinner might attend a prayer gathering and after being effected sentimentally may shed some tears or may cry. Then

Satan would say:

Great, wonderful! What a great thing have you done? You have already atoned and all your sins have been cleaned. While in reality, such a person neither is ashamed from sinning by heart nor has be decided not to commit sins any more, and to remit dues of the creditors. Such act does not constitute a real repentance and would not result one's attaining self-purification and eternal salvation. Such a person has not refrained from sins and has not returned to God-Almighty.

Things which Require Repentance

What is sin and what sins should be repented? The answer is that every thing which stops a man from journeying towards God-Almighty, making him attached to worldly-allurements, thus, preventing from repentance should be considered as sin, must be avoided, and self should be thoroughly cleaned from its contamination. The sins might be classified into following two categories:

Moral Sins

Moral abjectness and obscene characteristics results in self's contamination, thus, preventing him to follow the straight path of human exaltedness leading towards God's Nearness and Countenance. Moral abjectness if gets deep rooted within self gradually becomes his characteristic resulting in metamorphism of his inner essence. It even influences the ideal; of "what to be" for a human being. Moral sins, because of the excuse of their being only moral, should not be treated as smaller and in-significant, and, thus, being negligent for their repentance, instead self-purification for them is something necessary and of vital importance.

The moral-abjectness consists of: Hypocrisy, wrath, arrogance, egotism, harshness, oppression, deceit and treachery, back-biting, accusation, criticizing, fault-finding, slander, breach of promise, lying, love of world, greed stinginess, parents rights, cutting family ties, ungratefulness, extravagance, jealously, vilification, cursing, and other obscene characteristics. Hundreds of Qur'anic Verses and traditions condemn these characteristics and describe their prevention, treatment, symptoms and worldly and eternal punishments. Since this matter has been discussed in details in several books of ethics, it would not be appropriate for us to discuss here, rather the readers are advised to refer to the literature dealing with ethics.

Practical Sins

Consist of the following: stealing, murder, adultery, homosexuality, paying and receiving interest, usurpation of public property, cheating, running away from the battlefield in a mandatory crusade, breach of trust, drinking alcoholic beverages, eating pork and other forbidden meats, gambling, false testimony or oath, accusing some innocent person for adultery, refraining from offering mandatory prayers and fasting, refraining from Haj Pilgrimage, refraining from the duty to encourage good and forbid evil (*Amr bil-Maroof wa Nahi al-Munkar*), eating unclean food, and other forbidden things. These sins have been described in detail in the books of traditions and jurisprudence and therefore, it would not be appropriate to discuss them here in detail, rather the readers are advised to refer to the relevant literature.

These are some famous sins which should be avoided by a human being and in case of indulgence he should offer repentance and should return to God-Almighty. Apart from these there are some other types of sins which are not famous and have not been introduced as sins but for God's most favorite saints and exalted pious personalities they are counted as sins e.g.: refraining from recommended acts (*Mostahbbat*), performing acts which are supposed to be avoided although not absolutely un-lawful (*Makroohat*), sinful thoughts, attention towards other than God, and selfish whims and Satanic whispers which prevents them from God's Remembrance.

All of them are considered as sins for God's favorite saints and they offer repentance for them. Even higher than the above is their negligence and omission in true recognition of God-Almighty, His essence, Attributes and

Actions, which are the prerequisite for the existence of every created being is regarded as a sin for them and realizing this omission they tremble in fear, shed tears, and offer repentance to return towards God. The repentance offered by the prophets and Infallible Imams (A) might belong to this category. The Holy Prophet (S) had said:

"Sometimes it happens that the darkness approaches my heart, and because of this reason I offer repentance seventy times every day."

-Muhjatteh, vol. 7, p-71.

Imam al-Sadiq (A) said:

"The Holy Prophet (S) used to offer repentance seventy times a day, while he had not committed any sin at all."

-al-Kafi, vol. 2, p-450.

Nourishment and Perfection of Self (Tahliyeh)

Having cleaned and refined the self a wayfarer is ready for the next stage known as training and perfection of self (*Tahliyeh*). The logical sciences have confirmed that the human self is in the state of motion and growth gradually manifesting his hidden potentials. In the beginning the self is not complete and perfect, rather gradually develops his essence. If, he travels on the straight path gradually becomes perfect, eventually attaining his ultimate-perfection. But if deviates and selects the wrong course gradually takes distance from the ultimate human perfection, thus, eventually crashing into dark valleys of ignorance and brutality.

God's Nearness

It should be understood that human movement is a real one and is not a figurative thing; this movement is related to his Celestial Spirit and not to his body. Also, this movement takes place within his inner essence and is not an external phenomenon. In this movement his precious jewel of human essence moves and becomes metamorphosed. Therefore, the axis of human movement is also a real axis and is not something metaphorical, but the axis of movement is not separate from the mover's essence, rather the mover moves within his inner essence carrying the axis of movement along with him.

Now the question arises that every movement carries some goal. Therefore, the human beings in the world are moving towards which objective and what is going to be their eventual fate? The traditions and Qur'anic verses reveal that the ultimate objective or goal destined for human beings is God's Nearness, but all human beings do not travel on the straight path and do not attain the exalted position of God's-Nearness. The Holy Quran said:

> "And ye will be three kinds:
> (First) those on the right hand; what of those on the right hand? And those on the left hand, what of those on the left hand ? And the foremost in the race, the foremost in the race: Those are they who will be brought nigh, in gardens of delight."
> -the Holy Quran {56: 7-12)

The people on the right hand side are the ones who have received eternal salvation, the people on the left are the ones who have received adversity and the people foremost in the race are the ones who distinguished themselves in their journeying on the straight path and attained the exalted position of God's Nearness. This verse clearly indicates that the objective or goal behind human movement must be God's Nearness. And the following verse:

> "Thus, if he is of those brought nigh. Then breath of life, and plenty and a Garden of delight. And if he is of those on the right hand, {then the greeting) "Peace be unto thee " from those on the right hand. But if he is of the rejecters, the erring. Then the welcome will be boiling water and roasting at Hell fire."
> -the Holy Quran {56: 88-94)

Further, God-Almighty said in the following verse:

"It is not so (as understood by unbelievers), Nay but the record of the righteous is in Illiyin. Ah, what will convey unto thee what Illiyin is! A written record. Attested by those who are brought near (unto their Lord)."
   -the Holy Quran (83:18-21)

From the above verse it may be concluded that the exalted position of God's Nearness and attainment of absolute perfection is the ultimate goal of people's journeying and movement. Therefore, God's favorite servants are the most distinguished group among the people who have been bestowed eternal bliss. The Holy Quran said:

"And remember when the angels said: O Mary! Lo! God-Almighty giveth thee glad tidings of a word from him, Son of Mary, illustrious in the world and the Hereafter, and one of those brought near (unto God-Almighty)."
   -the Holy Quran (3: 45)

It can be inferred from traditions and Qur'anic verses that distinguished and deserving God's servants who have surpassed others in belief, faith, and righteous deeds shall be blessed with the most privileged and exalted position of God's Countenance, and in accordance to the in-terpretation of some verses has been also named "the Place of Nearness to the Most Magnificent King" (*Malik Muqtadar*). Also, the martyrs will be assigned this special position. The Holy Quran said:

"Think not of those who are slain in the way of God-Almighty, as dead. Nay, they are living with their Lord they have provision."
   -the Holy Quran (3:169)

Therefore, ultimate human perfection and the final destination of the wayfarers is Nearness of God-Almighty.

Meanings of God's Nearness

Now let us see what is meant by God's Nearness? And how could it be imagined that a person may reach closer to God-Almighty. The nearness means being close and could be defined as follows:

Nearness Relative to Place

The two existence which are closer physically are called near to each other.

Nearness Relative to Time

When two things are closer to each other relative to time are called near to each other. Of course, it is evident that nearness of (God's) servants with Him could not belong to the above mentioned two categories, because, God-Almighty is beyond the limits of time and place rather is the creator of them, therefore, it is not possible for any thing to have nearness with Him relative to time and place.

Metaphorical Nearness

Sometimes it is said that Mr. X is very close and intimate with Mr. Y, which means that Mr. Y Respects, likes, and accepts Mr. X's recommendations and suggestions. This sort of nearness is called metaphorical, figurative, and ceremonial but is not real.

Could this kind of nearness be possible between a servant and God? Of course, it is true God loves His deserving servants and accepts their prayers but still this kid of nearness could not be possible between a servant and God-Almighty, because as was pointed out earlier, that this has been proved by the logical sciences and Qur'anic verses, and traditions also support that the wayfarer, his direction, and straight path all are real things and are not figurative and ceremonial. Likewise, return towards God-Almighty which has been so much emphasized in plenty of Qur'anic verses and traditions is a real thing and cannot be metaphorical or figurative. For example: God-Almighty said in the Holy Quran:

> "O Thou soul at piece!
> Return unto thy Lord, content in his good pleasure."
> -the Holy Quran (89:27-28)

And said:

> "Whoso doth right, it is for his soul, and whoso doth wrong, it is against it.
> And afterward unto your Lord ye will be brought back."
> -the Holy Quran (45:15)

And said:

> "Who say, when a misfortune striketh them: Lo! We are God's and Lo! unto Him we are returning."
> -the Holy Quran (2:156)

Anyway, return to God-Almighty, straight path, way of God, and attaining self-perfection are real things and are not metaphorical. A human being's movement is an aware and optional act whose result will become manifested after his death. Since the very beginning of Human existence this movement begins and continues until death. The nearness to God is real thing and God's decent servants really become closer to Him and impious and sinner indeed take distance from God-Almighty. Therefore, let us see what is meant by nearness to God-Almighty. God's Nearness is not comparable to other types of nearness, rather it is a special kind of nearness which might be called nearness relative to perfection or relative to the rank of exaltedness of that particular existence. In order to further clarify let us refer to the following preface.

The books of wisdom and Islamic philosophy have confirmed that existence 'is real and consists of various rank and degrees. It may be compared to the analogy of illumination which consists of various degrees of lights varying from low to very high. The lowest degree of a lighting lamp could be one watt which is also illumination till the lamp with infinite brightness which is nothing other than illumination. In between the lowest and highest limits of illumination there exists various intermediate degrees of light differing relative to extreme limits in proportion to their weakness and strength.

Existence too consists of various ranks and positions differing in proportion to their weakness and strength. The lowest degree being the existence of nature and matter till the highest rank of existence the essence of God-Almighty which from the point of view of perfection is infinite and absolute. In between these two extremities there also exists intermediate degrees of existence varying in proportion to their weakness and strength. Here it becomes clear that as much as an existence is stronger and holder of higher rank, in perfection would be closer relative to the most supreme existence and the source of absolute perfection -the Essence of God-Almighty, and opposite to that the weaker an existence would be, the farther it will be relative to the Essence of Self Existent (*Wajib al-Wajoud*).

Now in the light of above explanation the meaning of nearness of servants to God and distance from Him could be imagined. As for as the Celestial spirit is concerned, a human being is an abstract reality, which from the point of view of manifestation is related to matter, and because of that is capable to grow, becoming perfect until attaining the ultimate degree of his existence. From the beginning of his movement until arriving at the final destination he is not more than one person and one reality, but as much as he achieves perfection and ascension in his journey-ing with in his essence, in the same proportion becomes nearer to the source of all Creation, the Absolute and Infinite Perfection -the Holy Essence of God-Almighty.

A human being through belief and righteous deeds can make his existence complete and perfect so that he could attain God's Nearness, thus, being able to utilize divine blessings and favors to his maximum advantage and therefore, making his own essence a source of further benevolence and goodness.

Faith – the Foundation of Spiritual Perfection

Faith and enlightenment are the basis for self's perfection and journeying towards God-Almighty. Before starting this journey a wayfarer must decide about his final destination, must know where is he going, and which path he must select, otherwise he would get lost and would never reach to his final destination. Faith in God-Almighty induces courage for movement, search and endeavor, as well as clearly demarcates his path and final destination. Those who lack faith are helpless to walk upon the straight path of perfection. The Holy Quran said:

> "And Lo! those who believe not in the Hereafter are indeed astray from the path."
> -the Holy Quran (23: 74)

And said:

> "Nay, but those who disbelieve in the Hereafter are in torment and for error."
> -the Holy Quran (34:8)

An unbeliever who does not believe in the existence of God-Almighty and Hereafter becomes absolutely cut off from the world of perfection and his activities are limited to follow his material and animalistic requirements. Therefore, his arms and objectives for movement could not be any thing else other than material world.

He is not journeying on the straight path of perfection and therefore, can never attain God's Nearness .The direction of his movement is world and therefore, continuously becomes farther away from the straight path of human exaltation. Evan if an unbeliever performs a righteous deed it would not become a means for his self-perfection; because, he has not done it with the intention for God and his Nearness (*Taqarrub*), so that it becomes beneficial for him, rather has done it for the sake of this world and, therefore, will see the result in this world but nothing will be left for him in the Hereafter. God-Almighty said in Holy Quran:

> *"A similitude of those who disbelieve in their Lord: their works are ashes which the wind bloweth hard upon a stormy day. They have no control of aught that they have earned. That is the extreme failure."*
> -the Holy Quran (14:18)

Anyway, faith is the foundation of deeds and bestows upon them merit. If, a believer's soul gets intermingled with faith (*Iman*) and the phrase of Monotheism (*Kalma-e-Towheed*) would become illuminated and would ascend towards God-Almighty. Of course, righteous deeds too helps him in this ascent. The Holy Quran said:

> *"Whoso desireth power (should know that) all power belongeth to God-Almighty. Unto Him good words ascend and the pious deed doth He exalt."*
> -the Holy Quran (35:10)

The righteous deeds carry a human soul upward enabling him to attain the exalted position of God's Nearness and providing him a sacred and beautiful existence subjected to his possessed with the faith (*Iman*). An unbeliever's soul is dark and does not have the decency of possessing God's Nearness and delightful existence. The Holy Quran said:

"Whosoever doth right, whether male or female and is a believer, him verily we shall quicken with good life."
   -the Holy Quran (16:97)

Therefore, a wayfarer from the very beginning must strive and endeavor to strengthen his faith because the stronger and superior will be his faith the higher will be his ascent and rank. Holy Quran said:

"God-Almighty will exalt those who believe among you, and those who have knowledge, to high ranks, God is informed of what you do."
   -the Holy Quran (58:11)

The Means of Perfection and God's Nearness

In order to attain self-perfection and God's Nearness one may resort to various means. Here we will point out some of the important means as follows:

1. God's Remembrance.
2. Nourishment of Moral Virtues.
3. Righteous Deeds.
4. Martyrdom and Struggle.
5. Benevolence and Service to Mankind.
6. Supplication and Prayer.
7. Fasting.

All of the above means shall be described in details as separate chapters in this book.

First Means - God's Remembrance (Dikhr)

God's-remembrance or invocation (*dhikr*) could be regarded as a starting 'point for the esoteric movement or spiritual migration, of a wayfarer towards the Nearness of the Lord of Universe. A wayfarer through invocation gradually lift himself above the horizons of material world stepping inside the Celestial World of beauty and illumination, becomes complete and perfect eventually attaining the highest exalted position of God's Nearness. God's invocation is the soul behind all the worships as well is the greatest aim behind their explanation, because the merit of each worship depends upon the degree of attention paid by the worshiper towards that particular act. The Qur'anic-verses and traditions have made plenty of recommendations about the importance of invocation. For example the Holy Quran said:

> *"Oh ye who believe! Remember God-Almighty with much. Remembrance."*
> *-the Holy Quran (33: 41)*

And said:

> *"(such as) Those who remember God-Almighty, standing, sitting; reclining, and consider the creation of the heavens and the earth (and say): Our Lord! Thou createdst not this in vain. Glory be to thee! Preserve us from the doom of fire."*
> *-the Holy Quran (3:191)*

And said:

> *"He is successful who groweth, and remembereth the Name of his Lord, so prayeth."*
> *-the Holy Quran (87:15)*

And said:

> *"Remember the Name of the Lord at morning and evening."*
> *-the Holy Quran (76:25)*

And said:

"Remember thy Lord much. and praise (Him) in the early hours of night and morning."
   -the Holy Quran (3: 41)

And said:

"When ye have performed the act of worship. remember God-Almighty standing, sitting. and reclining."
   -the Holy Quran (4:103)

Imam al-Sadiq (A) said:

"Whoever offers a lot of invocation. God-Almighty will reward him Paradise where he would live forever happily under the shadow of His grace."
-Wasail al-Shi'a, vol. 4. p-1182.

'Also, he said to his companions:

"As much as it is possible do remember God-Almighty at every hour during day and night because He has ordered His servants to offer a lot of invocation. Whoever remembers God-Almighty is reciprocated by him. Know that there is not a single believer who does not remember God-Almighty but that God-Almighty too remembers him with goodness."
-Wasail al-Shi'a, vol. 4. p-1183.

Imam al-Sadiq further said:

"God-Almighty said to Moses (A): 'to remember Him a lot throughout the day and night. During invocation be humble, during calamity be patient, and during My Remembrance be calm and relaxed. Worship Me alone and do not associate any partner with Me. Every body shall have to return towards Me. Oh Moses! Regard me as your provision of the Hereafter and deposit the treasurers of your righteous deeds near Me."
-Wasail al-Shi'a vol. 4, p-1182.

At another place he said:

"For every thing there is a limit except God's Remembrance which is infinite and beyond limits. There are religious mandatory obligations which are performed in accordance to prescribed limits. e.g.: The fasting during the month of Ramadhan is limited to thirty days, and similarly the Hajj Pilgrimage is limited to performance of certain prescribed Hajj rituals , but contrary to all of them God's-Remembrance does not has any limits and He has not limited himself to a prescribed or minimum amount of invocation. Then he recited the following verse:

"Oh ye who believe! Remember God-Almighty with much remembrance and glorify him early, and late." [27]
-*the Holy Quran (33: 41-42)*

"In the above verse God-Almighty has not fixed a limit for His Remembrance. Then he said: 'My father (Imam al-Baqir A.S.) used to offer a lots of invocation, while walking with him I found him remembering God, when we used to sit together for eating he was still busy with invocation, and even while talking to the people he was not negligent from invocation. I could see his tongue almost attached to his throat while chanting: there is no god except God-Almighty (la illahi Illallahu). After the morning prayer he used to assemble all of us together and ordered to offer invocation until sun rise.

"Then he quoted from the Holy Prophet (S) who said: shouldn't I inform you about your best deeds which would bring for you more distinctions as compared to any other deed ? Which is purest and most desirable before God-Almighty. Is much better for you as compared to silver, and gold even is superior than the Holy crusade for the sake of God-Almighty.'

The people asked: "Oh Prophet of God! Please tell us."

"Do a lots of God's Remembrance." Replied the Holy Prophet (S).

"Then the Imam said: A man asked the Holy Prophet (S): "Who is the best among the believers ?" "The one who offers a lot of invocation." Replied the Holy Prophet (S). He further said:

"Who possesses a invocating tongue has indeed been blessed with the goodness of this world and the Hereafter."
-Wasail al-Shi'a, vol. 4, p-181.

---

[27] The Holy Quran (33: 41-42)

The Holy Prophet (S) said to Abu Dhar:

"Recite the Holy Quran and do a lots of invocation, which will became a means for your remembrance in the Heavens and will produce illumination for you upon the earth."

-Bihar al-Anwar, vol. 93, p-154.

Imam al-Hasan [28] (A) quotes from the Holy Prophet (S)

"Take lead towards the Gardens of Paradise. 'Which are the Gardens of the Paradise? Asked the companions ? 'The rings of invocation Replied the Holy Prophet (S)."

-Bihar al-Anwar, vol. 93, p-156.

Imam al-Sadiq (A) said:

"The one who is a reciter of God's invocation among negligent is like a crusader waging war in the battlefield alone, while the others are fleeing away. Paradise for such a combatant is compulsory."

-Bihar al-Anwar, vol. 93, p-163.

The Holy Prophet (S) said to his companions:

"Do utilize the gardens of the Paradise." Which are these gardens of the Paradise

---

[28] Imam al-Hasan ibn 'Ali: The eldest son of Imam' Ali and Hadhrat Fatimah was born on Tuesday, 15 Ramadhan 3 AH in Madina. When the Holy Prophet received the happy news of the birth of his grandson, he came to the house of his beloved daughter, took the newly born child in his arms, recited adhan and iqamah in his right and left ears respectively, and in compliance with Divine command named him al-Hasan.

The martyrdom of his father Imam 'Ali (A) on the 21st Ramadhan marked the inception of Imam Hasan' s imamate. The majority of Muslims pledged their allegiance to him and finalized the formality of oath of allegiance (*bayah*). No sooner had he taken the reins of leadership into his hands then he had to meet the challenge of Mu'awiyah the Governor of Syria who declared war against him. In compliance of Div-ine will and in order not to refrain from bloodshed of Muslims he entered into a piece treaty with Mu'awiyah whose terms were not re-spected and carried out by Mu'awiyah.

Mu'awiyah's malice against Imam Hasan led him to conspire with Imams wife Ja'dah the daughter of Ash'ath. She was made give the Imam some poison which affected his liver. Imam Hasan, thus, succumbed to Mu'awiyah's total mischief and attained his martyrdom on 28th (Safar) 50 A.H. His funeral was attended by Imam al-Hussein and the members of Hashimite family. His bier while being taken for burial to the Holy Prophet's tomb was shot at with arrows by his enemies, (under the direct supervision and consent of A'ishah), and it had to be diverted for burial to Jannatu'l-Baqi' at Madina.

? Asked the companions.

> 'The assemblies of invocation; remember God-Almighty at morning and evening. 'Whosoever wants to know about his rank and position before God-Almighty, must see how is the position of God in his own life. Because, 'He elevates a servant exactly to the same position -which was assigned to God-Almighty by the servant in his own life. Know that your best and the most purest deeds which will elevate your rank and position before the Lord and is better than any thing else of this universe is -God's-Remembrance, because God-Almighty had said: **"Whoever remembers me -I become his companion."** -Bihar al-Anwar, vol. 93, p-163.

The above Qur'anic verses and traditions presented here as examples of invocation show its importance clearly. Now let us investigate what is the aim behind the invocation.

The Aim of Invocation (Dikhr)

Earlier, it was clearly demonstrated that God's Remembrance is a great worship and is one of the best method of self-building, self-perfection and spiritual migration towards God-Almighty. Now let us examine what is really meant with invocation whose importance has been so much emphasized in traditions and Qur'anic verses. Does it means
 simply recital of sentences like: Glory to God, All praises belong to God and there is no god but God (subhan allahi, walhamdu lillahi, wala ilaha illal-lahu) or is there any other aim behind this?

Do these sentences without paying any inner attention towards their esoteric meanings could still provide such important effect? The phrase invocation in the dictionary has been defined in the sense of simply recital as well as in the sense of recital with heart's presence. Similarly, is the case in traditions where this phrase has been used with both meanings i.e. recital with tongue as well recital with heart's presence.

In traditions it has been narrated that Prophet Moses (A) while reciting hymns, asked God-Almighty:

"Oh God! What is the reward for some one who remembers you by tongue and heart? 'I will place him under the shadow of My Thrown and My Own Protection on the Day of Resurrection."

-Bihar al-Anwar, vol. 93, p-156.

Therefore, as could be seen in the tradition the phrase invocation has been used in both senses i.e. invocation by means of tongue as well as invocation by means of heart. Also, there are plenty of traditions in which invocation has been used in both meanings, but mostly it has been used in the sense of heart's presence with esoteric attention -which is indeed true and perfect invocation.

God's Remembrance may be defined as a state of spirituality and discerning the truth with esoteric attention towards the Lord of Universe, and knowing that He is the Overseer and Supervisor of all our actions at all times. Someone who remembers God-Almighty in such a manner, acts according to His commands, performs compulsory obligations and sustains himself from forbidden acts. Therefore, from the point of view of these considerations we may conclude that invocation is not an easy thing. The Holy Prophet (S) said to Imam' Ali (A):

"There are three things of special strength for my Ummah: First: Fellowship and equality with brother believer in wealth. Second: Treading others justly against the self Third: God's Remembrance in all situations.

"What is meant with invocation is not simply recital sentences life: Glory to God; All praises belong to God; and there is no god but God (Subhan allahi, Wal hamdu lillahi wala ilahi illallahu), rather invocation is defined as the state of being so much in remembrance of God-Almighty that whenever one is encountered with a forbidden act, he should fear God-Almighty and should refrain himself from its commitments."

-Bihar al-Anwar, vol. 93, p-151.

The Commander of the Faithful Imam 'Ali (A) said:

"Do not engage your self in invocation in the state of negligence and never forget

God-Almighty. Remember Him with perfection so that your tongue and hearts become synchronized and your esoteric and exoteric affairs are in conformity with each other. One cannot engaged himself in real invocation but to forget his self completely and while performing deeds he should think of only God-Almighty and 'should not notice his own existence." -Gharar al- Hukm, p-817.

Imam al-Sadiq (A) said:

"Whoever remembers God-Almighty truly will become obedient; whoever is negligent of Him will certainly indulge into sins, His obedience means guidance and sinning indicates deviation. The invocation and negligence are the roots of obedience and transgression respectively. Therefore, consider your heart as the worshiping point (Qibla), and keep your tongue still without motion except by permission of heart, by approval of wisdom, and with the consent of belief because, God-Almighty is aware of your apparent and hidden affairs."

"Be like some one whose soul is being confiscated from his body or like some one who is standing before the Lord to be questioned about his deeds. Don't let the self-engaged into any other thing except discharging Divine obligations which are important for you. With the tears of shame, and grief cleanse and purify the contamination of your heart."

"Know that God-Almighty has remembered you therefore, you should too engage yourself in invocation, because, He remembered you while being absolutely needless of you. Therefore, yours remembrance by God-Almighty will make you more perfect, exalted, acquainted, and delightful as compared to God's Remembrance by you. Acquaintance with God's Remembrance will increase your humility, courtesy, and decency in front of Him, resulting in your being able to witness His past benevolence and blessings bestowed upon you. At this stage your obedience might appear to you as more but in front of God's favors to you, it will be something very small."

"Therefore, do perform your deeds strictly for the sake of God-Almighty only. If you perceived your invocation as big it will result in hypocrisy, egotism, ignorance, harshness, and negligence in appreciation of Divine blessings and favors. Such invocation will not bear any fruits except innovator's becoming farther away from the God-Almighty and with the passage of time will not produce any positive effect except fear and sorrow."

"As the Holy Prophet (S) said: 'I am helpless to hymn your praise (the way you truly deserves). Your essence is such -the manner you praised yourself. Therefore, the Prophet (S) did not attach any wo11h to his invocations because, he was aware of the fact that remembrance of His servants by God-Almighty is far superior than the God's Remembrance by His servants. Therefore, those whose rank is much lower than the Holy Prophet (S) better consider their invocation as insignificant. Because of these considerations some one who really wants to recite God's Invocation must understand that unless and until God-Almighty remembers him and bestow upon him His special grace –he would not be in a position to offer God's Invocation."

-the Bihar al-Anwar vol. 93, p-158.

As could be seen from these narrations that hearts attention and esoteric presence have been defined as the real meanings of invocation. Further simply heart's attention and esoteric presence but ineffective is not enough, rather what is required is effective esoteric presence whose indications have been identified as obedience of mandatory obligations and avoidance of forbidden things. But it does not mean that only oral recital of sentences like: "There is no god but God"; "Glory to God". And "all praises to God," (la ilahi illallahu, subhan allahi, and al hamdu lil-lahi) is not the evidence of true invocation, because these sentences in themselves reflect degrees of God's invocation.

Apart from that even this invocation by tongue flows from the heart's fountainhead. Someone, who recites these invocation by tongue certainly is having some attention by heart towards God-Almighty however small it may be, and because of this he is reciting these sentences by his tongue. From the point of view of Islam, simply recital of these sentences and other invocations is desirable and carries spiritual reward subjected to it being performed with the intention of God's Nearness. Incidentally we may mention that in case of daily prayers we are strictly obliged to recite similar sentences by tongue and to perform other related rituals outwardly while we know that the heart's presence and esoteric attention is the real spirit behind the daily prayers.

The Degrees of Invocation (Dhikr)

Invocation consists of various degrees or ranks the first and lowest of them begins with the recital of invocation by tongue, and continues till the degree of absolute perfection, which terminates into attaining the stage of feeling being ceased to exist, witnessing the supreme reality and becoming annihilated into His Essence (*Shahood* and *fana*). At the very first stage, since the invocator pays heart's attention towards God-Almighty, starts reciting special invocation by tongue with the intention of God's Nearness, without paying any attention to their meanings.

At the second stage, although he, recites invocation by tongue with the intention of God's Nearness, but at the same time also convey their meanings to his mind. At the third stage, the tongue follows the heart, since the heart pays attention towards God-Almighty and in his esoteric essence believes in the meanings and contents of invocations, therefore orders the tongue for their recital.

At the fourth stage, the wayfarer attains esoteric presence, and perfect heart's presence with respect to God-Almighty, considers Him as an overseer of his actions and witnesses his own existence under God's exalted presence. At this stage the experiences of wayfarers differs widely in accordance to the degree of perfection achieved by them. As much as they become detached from other than God, in the same proportion they become attached to God-Almighty ultimately achieving the highest and most exalted positions of being ceased to exist (*inqata*), countenance (*laqa*), and annihilation (*fana*).

The wayfarer at this stage -which is the most exalted position has teared off all the veils of ignorance and falseness and has attached himself to the Supreme Source of all Blessings and Perfection. He has removed himself from every thing including his self and has returned towards God-Almighty by cutting all his ties with other than God and reserving his pure love and affection for God-Almighty. He does not see any perfection except God-Almighty so that he could become attached to him, and does not find any companion to become intimate with him.

These purest servants of God have made their access into the supreme Infinite Source of Grandeur, Majesty, Perfection, Blessings and Illumination and ate able to witness the Beauty and Illumination of God's Essence with their esoteric eyes. They are not ready to attach their heart and pay attention towards the metaphorical phenomenon of this world even for an instant.

Because they have reached to the Fountain Head of Absolute Beauty and Perfection and, therefore, metaphorical and fictitious perfection do not have any worth in their eyes. They burnt in the love, affection and countenance of their beloved and are not ready to exchange this pleasure even if they are offered both the worlds, and if they encounter world's phenomenon, regards them as reflections of Divine Illumination and signs of God's Perfect Existence.

The Commander of the Faithful Imam Ali (A) was asked:

"Have you seen the God to whom you worship"?

'Woe, be upon you! I do not worship a God who could not be seen '. Replied the Imam. ' How did you see Him' ? He was asked. 'Woe be upon you! God-Almighty could not be seen with physical eyes rather hearts witness His exist-ence through the reality of their faith." Replied the Imam."

-Haqayaqe Faiz, p-179.

Imam al-Hussein (A) [29] said:

"In order to prove Your Existence how can a thing could be referred as an argument which in itself is dependent upon You? Is there exist any manifestation for other than You which You lack, so that he would make You revealed? When were You absent so that an argument will be required? When were You away so that the indications and circumstances of Your reappearance would be needed?

---

[29] Imam al-Hussein: The younger son of Ali by Fatimah was born in Medina on Thursday 3rd Sha'ban 4 A.H; like his brother he lived most of his life quietly in Medina under the watchful eyes of the caliph's officials and spies. When Mu'awiyah's son Yazid became caliph, he demanded al-legiance from al-Husayn, who refused to give it. Finally al-Husayn felt it necessary to go into battle against Yazid to protest against the injustices which were being carried out in the name of Islam. He and a small group of followers including most of his immediate family were cruelly mas-sacred at Karbala. The day of his martyrdom l0th Muharram ' A.H.(Ashura) has become the most solemn day of the Islamic calendar, marked by processions and universal mourning. He is buried in Karbala in Iraq [Tr].

Blind is the eye which does not see You as an Overseer upon his deeds. And how unfortunate looser is your servant, who have been deprived of Your Love."

-Iqbal al-Amal, Prayer for the Day of Arafah.

The Commander of the Faithful Imam' Ali (A) in his hymns for the Holy Month of Shaban said:

"Oh God! Bestow upon me absolute separation from every thing except You, enlighten the esoteric eyes of our hearts with Your Beauty and Grandeur ,so that they could tear off the veils of light and become attached to the Supreme Source of Absolute-Perfection. May our souls become united with Your Holy-Essence."

-Iqbal al-Amal, Monajat-e-Shabanyeh.

Imam al-Sajjad (A) describes God's righteous servants as follows:

"Oh Lord! The tongues are helpless to offer Your Praise and Adoration, worthy of Your Majesty and Splendor," the faculties of wisdom cannot comprehend Your Beauty and Glory; the eyes are powerless to be able to witness the manifestation of Your Beauty. For your servants, in their search to attain the exalted position of Your Enlightenment, You have closed all the avenues except to admit their impotence and helplessness."

"Oh Lord of the Majesty and Splendor! Please consider us among Your those servants in whose hearts the sapling of Your Countenance has been planted and whose hearts are saturated with the grief and sorrow of Your Love. Thus, they are moving towards the nest of most tender and sublime thoughts with the hope of living in pleasure forever in the most magnanimous and splendid garden of manifestation and nearness of their God. They drink the cups of Your Grace from the Fountain Head of Your Love and entering the wide freeways of fraternity and pleasure."

"The curtains have been rolled up from their esoteric eyes, the darkness of doubt has been removed from their beliefs and the palpitations of contradiction have been calmed down in their hearts. Certainly of Your Knowledge have made them as large hearted," strive to surpass others in the race of piety, in their trade with God-Almighty, have been rewarded with the most delicious and pleasurable drinks," In their union with their beloved possess a clean and pure inner self while encountering fearful situation are assured with the Divine guidance to-wards safety" In their return to God-Almighty have attained the most tranquil state,.

In their journeying towards eternal prosperity and salvation have attained the stage of certainty; In witnessing the glory of their beloved their eyes shine with joy, because of accomplishing the cherished goal, they now possess a peaceful inner self and have profited themselves in their bartering this world with the Hereafter."

"Oh God! How pleasing are the memories of inspiration relevant to Your Invocation for the hearts! How sweet is the journeying towards you by means of pondering about the unseen! How much delicious is the taste of Your Love! And how much pleasurable and gratifying is the drinking of drinks of Your Nearness !"

"Therefore, oh God! we seek Your shelter again banishment or getting lost. And accept us among the most distinguished gnostics, most righteous servants, most veracious obedient, and most sincere worshippers. Oh Lord of Majesty and Splendor, and Oh God of Mercy and Compassion we swore you of your Blessing, oh Thou Who are the Best of Blessers."

-Bihar al-Anwar, vol.93, p-163.

In summary, the fourth position is a position which is most distinguished and exalted and in itself consists of various degrees and ranks which are infinite and continue till the very Holy Essence, Self-Existent (*Wajib al-Wajood*), the Source of Absolute Perfection and Infinite Beauty. In the language of Godly people these stages are called namely: the position of invocation (*dhikr*) the position of love, (*uns*), the position of being, ceased to exist (*inqata*) the position of intense desire (*shouq*), the position of pleasure (*raza*) the position of fear (*khouf*), the position of witnessing, (*shahood*) the position of absolute certainty (*ain al-yaqin*) the position of assurance (*haq al-yaqin*) and the eventual position of becoming annihil-ated in God-Almighty (*fana wa baqa billah*). These interpretations most probably have been inferred from traditions and Quranic verses and each one of them requires a commenty e.g.:

When the worshipper pays attention towards the Glory, Splendor, Majesty and Infinite Perfection of the Holy Essence of Self Existent (*Wajib al-Wajood*), considers His Love, Favors, and Blessings and realizes his own helplessness and negligence, and looks at the distance between him-self and that Holy Exalted Essence; it causes .a feeling of love, eagerness, and sorrow within his existence which is known as the position of strong desire (*shouq*).

When the wayfarer thinks in retrospective about his gnostic spiritual journey and discovers the spiritual stations and perfection attained by him -this revelation makes him happy and pleased, which is known as the position of affection or love (*uns*). When the wayfarer pays attention towards the Splendor, Majesty, Glory, and Absolute Perfection of God's Essence and opposite to that realizes his own helplessness and shortness for attaining the Nearness of that Supreme-Reality -his hearts trembles with fear. The agony and grief overtakes his entire existence, whereby he cries bitterly and sheds tears. This stage is known as the position of fear (*khouf*), and similar is the case with other positions.

It would be better if this God's servant -the prisoner of self's passions, captive of darkness of materialism, deprived of attaining higher spiritual stations -does not put his feet inside this profound and infinite ocean, and let the explanation of these sublime spiritual stations be left for these who have reached there. Because, so for one has not tasted the deliciousness of God's Love, Affection, and Countenance, he is helpless and powerless to explain them.

"Oh God! I do like the righteous ones, although, I myself is not one of them, Oh God! Bless me with the sweetness of your invocation and please do include me among them! "

Let us hear the words of those who are qualified to speak in this field.

The great philosopher and divine gnostic Sadrudin Shirazi writes:

"If a ray of Divine illumination falls upon a servant, makes him awakened from the sleep of ignorance and nature, thus, his becoming aware of the fact that apart from this perceptible world there also exists another world, and higher than the animalistic pleasures there also exist other satisfactions. With this realization he refrains himself from indulging into false and worthless amusements and returns towards God-Almighty by offering repentance for his past omissions. Thus, he starts pondering about Quranic verses, listening Divine admonitions, deliberating upon the Prophet's (S) traditions and performing deeds in accordance with Divine commands."

"In order to attain the eternal perfection he restrains himself from following the worldly allurements such as wealth, power, and positions. If he is lucky to receive further Divine Guidance and Blessings – decides seriously to disassoci-ate himself from other than God, starts journeying towards Him and leaving the habitat of self, his whimsical attractions ascends towards God-Almighty. At this stage, a ray of Divine illumination enlightens his horizons; a door from the unseen world opens for him and gradually the pages from the Holy Kingdom become apparent for him enabling him to witness the affairs of unseen."

"When he tastes these special pleasures of the unseen affairs, starts liking seclusion and engages himself into invocation continuously. His hearts becomes detached from material involvement and pays absolute attention towards God-Almighty with his entire existence. At this juncture mystical knowledge is gradually bestowed upon him and spiritual illuminations become occasionally manifested for him, until he attains absolute certainty in his search discovering the Supreme Reality whereby, all contradictions, doubts are vanished and a special tranquility engulfs his entire existence."

"At this stage he enters into the Celestial Kingdom and after witnessing the existence of "Ten-wisdoms." [30] (Uqool-Mufarqeh) becomes united with their Celestial Lights and, thus, become enlightened. Eventually, the Glorious Illumination of the Lord of Majesty and Splendor becomes manifested upon him, thus, making his existence and egotism shattered and he surrenders in front of the Glory and Exaltedness of the Lord of the Heavenly Kingdom. This stage is known as the position of Monotheism (Towheed) in which any thing other than God-Almighty becomes amortized in the wayfarer's eyes and he listen to the sound of:

"Whose is the sovereignty this Day? It is God's the One, the Al-mighty." [31]
-Mafateeh al-Ghaib, p-54.

---

[30] Ten-Wisdoms (*Uqool Mufarqheh*):

Sardar al-Mutalihin and other Islamic philosophers, regarding the cre-ation of universe, have confirmed the existence of Ten-Wisdoms (*Uqool-Mufarqeh*) before the creation of natural world. And the Divine blessings upon the material world are bestowed through their means [Author].

[31] The Holy Quran (40:16) [Tr]

The most famous and eminent gnostic late Faiz-e-Kashani writes: *"The way for acquiring God's Love and its further strengthening to be worthy of witnessing His Manifestation and Countenance is -to attain enlightenment, (marefah) and its further strengthening. The way of acquiring enlightenment consists of purifying hearts from worldly occupations and being attached to its allurements through paying absolute attention towards God-Almighty by means of invocations and pondering, and cleansing of heart's dwellings from all sort of attachment towards other than God. Because, the heart is like a pot, which if filled with water completely would not have any space left to be filled with vinegar. In order to fill this pot with vinegar first it must be emptied with water. God-Almighty has not created anyone with dual heart."*

"Perfection in love demands that one must love God-Almighty with the entire existence of his heart, because so for as the heart continues to pay attention towards other things at least a part of it shall remain occupied with other than the

God-Almighty. Therefore, as much as one is attached to other than God -his love towards Him will be decreased in the same proportion, except where, this attention towards other than God is related to a situation, whereby " an act of God and His created being " are reflections of one of the manifestations of God's sacred names and Characteristics."

God-Almighty in the following verse of Holy Quran, has pointed out about the same meanings:

"Say God: Then leave them", an stage which is achieved as a result of strong desire where a human being strives that whatever have been revealed for him should become further clearly manifested. While he should remain anxious towards what have not yet been accomplished, because, the strong desire is related to a thing which partly have been perceived from some aspects. but from other dimensions it has not yet been comprehended, and in between these two, there exists the reality, which is beyond the limits and infinite.

"Because, the degree and ranks of comprehension of what have been achieved -is infinite. Similarly, whatever magnification has been left from God's Splendor and Beauty is also infinite and having attained the real union with the sweet-

heart, one still desires strongly that pleasurable event which is free from all sort of pains. Therefore, desire never rests at any stage especially when he witnesses so many ranks and positions beyond the imagination of human intellect."

"There light will run before them and on their right hands: They will say: our Lord! Perfect our light for us." [32]

-Haqaiq, p-181.

---

[32] The Holy Quran (66:8) [Tr]

The Effects and Indications of Invocation (Dhikr)

As it was explained earlier that invocation (*dhikr*), witnessing (*shahood*), and countenance (*laqa*), are esoteric positions; and are genuine spiritual perfections, whereby a wayfarer really attains an exalted rank of existence which was not accomplished by him earlier. If it is said: the position of witnessing is real and similarly, if it is said: the position of love, the position of compliance, the position of desire, the position of union, and the positions of countenance are not metaphorical, rather are real positions; it means that the relevant position represents a rank and degree of a real existence, which naturally should be accompanied with new effects and indications, so that the existence of that perfection could be identified through them. Here, we would describe the details of the following effects:

Commitment for God's Obedience

When some one attains a position whereby in his esoteric essence witnesses God's Beauty and sees himself in His presence, without any doubt will obey His commands absolutely. Whatever, he has been commanded to do will be performed by him and will refrain himself from things made forbidden for him. If, a human being wants to know whether he has attained that position or not, he must evaluate his commitments towards Divine positive and negative commands and in accordance to his performance may determine his relative rank. It is not possible that a human being would have attained the exalted position of love and witnessing and would not have a total commitment towards Divine commands. Imam al-Sadiq has defined the invocation (*dhikr*) as follows:

"*Invocation is meant that when some one encounters an act which has been made mandatory by God-Almighty he performs it and if it is forbidden, he re-frains from it.*"

-Bihar al-Anwar, vol. 93. p-155.

Imam al Hussein (A) in his prayer of Arafeh said:

"*Oh God-Almighty! Thou are the One Who has poured the sweetness of Your love inside your friend's mouths so that they should stand in prayer in front of You and must adore You with humility. Oh Thou are the One Who has dressed your saints with the robe of fear so that they should stand and repent in front of you.*"

-Iqbal al-Amal-Prayer of Arafeh.

God-Almighty said in Holy Quran

> "**Say: If you do love God follow me: God will love you.**"
> **-the Holy Quran (3:31)**

Imam al Sadiq (A) said:

"*Whoever becomes a sincere invocator of God-Almighty, will also become truly obedient to Him, and whoever is negligent, will be a sinner.*"

-Bihar al-Anwar, vol. 93, p-158.

Humility

Whoever witnesses the Power and Majesty of God-Almighty would naturally humiliate himself in front of him, and will continuously lower his head in regret while realizing his omissions and negligence.

Imam al-Sadiq (A) had narrated in a tradition:

"Your enlightenment because of your being paid attention by God-Almighty will result in your becoming humble, modest and prudent."

-Bihar al-Anwar, vol. 93, p-158.

Excitement for worshiping

One of the indication of attaining the position of witnessing is the strong liking for worshiping and feeling intense pleasure during its performance, because, some one who has witnessed the Majesty and Splendor of the Lord of the Worlds and considers himself in the presence of God-Almighty -the Fountainhead of All Magnanimity and Perfection –would prefer the pleasure of hymns and humming communications with Him over any other enjoyment. Those who are deprived of spiritual pleasures keep themselves amused with transient worldly amusements which in reality are no more than a pain killer, but those who have tasted the real pleasure of worshiping and hymns of the Lord of the Worlds would never exchange their pleasant state and beauty with any other enjoyment.

These are the purest God's servant who worship him only for the sake of his worthiness to be worshipped and not for the sake of any reward and punishment. In this regard, you must have heard about the melting and burning worshiping and intimate humming communications of the Holy Prophet (S) Imam' Ali (A) Imam al-Sajjad and other Imams of Prophets (Ahlul Bayt) with their Lord.

Tranquility and Assurance

The world is a place of pains, sorrows, and sufferings, which can be classified into the following three categories:

1. First type: Tragedies like sickness of self or relatives death of self or next of kills, oppression, prejudices, injustice, discard, and interference etc.

2. Second type: Regret and annoyance for lack of worldly things which are beyond one's reach.
3. Third type: Fear of loosing whatever have been accumulated, fear of theft or loss of wealth, fear of loosing children because of accidents, and fear of getting sick and possibility of death.

All of the above most probably takes away ease and comfort from a human being, whose roots could be traced to strong attachments to world and avoidance of God's remembrance. The God-Almighty said in the Holy Quran:

"But he who turneth away from remembrance of me, his will be a narrow life."
   -the Holy Quran (20:124)

But God's sincere servants who have reached the Source of all Blessings and Perfection, have witnessed the Absolute Beauty and Splendor, are contented because of God's Remembrance and Affection. They are free from all sort of worries and sorrows, because of their having God-Almighty, they possess every thing. They do not become annoyed or it worried for lack of worldly things because they do not have any inclinations towards them, instead, they have attached themselves to the Foun-tainhead of all Blessings and Perfection, which lacks nothing. Imam al-Hussain (A) in his prayer of Arafeh had said:

"Oh Lord! Thou are the one who has removed the love of others from the hearts of your favorite saints, so that they are not attached to any body except You, and do not seek any other shelter except You. While encountering terrible calamities they seek refuge in You. If Your Enlightenment and Nearness have been achieved by them -it was only because of Your-Guidance."

"Whosoever does not find You what else there remains to be found? And whoever has found You what else would he be lacking? How much looser is the one who chooses other than You and how unfortunate is the one who deviates from You. How can a human being expect thing from others while Your Favors never get cut off from him? How could one pray for his need before others, while knowing that Your Generosity and Benevolence surround him."

-Iqbal al-Amal, Prayer of Arafah.

Any how, the most important effect of one's attaining the position of invocation, witnessing, and love is the attainment of heart's peace and tranquility, because, in principle, nothing can rescue the heart's boat inside the stormy oceans of the life except God's Remembrance. God-Almighty said in Holy Quran:

> "Who have believed and whose hearts have rest in the remembrance of God.
> Verily in the remembrance of God do hearts find rest!"
> -the Holy Quran (13:28)

The stronger will be the belief of a person the greater will be his heart's degree of assurance and tranquility.

God's Attention towards the Servant

When a God's servant remembers God-Almighty, reciprocally He too bestows special favor and blessing upon His servant. This matter has been mentioned in the following verses and traditions, God-Almighty said in Holy Quran:

> "Therefore, remember me, I will remember you."
> -the Holy Quran (2:152)

Imam al-Sadiq {A,S,) said:

"God-Almighty had said: 'Oh son of Adam! Remember me in your self so that I would remember you in My Self;. Oh son of Adam! Remember me in solitude so that I may remember you in solitude; Oh son of Adam! Remember me in congregation so that I remember you in a congregation much better than yours," and said: 'Every servant who remembers God-Almighty among the human beings,

God-Almighty remember him among the angels."
-Wasail al-Shi'a, vol 4, p-1185.

God's attention and special blessings towards a servant is not a metaphorical thing, rather is a reality whose reasons may be explained as follows:

1. First Reason

When a servants remembers God-Almighty and with this means makes himself readied for acceptance of His special favors, God-Almighty increases the level of his perfection and elevates him into high-er spiritual positions.

1. Second Reason

When a servant recites God's invocations and spiritually migrates towards Him, he is blessed with God's attention and special favors, whereby He bestows upon him exalted spiritual positions and takes over the control of his heart, The Holy Prophet (S) said:

"God Almighty said: 'When I find a servant sincerely engaged in my invocation -makes him further interested into hymns and worshiping, and if occasionally negligence dominates over him, I prevent such occurrence, These are my real saints and heroes, If I want to annihilate all the earthly creations, it is because of their distinguished existence that My punishment does not descend towards earth."
-Bihar al-Anwar, vol, 93, p-162.

God's Love towards the Servant

One of the effect of invocation is the God's love towards the servant. It has been inferred from various Quranic verses and traditions that when a person engages himself in God's remembrance and obeys His commandments, He too reciprocates and starts loving that person, The Holy Quran said:

"If you love God, follow me, God will love you."
-the Holy Quran (3:31)

Imam al-Sadiq had narrated from the Holy Prophet (S)
"Whoever offers lots of God's invocation will achieve God's affection towards him, whoever continuously remembers God-Almighty will have two letters written for him letter of immunity from Hells' fire, and letter of immunity from discard."
-Wasail al-Shi'a, vol. 4, p-181.

God's affection towards a servant is neither a ceremonial act nor it could be compared to the meanings of love as related to human beings. In case of human beings love is meant as heart's attachments and inclinations towards a desirable object, but for God such interpretation of love is not correct.

Love of God must be interpreted as His special favors and graces which further enhance a servants sincerity, attention, and worshiping, towards Him, and through these means attracts him towards the higher stages of perfection and nearness. Because, He loves the servant and likes hearing his humming hymns -bestows upon him the special favor of motivating further towards prayer, invocation, worshiping, and supplications. Since, He likes servant's nearness, accordingly provides the required means for his perfection, and in nutshell because of His affection towards the servant -takes over his heart's control, thus, providing him the opportunities for better and speedy ascent towards His nearness.

The Most Important Effects

At this stage the wayfarer is blessed with most special benefits and privileges whose explanation is not possible through the pen and tongue of strangers, and except the recipient of these positions no one knows any thing about these affairs. Because, of the effects of self-purification, esoteric cleansing, worshiping, asceticism, thinking, and continuous recital of invocation, the wayfarer attains on exalted spiritual rank where, by means of his esoteric eyes and ears is able to see and hear the most sublime realities which can not be seen and heard by the apparent eyes and ears. Sometimes he hears the praise and hymns of other creatures including angels and joins them.

While he lives in this world and socialize with its people but in his esoteric essence looks towards upper horizons living in an another world as though he does not belong to this world. In that World he witnesses the Hell and Paradise and keeps in touch with angels and spirits of God's righteous saints. He is familiar with other World, and utilizes its blessings but does not want to speak about it, because such persons prefers seclusion and strictly sustain themselves from fame and popularity.

The higher Divine learning are descended upon the gnostics heart, and mystical-sciences which are not customary with conventional learning are witnessed by him. The wayfarer ultimately achieves an exalted spiritual position whereby he forgets everything including his self and does not pays attention towards anything except the Holy Names and Characteristics of God-Almighty. He sees the Lord of the Universe as Over seer of every thing and every where, Who had said:

"I am the first, the last, the hidden and the apparent."

He sees the world as a manifestation of God's characteristics and considers every perfection and beauty from God-Almighty. The depravity of essence of all creatures, the absolute richness of the Self Existent (*Wajib al-Wajood*) becomes apparent for him and in witnessing the Supreme Source of Absolute Beauty and Perfection feels fascinated and absorbed.

Here it should be pointed out that the position of annihilation (*fana*) in itself consists of various degrees and ranks, and it would be appropriate if this deprived servant should better refrain himself from entering into these privileged positions.

The Means of Attainment

In order to achieve faith's perfection and attaining higher spiritual positions of God's Remembrances (*Dhikr*), Witnessing, (*Shahood*), and Coun-tenance (*Laqa*), the following means should be utilized:

Meditation and Reasoning

The reasons and arguments presented for the proof of God's Existence might be of some help in this regard, because, the reasons presented in the Holy Quran and other books of wisdom and gnosticism confirm that all the worldly phenomenon are needy and deprived rather in their essence are absolute indigence and deprivation. In order to exist, and for continuation of their actions and movements they all are related to a -"Free from Want Existence", rather in essence are related and dependent upon Him. All are needy and limited.

In the entire circle of existence there does not exist more than one-"Free from Want", Self Sufficient and Infinite Existence and that is the Essence of Self Existent (*Wajib al-Wajood*), Whose Existence is absolutely free from defects, limitations, and needs. He is the Source of all Perfection Whose Power, Knowledge, Life, and Other Characteristics are Absolute and Infinite; is present everywhere and is the overseer of all things, nothing is hidden from Him, is closer to all the creatures, even is nearer to man than his jugular vein. The Quranic verses and traditions have ex-plain this in detail. Following are some examples:

> *"To God belong the east and the west: Withersoever ye turn, there is the pres-ence of God."*
> -the Holy Quran (2:115)

And said:

> *"And He is with you wheresoever ye may be. And God sees well as that ye do."*
> -the Holy Quran (57: 4)

And said:

> *"We are nearer to him than (his) jugular vein."*
> -the Holy Quran (50:16)

And said:

> *"For God is witness of all things."*
> -the Holy Quran (22:17)

Therefore, pondering and reasoning over the Divine proofs helps man's exit from the intense darkness of unbelief, makes him enter inside the boundaries of faith, opens the path of perfection, and invites him towards action which is the prerequisite of belief.

Deliberations over the Quranic Verses

The Holy Quran regards all worldly phenomenon as sign and indications of the existence of the World's Creator. The Quranic verses emphasize repeatedly to deliberate and think about God's signs, and the beauties, wonders, rhythm, and coordination which is controlling them in order to discover the existence of a Learned, Wise and Omnipotent God.

The human beings have been asked to deliberate deeply about their own creation, mysteries, and wonders incorporated within the structures of their sprit and body, the differences of colors and languages, and the crealtion of their spouses. Similarly, they are asked to ponder about the creation of sun, moon, stars, and their wonderful movement. Further they are encouraged to look and think about the creation of earth, mountains, hills, trees, plants, and animals living inside, the water and over land. Also, the Holy Quran has described a lot of examples from these creations.

The world indeed is beautiful and fascinating, arid a little bit pondering would reveal hundreds of hidden wonders and mysteries within its creatures. Starting from sun, moon, stars, milky ways, and clouds till the fascinating and mysterious world of atom; from the great forests till different types of plants and smaller and larger trees; from the great animals like elephant and camel till the tiny ants, mosquitoes, bacteria, and viruses all of them reveal a special beauty and elegance.

By witnessing the wonders of these worldly phenomenon and the most accurate precise coordination prevailing upon them, a human being may discover the Infinite Grandeur, Majesty, Wisdom, and Knowledge of the Creator and, thus, becomes astonished and fascinated crying from the inner depths of this heart.

> *"Our Lord! Thou createdst not this in vain."*
> *—the Holy Quran (3:191)*

Look at the brightening sky full of stars and deliberate deeply over their creation; sit near the edge of a forest and see the Majesty and splendor of God-Almighty. Alas! The world is so beautiful!

worshiping

After being blessed with faith (*iman*) and enlightenment (*marefah*) a human being must strive and endeavor to perform righteous deed and must discharge his religious obligations. Because, it is through the performance of righteous deeds that the belief and enlightenment achieve perfection, ultimately ascending towards God's Nearness. It is True that belief, enlightenment and the words of purity (Monotheism) ascend towards Him, but in this movement they are assisted by the righteous deeds. The God-Almighty said in Holy Quran:

> *"Whoso desireth power (should knew that) all power belongth to God. Unto Him good words ascend, and the pious deed doth He exalt."*
> -the Holy Quran (35:10)

The righteous deeds may be compared to the fuel in an airplane. So for it contains fuel it may continue to ascend, but the moment its fuel is finished it crashes immediately. Likewise, belief, ,and enlightenment so for are accompanied by righteous deeds they help ascend the human being towards Upper Heavens, but without the assistance of righteous deeds a human being crashes like an airplane without fuel. God-Almighty said in the Holy Quran:

> *"And serve thy Lord till the inevitable cometh into thee."*
> -the Holy Quran (15:99)

The only way for achieving self-perfection and attaining the state of certainty (*yaqeen*) is to strive seriously to discharge obligations, worshiping , and servitude of God-Almighty. If some one imagines that he may attain exalted spiritual position through means other than worship -is in gross error. [33] If God willing (*inshaAllah*) the discussions regarding righteous deeds will be continued later on.

Invocations and Supplications

Islam, especially has emphasized the importance of continuous recital of invocations and in this regard special invocations and supplications have been prescribed by the Holy Prophet (S) and Infallible Imams (A) whose recital earns a special reward. Invocation in Islam is considered as a type of worship which helps one to achieve self-perfection and God's Nearness. For example The Holy Prophet (S) had said:

"There are five things which makes a human being's deeds heavier: Glory to God (*Subhan Allahi*), All praises belong to God (*AlhamduLillahi*), there is no God but god (*La ilahi-illallahu*), God is Great (*Allahu Akbar*) and to remain patient at the demise of a righteous offspring."

---

[33] According to a tradition narrated by Imam 'Ali bin al-Hussein (A), since God was aware that the later period of history, would produce curious people, and therefore: He revealed the verses of Surah Iron till verse "knower of all that is in the breasts, " in order to define the boundaries for investigating His essence and characteristics. Therefore whosoever has allowed himself to ponder over beyond these prescribed limits is bound to be doomed.

As if the Surah al Ikhlas, "Say God is One" says to the prayer offerer: God is unique Supreme Power, the Most High, Exalted, the Needless, His essence beyond description, neither Begets nor Begotten, and there is no one similar to Him or His equivalent. Learned, Seer, Wise etc., and other characteristics of God's essence whose knowledge and awareness is obligatory for Muslims, and are regarded influential and effective in shaping their lives, and ascension of their spirits, have been repeated in other surahs of the Holy Quran. Do not think beyond the limits as already defined in this surah about God's essence and know-how about His characteristics. Rather, concentration should be exerted for performing deeds, which would eventually enlighten the believer in knowing God better . Do not think that by engaging in lengthy mental debates about His essence you will achieve more enlightenment. It is not so! In-stead, try to. achieve this desired enlightenment by bringing purification and spirituality to your inner self, and by practicing the principles of Monotheism in your deeds and action; and that is the way the prophets, saints, righteous servants of God, pure Monotheists, and gnostics were.

-Profundities of Prayer, Ayatullah Sayyed ' Ali Khamenei, pp-45, 46 [Tr].

-Bihar al-Anwar, vol. 93, p-169.

And said:

"When on the Night of-Ascent (Mairaj) I was taken into the paradise I saw the angels busy in building the palaces of silver and gold but occasionally they suspended the work. I asked them: 'Why do you work intermittently?' 'When we do have construction material, we continue work but when the material is consumed we are forced to terminate the work.' Replied the angels."

"What sort of material you require ? I asked. "Glory to God," "All praises belong to God", "There is no god but God" and "God is Great"; when a believer is busy in invocation -we receive the material and start to build, but when he forgets to offer invocation, we too are forced to terminate the work." Replied the angels."

-Bihar al-Anwar, vol. 93, p-169.

The Holy Prophet (S) said:

"Whoever recites: "Glory to God", a tree is planted for him in the Paradise, similarly God-Almighty orders plantation of a tree for a believer inside the Paradise for each recital of" All praises belong to God" or "There is no god but God or "God is Great". "Then a Qureshite man asked: 'Oh Prophet of God! Then we will have plenty of trees in the paradise.

'Yes it is so! But be careful not to send the fire which will bur" all the trees, because God-Almighty had said in the Holy Quran: O Ye who believe! Obey

God and obey the Messenger and render not your actions vain. ' Replied the Holy Prophet (S)."

-Bihar al-Anwar, vol. 93, p-168.

Each phrase which induces God's Remembrance in a human being and whose meanings are related to praise, supplication, and adoration of God-Almighty -is called invocation (*dhikr*). But traditions have prescribed special invocations whose recital brings special rewards. Some of the important invocations are as follows:

(La ilahi illallahu)

"There is no god but God."

(Subhan allahi)

"Glory to God"

(Al hamdu lillahi)

"All praises belong to God."
(La hol wala quwwateh illa billah)
"There is no power except God-Almighty."
(Hasbanallahi wa nemal wakil)
"God is sufficient and He the best defence."
(La illahi illallahu subhanak inni kuntu min al zalimin)
"There is no God save Thee. Be thou Glorified. Lo! I have been a wrong Doer."
(Ya hayyu ya qayoom ya min la ilahi illa unt)
"Oh Self-Existent, Eternal these is no God except Thee."
(Afwaz amri illallahi innalahi basir bil ibad)
"Leave the affairs to God, He is aware and knowledgeable about His servants."
(La howlwala quwwateh illa billah il 'ali ul azim)
"There is no power except God the Exalted."
(Ya Allah)
"Oh! God."
(Ya Rab) "Oh! Lord!"
(Ya Rahman)
"Oh! Merciful!"
(Ya arhamar rahimin)
"Oh! The Merciful and Compassionate."
(Ya zul jalale wal Ikram)
"Oh! The Majestic and Magnanimous."
(Ya ghani ya mughni)
"Oh! Thou Who is free from needs, and oh! Thou Who is the Granter of our needs."

Similarly there are other Holy attributes of God-Almighty which have; been mentioned in the traditions and supplications. All of them are invocations, motivates a man towards God's Remembrance, and. are means of His-Nearness.

A wayfarer may select any one of the above mentioned invocations and should recite them continuously. But some enlightened gnostics preferred certain special invocations. some of them recommended: "there is no god but God" (La ilahi illallahu), while others selected: "glory to God" all praises belong to God; there is no god but God; and God is Great; (Subhan allahi, wal hamadu lillahi wala ilahi illallahu walahu akbar).

But according to some traditions it may be concluded that the invocation: "there is no god but God " " (La ilahi illallahu) " possesses distinction over other invocations. The Holy Prophet (S) had said:

"The best worships are the recital of invocation 'there is no god but God.'"

-Bihar al-Anwar, vol. 93, p-195.

And said:

"The phrase -"there is no god but God " -is the chief and most distinguished among all other phrases of invocations."

-Bihar al-Anwar, vol. 93, p-204.

The Holy Prophet (S) had narrated from Arch Angel Gabriel that God-Almighty said:

"The phrase -There is no god but God -is the most stable shelter of Mine. Whoever entered in it shall be immune from My Punishment"

-Bihar al-Anwar, vol. 93 p-192.

Since the aim of invocation is attention towards God-Almighty, therefore, it may be concluded -that every phrase which improves and increases a person's motivation to remember God-Almighty is indeed the most suitable invocation for that person.

Generally speaking individuals, conditions and their spiritual ranks differ. It is quite possible that the phrase "Oh! God" (Ya Allah!) under certain conditions might be interesting and suitable for some one, while the phrase- "Oh Thou the Granter of the prayers of the depressed." (Ya Muji bud dawatul Muztarin) may suit some other individual. For some individuals the phrase -"there is no god but God. " (La illahi illallahu) may suit, while for some others the phrase-"Oh Merciful", Concealer of faults" (Ya Ghafar! Ya Sattar!) might be more suitable, and similar is the case with other invocations.

It is because of these considerations that if a wayfarer has access to perfect teacher, it would be better for him to seek his guidance in this regard. But if one does not bas access to such learned teachers he may resort to supplication books, traditions and guidelines left by the Holy Prophet traditions and guidelines left by the Holy Prophet (S) and Infal-lible Imams

(A) of Prophets (Ahlul Bayt).

All invocations and worships are good and if performed correctly may help a wayfarer to attain higher gnostic stations. A wayfarer might utilize some or all of them but the learned teachers of gnostics recommend that in order to attain the positions of invocation (*dhikr*) and witnessing (*shahud*), a wayfarer must select a special invocation and then must undertake its recital for a certain fixed numbers in a special manner in order to accomplish the desired goal.

Here it is important to point out that invocations and supplication prescribed in the religious law, although are worships and could be a means of achieving God's Nearness but, their main aim is attaining the stage of absolute cut off from other than God, and absolute attention and heart's presence towards God-Almighty. Therefore, simply recital of phrases without paying attention towards their meanings and remaining negligent towards the real aims behind them would not produce any result. Because, recital of invocations and even their continuous repetition is not so difficult but this action alone may not help a wayfarer attaining his cherished goal.

What is useful is concentration and heart's presence towards God-Almighty, and negation and complete cut off from every thing other than Him, which is extremely difficult. So far as one does not achieve negation of others than God, he does not attain the worthiness and decency of receiving God's blessings and illuminations. Only a heart absolutely and thoroughly cleansed from all existence other than God -has the honor of becoming a sacred place for the illumination of Divine light. Attaining concentration of thoughts and negation of things other than God require !' serious decision, perseverance, supervision, and constancy. It is not so that one will achieve it during the first attempt without practice and undertaking exercises. We must treat the self cautiously and should make him habitual of this act gradually.

Instructions

~~~❦~~~

Some of the enlightened gnostics have recommended the following instructions for a wayfarer before starting his spiritual journey:

1. First: Before every thing else a devotee must purify his self from sins and moral abjectnesses by means of repentance. In the beginning with the intention of repentance (*towbah*) take a bath (*ghusl*) and during bathing, think about your past sins and esoteric contamination and then with a feeling of shame, present your self before the Most Merciful and Most Compassionate Lord saying: Oh Lord! I have repented and have returned to you. I have taken a firm decision never to sin again. As I cleaned my body with water, I have also cleaned my heart from sins and moral abjectnesses.
2. Second: Consider yourself all the time under the presence of God-Almighty. Try your best to remember God in all circumstances and if once in a while negligence overtakes you try to return to the previous state immediately.
3. Third: Must be strict in guarding his self against contamination with sins. During a period of twenty four hours he must fix a time for self scrutiny and with extreme accuracy should review his daily deeds and should seriously remonstrate his self.
4. Fourth: Should remain silent and should speak whenever it is

absolutely necessary to speak.
5. Fifth: Should eat moderately to meet his physical needs and should strictly avoid overeating and becoming a slave of belly.
6. Sixth: Should maintain his ablution all the times i.e. whenever he terminates ablution he should perform it again. The Holy Prophet (S) narrated a tradition:

"The God-Almighty said: 'Whoever after termination of ablution does not perform it again has been unfaithful to me,' whoever after performance of ablution does not offer two units of prayer has done oppression, and whoever after performance of ablution offers prayer and requests for his worldly and spiritual needs -if I don't grant them, I have oppressed him. But I am not the oppressor God."
-Wasail al-Shi'a, vol. 1, p-268,

7.Seventh: Should fix a time during 24 hours preferably during night before down for practicing concentration and presence of heart, by sitting alone in an isolated place, lowering his head upon knees, concentrating all the senses towards face and strictly avoiding entry of all external thoughts and memories. One should remain in this state for a while. May be this action would result in some spiritual contemplation for the wayfarer.

8.Eight: Invocation: "Oh Self-Existent, Eternal, there is no god save Thee," (Ya Hayyu ya Qayum ya man la ilahi illa unt), should be recited continuously by tongue together with heart's presence i.e. whatever is being chanted by tongue is also comprehended by the heart.

9.Ninth: During a period of 24 hours one must perform a prolonged prostration with concentration and presence of heart in proportion to one's strength and should repeat the invocation: "There is no god save Thee. Be Thou Glorified. Lo! I have been a wrong Doer." (La ilahi illal-lahu Subhanak inni kuntu min az zalimin). The prolongation of prostration has been proved as very effective and produces good spiritual revelations. Some of the devoted wayfarer are reported to have repeated this invocation as much as four thousand times during a single prolonged prostration.

10. Tenth: Fix a certain time during 24 hours and with presence of heart should repeat the invocation, "Oh! Thou Who is free from needs, and Oh Thou Who is the Granter of Our needs." (Ya Ghani Ya Mughni!)

11. Eleventh: Recite the Holy Quran with presence of mind daily, preferably in the standing position and should ponder over the meanings of its verses.

12. Twelfth: Awake a little before the call of Adhan for the morning prayer, after performing required ablutions should offer Night Prayer (*Namaz-e-shab* or *Salatul-lail*), and after finishing it should recite the following verses of Surah Heights (*al-Araf*) with heart's presence, which is useful for attaining certainty and negation of external thoughts.

"*Inna Rabbokumul lahu lazi khalaqas samawate wal arzfi sittate ayyame summastavi ala arsh yaghshil lailin nahar yatlebo hasisan washamso wal qomro wal najoom muskharat be amrehi. elahul khalqo wal amr tabarkallaho rabbul alamin adava rabbokum tazraun wa kafitan nahu la yohubbul moatadin wala tafsodu fil arz bada islaha wa ada wa ho khofan wa tamum un rahmatullahi qarib minal mohsenin."*

"Lo Your Lord is God who created the heavens and the earth in six days, then mounted He the thrown. He covereth the night with the day, which in haste to follow it, and hath made the sun, the moon and the stars subservient by His command. His verily is all creation and commandment Blessed be God, the Lord of the worlds."

"(Oh mankind!) call upon your Lord humbly and in secret. Lo! He loveth not aggressors. Work not confusion in the earth after the fair ordering (thereof, and call on Him in fear and hope. Lo! the mercy of God is nigh unto the good."

-the Holy Quran (7: 54-56), al-Kafi, vol. 1, p-344.

In order to achieve the desired result the above mentioned instructions should be practiced for a period of 40 days. It is possible that the way-farer may succeed in receiving God's attention and might be blessed with spiritual contemplation. But, if after passing forty days one is not fortunate enough to receive such blessings, instead of becoming disap-pointed, the program should be repeated again and again till the desired results are accomplished.

Without giving up seriousness, action, and struggle the wayfarer should remain seriously committed towards his spiritual migration and seek favor from the Most Merciful Lord. When ever, he develops the required decency and competency to receive God's special blessing -it will be bestowed upon him.

In case a wayfarer in the beginning does not have the strength to perform all of the above mentioned guidelines, he may begin with few gradually adding others. But most important among these deeds are pondering, self-control, heart's presence, and attention towards God-Almighty. It is crucial that a wayfarer should thoroughly negate all sort of external thoughts and should pay absolute attention towards God-Almighty, which is a difficult task indeed. The negation of other than God could be achieved gradually in three steps:

1. First: During first stage while reciting invocation try your best to concentrate all your thoughts towards the invocation while strictly pre-venting the entries of all external thoughts.
2. Second: During this stage one should recite invocation exactly like the first stage with the exception that, while reciting complete attention should be paid towards its meanings and contents, in a manner that mind should become clearly aware of this occurrence. At the same time efforts should be made to strictly prevent the attack of all sorts of external thoughts and memories. is program should be exercised until one is able to prevent the attacks of all external thoughts during the entire period of invocation, while being remained attentive to their meanings and contents.
3. Third: During third stage, try your best first to memorize the meanings of invocation inside the heart, and since it has accepted their meanings and believes in them, orders the tongue to recite them. In this case the tongue actually follows the heart.
4. Fourth: At this stage try your best to negate all the meanings, contents, interpretations, and even the imaginations of invocations from the heart, thus, making it readied for receiving Divine blessings and

illuminations. Try to pay absolute attention towards God-Almighty with your entire existence cleansing your hearts thoroughly from all sorts of external existence, opening its gate for the entrance of God's-Celestial Light. At this stage it is quite possible that one might succeed in receiving God's special attention, may utilize His grace and illuminations, and sub-merged with His attraction may ascent further higher and higher upon the ladder of perfection in his spiritual migration towards God-Almighty.

At this station of his gnostic journey the wayfarer might become so much absorbed that he would be seeing nothing except God-Almighty even forgetting his own self and actions. It is better for me to leave the description of these most sublime realities for the God's favorite saints who had seen the end of journey and have tasted the most delicious taste of the stages of Desire (*Shouq*), Affection (*uns*), and Countenance (*Laqa*).

Instructions of the Commander of the Faithful Imam ' Ali (A):

Nouf had narrated:

"*I saw the commander of the Faithful Imam' Ali (A) while passing by with speed, I asked him. 'Oh my master! Where are you heading for?' 'Nouf, leave me alone, my desire is forcing me towards my Beloved. ' Replied the Imam. 'Oh my Master! What is your desire.' I asked him. 'the one who is supposed to know about it -already knows, and there is no need to describe it to some body else. The decency demands that a servant of God should not include others (as partner) as for as the blessings and wants are concerned." Replied the Imam.*

"*'Oh commander of the Faithful! I am afraid of being dominated by selfish whims and greed in my worldly affairs. ' I said. 'Why are you negligent towards the Saver of afraid ones and Protector of pious ones ?' Said the Imam.*

"*'Introduce Him to me.'' I requested. 'He is the God-Almighty the Magnanimous through whose special benevolence your wishes are granted. Pay attention towards*

Him with your full strength and do not allow Satanic whispers to enter inside your heart, and if you find it difficult then consider me as your guarantor. Return to God and pay absolute attention towards Him. The glor-ious God has said:

"'I swear to My Majesty and Splendor that: Whoever puts his hope in some one other than Me, I will cut off his hope, will dress him in the robe of disgrace and wretchedness, will deprive him from My Nearness, will cut off communication with him and will hide his memory. Woe be upon him, who takes shelter in other than Me during difficulties, while the solution of difficulties rests with Me. Does he hope in others while I remain Living and Eternal ? Does he go to the homes of human beings for solution of his problems while the gates of their houses are closed? Does he leave the door of My house while its gate remains always open ?

"'Was there anyone who trusted Me and was betrayed? The hopes of My servants are tied to Me, and I take care of their hopes. ' I have filled the sky with those who never get tired of My praise, and have ordered the angels never to close the door between Me and My servants. Does not, the one who face the problem, know that no one can solve it except with My permission ? Why does not the servant approach Me for his needs, while I had already blessed him with favors without his being asked for them ?"

"Why does not he ask me instead of asking others ? Does he imagine that in the beginning I bestow My favors upon the servant and will now deprive him after his request? Am I miser that My servants regard me as miserly ? Do not the world and Hereafter belong to me ? Do not the merry and benevolence are my characteristics ? Do not the blessings and favors rest in My hand ? Do not all the desires end with Me ? Who has the power to terminate them ?"

"'I swear with My majesty and splendor that if all the needs of all of the world's habitants are summed up, and if I bestow upon them in accordance to their wants, not equivalent even to the weight of a tiny particle will be decreased from My kingdom. Whatever is bestowed by Me, how could be it susceptible to loss or reduction ? How destitute and wretched is the one who is hopeless of My Blessings ? How helpless is the one who disobeys me, indulges into forbidden deeds, disregards My limits and transgresses?" The Commander of the Faithful after narrating this narration said: 'Oh Nouf ! recite the following prayer:

Arabic Pronunciation:

Elahi in hamad tokafa be mawahibe ka, wa in ma Iiattoka fabeh moradeka, wa in qaddastaka fabe qu"vwateka wa in hallatoka fa be qudrateka, wa in naazrto fa iIIa rahmateka, wa in uzuzto fa ala nemateka, ilahi innahu man lam yashqalhul wa luo be zikneka, wa lam yaz wehis safaro be qurbeka, Kanat hayatohu aleyhe maytatan wa maytatahu aleyhe hasratan, llahi tanahat ubsarub nazirina elayka be sarai ril quloobe wa talaat asgas sameyeena laka naj yato sudoor, falam yalqa absarahum raddo duna ma yoriduna, hatak ta baynaka wa baynahum hojobal ghaflate, fasakanufi nooreka, wa tanaffasu be roheka,fasarat qulubohum maqaresan ley habatatika wa absarohum maakefan lequdrateka.

Wa qarrabta ar wa ha hum min qudseka, fajalasu ismaka be waqail mu-jalasate, wukhuzuil mukhatabate, fa aqbalta ilayhim iqbalash shafiqe, wa unsat-ita lahum insator rafiqe, wa ajabtahum ijabatil ahibbai wa najaytahum mun-ajatal ekhil lai, fo ballagh bill mahallallazi ilayhe wasalva, wan qulni min zikri ela zikreka, wala tatruk baini wa baina malakute ezzeka baban illafatehtah wala hijaban minjuhobil ghaflate illa hatakta, hatta toqima.

Ruhi haina ziae arsheka wa taj-ala laha maqarman nasba nooreka innaka ala qulle shyin qadir. Elahi ma aw hasha tariqan layakuno rafiqi fehay amali fika, wa abada safaran la yakuna rajai minho dalili minka, khoba mane etasama be hablay ghayreka, wa zaofa rukno man istanada ila ghayre rukneka, fayar mual-lama muammali hil amalafayaz habo un-hum kabatul wajale, la tahrimni sale-hal amale, wak la ani kal ata man faragatful hiyalo, fa kaifaa yal hoqo muamma-lika zullul faqre wa antal ghani yo un mazaril muznebina.

Elahi wa inna qulla halawatin munqate atun, wa halawatul imane tazdado halawatoha ittasalan beka, Elahi wa inna qalbi qad basata amalahu fika, fa aziq ho min halawate basteka iyyahul buloqa lema ummala, innaoka ala kulla shain qadir, Elahi usaloka mas alata man yarifoka kun ha marefateka min kulla khyrin yanbaqi lil momine us yaslokahu wa auzo beka min kulla sharran wa fi.fnatin aazta beha ahibaka min khalqeka, innaka ala kully shayin qadir.

Elahi asaloka masalatal miskinei lazi qad tahoiyerafe rajahe, fala 'jajdo maljaun wala musnedan yasillo behi elayka, wala yastedillo behi alaika ma beka wa be arkaneka wa magamate kallati la talita laha minka, fa us alo ka bis me kallazi zaharta behi lekhasate oliyaeka fa wahad wo ka wa arafuka fa abaduka be haqiqateka un to arifni nafsaka lay aqir ra laka be rabubiyateka ala haqiqatil imane keka wala toj alni ya Elahi min man yabudul isma dunal mana wal hazni be lahzatin min lahzateka tannavaro beha qalbi be marfeteka khasatan wa mara-fate oliyaika innoka ala kulle shayin qadir.

"Oh God! If I adore you -it is because of Your Mercy and Compassion,. if Glorify you -it is because of Your commandments, if I sanctify and attribute inviolability to you -it is because of your energy, if I chant the world of Monotheism with my tongue -it is because of Your Power. If I raise my eyes -see Your Blessings all over, if I practice thriftiness, it is because to save Your Bounties,. oh Lord! Whoever, You do not engage in Your invocation, and bestow upon him the grace of journeying towards Your countenance -life becomes for him like death, and death becomes for him a regret and disaster.

"Oh Lord! Those who are able to see -look towards You with their esoteric eyes, mysteries of their hearts became manifested and their wants are granted,. the veils of ignorance have been removed between You and them,. your Divine illumination has enlightened their hearts, they breath the breeze of Your Blessings,. Your Majesty and Splendor has overwhelmed their hearts,. they witness the signs of Your Absolute Power every where,. there souls have reached near Your Sacred Thrown and with dignity, tranquility, and humility engage themselves in Your invocations. Like a friend You pay attention towards them, listen to their words, grant their, wants, and communicate with them.

"Please bestow upon me similar positions as attained by them, let the veils of ignorance be uplifted so that my soul could see the Divine illumination of Your Celestial Kingdom, and may receive an exalted position therein. Indeed You have the absolute power over all things. 'Oh God! how fearsome and terrible is journeying on the road which does not terminate in you. Whoever, chooses a shelter of other than you -would certainly be disappointed. Whoever puts his trust in other than you is like sitting upon an unstable base."

"Oh God! who had induced hope within the hearts of all the hopeless ones and have removed their pains and sufferings, please do not deprive me from the grace of performing righteous deeds and preserve me -the shelter less and destitute-in your shelter. How come those, who put their trust in Your Mercy could be inflicted with deprivation? While you remain absolutely free from the need of inflicting loss upon sinners."

"Oh God! All sweetness and pleasures eventually get terminated except the pleasure of faith which increases every day. Oh god! my heart is looking towards You with plenty of desires, please let my heart taste the sweetness of seeing those desires granted. Indeed You have absolute power over all things."

"Oh God! As some one who has reached near the enlightenment of Your Essence, I beg You, to bestow upon me all the blessings which are worthy of a believer. And protect me from all sort of evils and calamities the way You protect all Your favorite servants. In deed You have absolute power over all things."

"Oh God! My request to you is like the request of a confused beggar who does not have any shelter or support and except from you does not seek the help of any other helper. I request by the name, which became manifested for Your favorite saints, thus, enabling them to become enlightened about Your Holy Essence, comprehended You as One, and worshipped You with sincerity indeed; please bestow upon me too the learning to comprehend Your Holy Essence, so that I may admit the reality of Your Divinity and Godhood, and do not include me among them who worship Your Name only without paying attention to its meanings."

"And allocate at least a certain moments (among various moments) to pay attention towards me thus, enlightening my heart about Your Sacred Essence as well as the essence of your favorite saints. Indeed you have absolute power over all things."

-Bihar al-Anwar, vol. 94, p-94.

Instructions of Imam al-Sadiq (A)

Unwan Basari, an old man of ninety-four years has narrated as follows:

"For the sake of acquiring knowledge I used to visit Malik bin Anas. When Ja-far bin Muhammad (A) came to our city I went to visit him, because I wanted to acquire knowledge from his distinguished and eminent personality. One day he said to me: 'I am a person who had received God's special favor and attention and have incantation and invocations for every hour during day and night, therefore, you should not prevent me from their recital and like before continue to visit Malik bin Anas for learning knowledge."

"Hearing these words I become sad and disappointed and left his company. I said to myself. 'If Imam had discovered some goodness within me, certainly he would not have deprived me from his company. Then I left for the Prophet's mosque and offered salutation to him. Next day, I went to the Holy Prophet's tomb and after offering two units of prayer raised my hands up and said:

"Oh God! Oh God! Make Jafar's heart soft for me so that I could utilize his knowledge, and guide me towards straight path." After that with a heavy broken heart returned home as well as visited Malik bin Anas, because love and affection for Jafar bin Muhammad had penetrated far deeper inside my heart. For a long time I confined myself within the four walls of my home and did not come out except for offering mandatory daily prayers till my patience was exhausted one day I went to Imam's house and after knocking the door asked permission to enter inside. A servant came out and asked me."

"What do you want?' 'I would like to see the Imam and offer a salutation.' I replied. 'My master is offering his prayer, replied the servant and returned in-side the home, while I kept awaiting outside the door. After a little while the servant returned and said: 'You may come in."

"I entered inside the house and offered salutation to Imam. He replied my salutation and said: 'Please be seated, may God-Almighty bestow upon you forgiveness.' Then he lowered his head and after a prolonged silence raised his head and said: 'What is your name?' 'Abu Abdullah,' I replied. 'May God-Almighty bless you with His Special Grace and bestow upon you firmness. What do you want?'

"In this meeting i/there is no any other advantage for me except this prayer -even this much is going to be extremely precious for me.' I said to myself Then I said: '1 asked God-Almighty to soften your heart for me so that I may utilize your knowledge. I hope my prayer would have been granted by him.

"Oh Abu Abdullah! Knowledge cannot be acquired by learning rather real knowledge is the light which illuminates a person's heart who is blessed with His guidance. Therefore, i/you are seeker of the knowledge, first make your heart comprehend the reality of (God's) serventhood, then request knowledge by means of deeds, and ask God-Almighty for comprehension so that he could make you understand.' said the Imam.

"I said. 'Oh! Honorable one!' 'Abu Abdullah !'" " Please continue.' said the

Imam. 'Oh Imam! What is the reality of servanthood?' I asked.
The Imam replied. "The reality of servanthood consists in three things as follows:

1. First: A servant should not consider himself the owner of things which have been bestowed upon him by God-Almighty, because servants never become owner of things rather consider all the wealth as God's property and spent it exactly in the same manner as prescribed by him.
2. Second: Should regard him as absolutely helpless in managing his own affairs.
3. Third: Should engage himself continuously in performance of deeds recommended by God-Almighty and avoidance of His forbidden deeds.

"Therefore, if a servant does not consider himself as the owner of the wealth, spending it for the sake of God's way would become easier for him. If he trusted God-Almighty as a competent manager for managing his affairs then tolerance of worldly hardships would become easier for him. If he kept himself engaged in performing Divine commands and sustained himself: from committing forbidden deeds his precious time would not be wasted in nonsense amusements.

"And if God-Almighty honored a servant with these three characteristics then dealing with world, people, and Satan would become easier for him. In that case, he would not endeavor for increase of wealth for self-glorification, and would not wish for things whose possession is con-sidered as means of prestige and superiority among the people and would not waste his precious hours in false pleasures. This is the first rank of piety which have been described by God-Almighty as follows:

> *"As for that abode of the Hereafter, we assign it unto those who seek not oppression in the earth, nor yet corruption, the sequel is for those who ward off evil."*
> *-the Holy Quran (28:83)*

"'Oh! Abu Abdullah! Please bestow upon me practical instructions.' I said. The Imam said: 'I recommend you to follow the, following nine items. These are my recommendations and instructions for all those wayfarers who are journey-ing towards God-Almighty, and I pray that may God-Almighty bestow upon you his special grace. The following are the guidelines: 'There are three guidelines for practicing self-asceticism (riyazat-e-nafs), three guidelines for for-bearance (hilm wa burdbari), and the last three guidelines are for education

{ilm). Preserve them and, be careful not act negligently in their practice'. Unwan Basari said: 'I was listening to Imam's instruction with my entire existence, then the Imam continued ': 'The three instructions recommended by me for self-asceticism consist of:

1. *Be careful, do not eat any thing until and unless you feel an appetite for it, because otherwise, it would be a matter of foolishness and ignorance.*
2. *Do not eat any thing until and unless you feel absolutely hungry.*
3. *When you eat always recite phrase in the Name of God (Bismillah) and eat only lawful (halal) foods.*

The three instructions recommended by me for forbearance consist of:

1. *Whoever tells you: 'For each sentence you speak to me, I will speak ten sentences in response.' You should say in reply: 'If you speak ten sentences to me, in reply you will not hear even one sentence from me.*
2. *Whoever threatens you with abusive language, you should promise him good wishes and advice.*
3. *Whoever accuses you, you must say in reply: 'If you said it right may God forgive me and if you lied then may God forgive you.*

The three guidelines recommended by me for education consist of:

1. *Whatever is unknown to you ask from the learned ones, but be careful not to question them with the intention of examining their knowledge or giving them hard time.*

2. Strictly avoid following your whims and as much as possible act prudently.
3. Strictly avoid issuance of religious decrees (fatwas) without religious documents. As much as you would like to run away while encountering a wild beast, similarly be careful not to offer your neck as a bridge for people's crossing.

"Then he said: 'Oh Abu Abdullah! You may leave now. I have given you sufficient advice. Do not disrupt me from continuation of my incantations and invocations, because, I believe in the dignity of my own self: Salutations be upon those who are obedient to guidance."
-Kashkul, Shaykh Bahai, vol. 2, p-184,
-Bihar al-Anwar, vol. 1, p-224.

Instructions of Allameh Majlisi (R.A.)

One of the most eminent wayfarer of gnostic journey -the great learned Divine Scholar Mulla Muhammad Taqi Majlisi writes:

"Whatever this servants has discovered during his period of self-building and gnosticism is related to the period when I was busy in studying commentary of the Holy Quran, one night, while I was in a state of partly slept and partly awakened I saw the Holy Prophet Mohammad (S) in a dream. I said to my self that it is a good opportunity to take a profound look about the perfection and moral ethics of the Holy Prophet (S) The more I paid attention towards him I found his splendor and illumination spreading till it brightened the entire space around me."

"At this moment it was revealed to me that the Holy Quran is the perfect manifestation of the Holy Prophet's moral ethics. Therefore, to know more about Holy Prophet's moral ethics I must ponder deeply about the Holy Quran. The more I paid attention upon the verses of Holy Quran the more I discovered the sublime realities till at one instant I felt that a lot of realities and learning have been descended upon my heart."

"After that whenever I pondered about a Qur'anic verse, I felt that a special talent for its comprehension has been bestowed upon me. Of course, appreciation of this incident by some one who has not been blessed with such a grace is natur-ally difficult rather impossible, but my aim was to advice and guide the fellow brothers for the sake of God-Almighty. The guidelines for asceticism and self-building consist of:

-Useless talks, rather any thing other than God's Remembrance should be strictly avoided.

-Living in luxurious, beautiful and comfortable housing as well as consumption of expensive foods, drinks and fancy clothing should be renounced. (one should limit himself to the extent of .fulfilling his genuine needs).

-Social mixing with other than God's most favorite saints should be strictly avoided.

-Excessive sleep should be avoided and God's invocation with complete dedication should be recited continuously.

"God's favorite saints by continuous recital of invocations namely: "Oh! Self-existent Oh! Eternal " (ya Hayyio ya Qayyum!) and "There is no god but God" (Ya man la ilaha illa ant), were able to obtain good results. I too have practiced the same invocation but perhaps my favorite invocation is "Oh! God"! (Ya Al-lah), with thorough cleansing of heart from all existence other than God, together with absolute concentration towards Him. Of course, what is important is that God's Remembrance should be accompanied with absolute concentration and heart's presence. Also, all other deeds do not come close to the importance assigned to invocation."

"If this is done for a period of forty day and night continuously then certainly the doors of wisdom, learning, and love will be opened for the wayfarer enabling him to ascent towards the most exalted gnostic positions of annihilation in God (fanafi Allah wa baqa billah), or achieving permanence with God-Almighty."

-Rozatehal-Mutaqin, vol. 13, p-128.

Letter of Akhund-Mulla Hussein Quli Hamdani

The most eminent learned Divine scholar and gnostic (late) Akhund Mulla Hussein-Quli Hamadani (R.A.) in his letter to one of the scholar in Tabriz writes:

(Bismillah ar Rahman ar Rahim, Alhamdulillahi rabal alimin was salat was salam ala Muhammad wa aleh al tahirin wa lantatullahi ala adaihim ajmaeen).

"In the Name of God, the Beneficent, the Merciful"

"Praise be upon God of the worlds, salutations be upon the Muhammad and his Holy progeny and may be the curse of God be upon their enemies."

"It should not remain hidden for religious brothers that there is no way to achieve the nearness of the Lord of Splendor and Majesty except strictly following the sacred religious law of Islam (Sharia) in all movements, pauses, conversations, and instances etc. Superstitious methods practiced by some pseudo mystics and ignorant ones in accordance to their intellectual taste do not produce any desired result except their taking farther distance from God-Almighty."

"Even a person who forbids upon himself meat and leaves the hairs of his mustache untrimmed is blessed with the blessing of faith, (i. e. belief about the immunity from sin for the infallible Imams of the Prophet's progeny) must understand, that unless and until he strictly practices their instructions and traditions for invocations, he would become farther away from God-Almighty."

"It is therefore, necessary that he must regard the sacred Divine Law (Sharia) with special reverence and should attach utmost importance for its execution. Whatever have been emphasized in the sacred religious law as well as whatever have been comprehended by this poor servant by using intellect and deliberating traditions may be concluded: "The fulfillment of the heartiest desire of all creatures -God's Nearness depends upon their making serious efforts and endeavors to quit sinning."

"So for this is not done recital of invocations and pondering over Qur'anic verses would not produce any useful result for heart, because the services rendered by some one who is in direct rebellion against the King would be useless. I don't know, what sort of King ? The exaltedness belong to that king of Splendor and Majesty, and which enmity could be more worst then enmity with such a King ?"

"You must better understand that your efforts endeavor for achieving God's Nearness -while still sinning and being contaminated is a serious mistake. How come this matter has remained hidden from your eyes that it is the sin of a sinner that causes the King to feel hatred towards him, and this hatred can never be summed up with His love."

"Since you know it with certainty that avoidance of sins is the beginning, end, apparent, and hidden of faith, therefore the sooner you engage yourself in self-struggle the better it would be. With absolute dedication from the moment you awake, all along the day till the time of sleep you must monitor your self strictly. Be careful to remain respectful because you are continuously in the presence of the Lord of Majesty al 1d splendor and know that all your body parts and members, including the finest particles of your existence are the prisoners of His Power, therefore, do not forget to observe the rules of etiquette. Worship him in a manner as though you are actually seeing Him, and if you do not see Him, any way He sees you."

"Be conscious about His Majesty and your humility, His Eminence and your lowness, His Magnanimity and your abjectness and His Freedom from needs and your neediness. Be aware that if you act negligently in remembering the Lord of Glory and Magnanimity but He does remember you, and in his presence stood like a helpless, wretched servant. Like a bony dog put your chin upon din before His feet. Is this distinction and honor is not sufficient for you that He has permitted you to utter His Holy Exalted Name by your filthy tongue? The tongue that had become unclean due to pollution of sinning."

"Oh dear! Since the Most Compassionate and Most Merciful Lord has made the tongue as the reservoir of the mountain of light, to be commissioned only for His Holy invocation it is indeed shamelessness that the King's reservoir be polluted by refuse and filth of lying, backbiting, cursing, teasing, and sinning. It should be a place full of perfume and rose water instead of being filled with filth and refuse. Beyond any doubt since you acted negligently in supervising your self strictly, you don't know what son of horrible sins and transgression have been committed by your body pans namely: ears, tongue, eyes, hands feet, belly, and sexual organs."

"What sorts of devastating fires have you ignited? How much corruption have you induced in your religion? How much prohibited wounds have you inflicted upon your heart through the tongue's swords and arrows? It will be surprising if it has not already been killed. If I want to comment about the details of these deviations even this entire book would not be enough, what can I do with one page? You, who have yet not cleaned your body pans from the filth, how do you expect someone to write for you about the heart's condition? Therefore, make *haste, hurry up to perform a true repentance and seriously guard your self."*

"In summary, after making his best endeavors for strictly guarding the self a wayfarer striving for God's Nearness should not be negligent about night vigil awakening before dawn and offering the night prayer (Namaz-e-Shab) with concentration and heart's presence. If time permits J he should engage himself in hymns and invocations but at least a pan of night should be spent in invocation with heart's presence. In all these situations the wayfarer should not be without grief and sorrow and if he is -he should acquire its causes."

"In the end recite the following:

1. The rosary of Hazrat Fatimeh al-Zahra (S.A.)[34]
2. Surah al-Ikhlas (surah no. 112)-12 times,
3. "There is no god but God. There is no partner, there is no kingdom except yours." (La illahi illahi wahdahu la sharika lah, lahu al-Mulk) -10 times,
4. "There is no god but God" (la ilahi illallahu) -100 times,
5. I Beseech God's forgiveness and offer repentance" (Astaghfarullahi rabi wa atuboh ilahe) -70 times,
6. A portion of Holy Quran and the famous prayer named Dua-i –Sabah [35] of the Commander of the Faithful Imam 'Ali (A).

"One should remain in the state of ablution continuously and it is preferred to offer two units of prayer after performing each ablution. Be careful not to inflict the least damage or hurt the feeling of fellow human beings and must strive sincerely in meeting the needs of fellow Muslims especially the scholars and pious ones. He should not attend any meeting where there is a possibility of sinning, even socialization with the negligent ones is harmful. Also, excessive involvement in world affairs –although permitted religiously, too much humor, nonsense talking, and listening to false rumors are injurious for the hearts con-dition ultimately making it a dead heart."

---

[34] Allahu Akbar 34 times, Subhan Allah 33 times, an Alhamdu lillah 33 times [Tr].

[35] For Dua-i Sabah refer to Mafateh al-Jinan of Haj Sheikh Abbas Qummi p-97 [[Tr].

"Without, practicing, strict self-control simply engaging in invocation and deliberations would be fruitless and would not produce the results even though if one succeeds in achieving ecstasy, because it won't be durable and one should not be fooled with ecstasy achieved without self-surveillance. I do not have lot of strength and I beseech you to pray a lot for me and do not forget this humble wretched sinner full of guilt. Do recite Surah Power (Qadr), one hundred times on Thursday night and Friday afternoon."

-Tazkirateh al-Muttaqin, p-207.

Instructions of Mirza Javad Agha Malaki Tabrizi (R.A)

[36] The most celebrated perfect gnostic Mirza Javad Agha Maliki Tabrizi writes:

"The Holy prophet (S) through his repeated recommendations have emphasized

---

[36] Mirza Javad Agha Malaki Tabrizi: The most distinguished jurispru-dent and perfect mystic late Mirza Javad Agha Malaki Tabrizi was born in Tabriz. After finishing has early education at his home town, he left for Najaf-e-Ashraf which at that time was supposed to be the most reputable religious learning center. At Najaf he attended the lectures of great learned jurisprudents such as Akhund Khorasani (writer of Kifayateh al-Usool) Haj Agha Ridha Hamadani (writer of Misbah al-Faqiyeh) and Muhaddith Nouri (writer of Mustadrak al-Wasail).

Also, during this period he came in contact with most celebrated mys-tic personality of that time -Akhund Mulla Husain Quli Hamdani, who was unique in knowledge, ethics, and mystics. Mr. Malaki spent 14 years with him and during this period acquired profound knowledge of moral ethics and Mysticism from his learned professor. Mr. Malaki attained such higher spiritual positions in gnosticism that a great jurisprudent and scholar like sheik Muhammad Hussain Isfahani famous as Kampani, himself an outstanding authority of learning and deeds, in a letter to Mr. Malaki, seeks his instructions regarding ethics and mysticism.

Mr. Malaki returned to his native home town Tabriz in the year 1320 or 21 A.H. and settled down there, but after few years due to constitutional revolution the conditions in Tabriz deteriorated facing him to migrate to Qum. Where he started teaching jurisprudence from Faiz Kashani's Book: Mafateeh as well as taught ethics (Akhlaque). Also, he kept himself busy in writing and had left many precious works.

Ultimately, after living a fruitful life full of learning, teaching, writing, refinement, and purification of self he left this transient world to join his beloved in the moving of 11th Dhill Hijjah 1343 A.H. His Holy remains were buried in the t Shaykhan-Qum Graveyard near the tomb of Mirzai Qummi. The following verse, written in Arabic reflects about his precious existence and the year of his demise.

"The world lost its soul, the Nation lost its shelter."

His virtues and mystical perfection are far greater to be confined in words. In order to satisfy the curiosity of our readers to know more about profundities of Islamic mysticism, the following reports narrated by authentic sources will through some light about the spiritual perfection of this great man.

1.One of his close friend and pupil had reported:

"One night in the city of Shahroud in a dream I found myself in a plain where Imam al-Mahdi (2) (A) the Lord and Master of the Age, together with a group of his companions, was leading the congregational prayer. With the intention of kissing his hand and salutations, when I approached him, I saw a sheik whose face was the manifestations of virtues and perfection sitting near the Imam. After awakening from this dream kept thinking deeply about the dignified sheik who is so close to the Imam. I was so much interested to identify and meet him."

the importance of prolonged prostration, which indeed is an extremely important matter. Prolonged prostration is the most nearest aspect of servanthood, and it is

---

"Searching for him, I went to Mash had hoping to locate him over these but could not; came to Tehran but still there was no news from him, ultimately, when I came to Qum, I found him in a small room at Faizyeh -school busy in teaching. Having inquired about him, they said: 'He is Mirza Javad Malaki Tab-rizi.' When I visited him he welcomed me worm I heartedly and with kindness, treated me in a manner as though he knows me, and was aware of that dream. After that I remained in his company and found him exactly the way I had first perceived him in that dream."

2. Another one of his intimate friend has reported. The following story: "One day after finishing the lecture late Malaki went to the room of a religious student in Dar al-Shafa School; he thanked and appreciated the inmate and after sitting over there for a while came out of the room. Since I was accompanying him, I asked the reason of visiting this student Mr. Malaki answered: 'Last night near the dawn I was bestowed with special Divine grace which I understood was not due my own deeds. When, I thought deeply, I discovered that this student is busy in night vigil and in his night prayer has prayed for me and those blessing were the result of his prayer. Therefore, I visited him for offering my appreciation and thanks.

3. "Late Malaki has a son who is the source of warmth and pleasure for his household. On the Day of Eid-e-Ghadir (3), when traditionally people visit the elderly personalities to offer greetings, his house is full of visitors. Suddenly, a female servant discovers the dead body of his son floating inside the yard's water pool. She starts crying; the others women folk of Mr. Malaki's household joins her in loud crying; having heard the loud screams Mr. Malaki comes to the back yard and sees the lifeless body of his dear one; he controls himself and asks the women folk to stop crying, the women stop lamentation and become silenced, the dead body is placed in a corner and they return inside the house in order to treat the visiting guests. Some of the guests remained for the lunch at his house. After lunch, when the guests asked permission to leave, Mr. Malaki says to some of his close friends:

'Please don't leave, I have some thing to tell you.' When all the guests left the house, he informed them about the tragedy of his son's demise and seeks their help in making the necessary arrangements for the funeral."

4. Late Hujjatul Islam Sayed Mahmood Yazdi, one of very close and intimate friend has narrated the following: "When the time of night prayer arrived he used to perform all the etiquettes recommended for awakening of heart namely prostration and special supplications, used to cry in his bed, then he will come outside in the yard and looking at the sky will recite the verse:

"(Lo! in the creation of earth and sky there are signs..." -the Holy Quran (2: 164)

and while placing his head against the wall, shedded tears. During ablutions sitting one the water pool continued crying and while standing upon the prayer rug used to become agitated and used to cry a lot during prayer and especially in Qunoots."

because of this consideration that two prostration have been incorporated in each unit of prayer. About the prolonged prostration of Infallible Imams

1. of the prophets progeny and their Shiite's, a lot of traditions have been narrated."

---

5. Late Haj Agha Husain Fatimi, a pious ascetic and an intimate friend of Mr. Malaki has narrated: "When I returned from the Jamkaran Mosque, I was informed that Mr. Malaki has inquired about me. Since, I knew that he is sick I rushed to see him. I presume it was Friday after noon, I found him laying upon a bad neat and cleaned, bathed, perfumed and hair dyed readied for Dhohr and Asr Prayer. He recited Ad-han and Aqameh upon his bed, recited supplications and as soon as raised his hands for Takbirteh al-Ahram and said Allahu Akbar (God is great) his sacred spirit ascended towards the celestial Kingdom thus, the meanings of narration: The Prayer is believers heavenly journey -become truly manifested for him. Also, the meanings of "Get readied for the Prayer" in accordance to traditions have been described as the time of meeting the Beloved, too become materialized for him because he rushed to meet his Beloved with prayer.

This was the brief life history of a perfect mystic. For the detailed biography the readers may refer to the following books:

Rehanateh al-Adab vol. 5 p-397, Naqba al-Beshar vol. 1 p-330, Ganjinai Danishmandan vol. 1 p-232, preface to Resala Laqa Allah and Simai Far-zangan pp. 60-70 [Tr].

(2)Imam al-Mahdi (A): The son of Imam Hasan Askari was born in Samarra on Friday, 15th Sha'ban 255 A.H. The twelfth Imam lives in hiding under the protection and tutorship of his father until the latter's martyrdom, when by God's command he went into occultation, during a period known as "lesser occultation" (al-Ghaybat as-Sughra). During this period, four special deputies in succession would answer the questions of the Shi 'ite and resolve their problems. After that in the year 329 A.H. the Imam went into the Greater occultation (al-Ghaybat al-Kubra), until a day when by God's command he will reappear to fill the world with justice as it is now filled with oppression.

(3).Eid-e-Ghadir: In the tenth year of the Hijra, the Most Noble Messenger (S) set out foro Mecca to perform his final, farewell Hajj. After car-rying out the rituals of the pilgrimage and imparting necessary teachings to the people, he set out for Medina. When he was returning on 18th Dhu' l-Hijja (10 March, 632), on the road at a locale known as Ghadir al-Khumm (Ghadir Pond), he ordered the caravan to halt. In the midst of one hundred twenty thousand pilgrims from all over the Arabian Peninsula, he took 'Ali's (A) hand, raised it aloft and declared:

"He of whom I am the mawla (the patron, master, leader), of him 'Ali is also the mawla (man kuntu mawlahu fa Ali-un-mawlahu).

Oh God! Be friend of him who is his friend, and be the enemy of him who is his enemy {Allahuma wali man walahu wa adi man adhau)"

In the one of his prolonged prostration Imam al-Sajjad has repeated the following invocation one thousand times:

(La illahi illahi haqan haqqa, la illahi illahi taubdan wa riqqa, la illahi illahi Imanan wa sadqa)

"There is no god but God-truly and Justly." "There is no god but God I bow in humility in front of him." "There is no god but God is the truth indeed and is my faith."

About Imam al-Kazim (A) it has been reported that some times he prolonged his prostration from morning till noon, and similar incidents have been narrated about his companions namely: Ibne abi Amir, Jamil, and Kharbouz.

"During my stay in Najafi-Ashraf, I had a learned pious scholar who was a Marjai-Taqlid for religious students. I once ask him: 'What special act have you tried in your own life which is effective for a wayfarer in his spiritual gnostic journey?' He replied: 'To prolong the prostration during a period of twenty four hours and reciting of invocation:

(La illahi illa ant Subahnak Inni Kunt min as Zalimin). "There is no God save Thee. Be Thou Glorified. Lo! I have been a wrong doer." While reciting this invocation lie must pay attention to the fact that God-Almighty is for inviolable to oppress me rather I am the one who have oppressed my own self and have blamed

---

With this act, the question of the successor, who was to govern the affairs: of the Muslims, guard the sunnah (the body of customary behavior based on the Prophet precedent), and uphold religious customs and laws, was settled for the Islamic society. The intent of the noble verse, ' Messenger! Promulgate what has been revealed to you by your Lord. for if you do not. you will not have conveyed His message' (5: 67), was carried out. The Most Noble Messenger (S) died shortly after returning to Medina. The above traditions of al-Ghadir are so abundantly reported and so commonly attested by hundreds of different transmitters belonging to all school of thoughts that it be futile to doubt their authenticity. Ibn Kathir, a most staunch supporter of Sunni viewpoint has devoted seven pages to this subject and has collected a great number of different isnads from which the tradition is narrated. Also, Imam Ahmad bin Hanbal has recorded this event in his Musnad [Tr].

4While offering prayers in sitting positions the legs are bent in a
vertical, plane. Like sitting for Tashahud and Salutation. Squared position means a relaxed position in which the legs are bent in a horizontal plane [Tr].

Him for that."

"My teacher recommended this prostration to those who were interested in gnostic journey, and those who performed it obtained good results especially, those who prolonged it more. Some of them repeated this invocation in prostra-tion one thousand times, some of them a little more or less and about some of them I heard that they repeated it three thousands times in their prostration."

-al-Moraqebat, p-122.

Instructions of Sheikh Najmuddin (R.A)

Sheikh Najmuddin Razi writes:

"Know that engaging in invocations without paying due regards to recital manners and relevant etiquettes will not produce useful results. First of all a devoted wayfarer should prepare himself thoroughly to meet all the requirements of moral etiquette. When a true devotee is inflicted with the pain of desire for undertaking the spiritual journey, its symptoms are that he develops intense affection with invocations and feels frightened with the people until reaching to a point whereby he turns his face away from the people and takes shelter in invocation, as the Holy Quran says:

> *"Say God! Then leave them in the play of caviling."*
> *-the Holy Quran (6:91)*

"As he continues to guard his invocations he should not be negligent towards its basis which is true repentance (towbatun nasuh) and should not commit sins. While, engaging in invocations it is preferable to take a bath (ghusl) and in case it is not possible one must make ablutions, because invocation is tantamount of waging wars against enemies in the battlefield which cannot be done without armaments, and this is why the ablution has been called as the armaments of believers:

The clothing of devotee should be clean and should meet the following four requirements:

1. First: Cleanliness from impurities such as blood, urine and excrement etc.
2. Second: Cleanliness from oppression i.e. the clothing should not have been obtained through oppression.
3. Third: Cleanliness from sanctity i.e. it should not consists of forbidden (haram) Material such as silk (for men).
4. Fourth: Cleanliness from vanity i.e. its length should be short in accordance with Islamic traditions and should not be dress of vanity.

The place of invocation should be dark, clean, and isolated and it is preferred to make it perfumed by burning some incenses. He should sit in the direction of Mecca, sitting in a squared position [4] -a position which is forbidden all times except far recital of invocation because Khuwaja (A) after offering morning prayer used to sit in squared position until sunrise. He should place his hands upon his thighs, making his heart and eyes readied with all due respect

should, start reciting the invocation (la ilahi illallahu). "There is no god but God" -with his entire existence in a rhythmic cycle in a whistling manner without raising his voice.

"He should recite the invocation firmly and continuously pondering about its meanings within his heart as well as negating all the external thoughts. Like the meanings of "there is no god" (La illahi) he should negate whatever thoughts enter inside his heart, meaning that he would no longer desire any thing else and would not like to have any other beloved except God-Almighty. In totality he should negate other gods and should affirm the God-Almighty as the beloved and ultimate desired object."

"While chanting each phrase of invocation the heart should accompany the tongue from the beginning till end negating and affirming, and in this process whenever he looks inside his heart and if discovers his heart attached to something else -should discard it, returning the heart to God-Almighty. By negating -"There is no god." -must nullify heart's attachment towards other than God, thus, destroying the roots of his attachment to other objects and replacing it with God's love."

"In this manner the devotee should chant, invocation continuously, so that gradually heart becomes cleaned and purified from all sorts of usual desirable

objects achieving an state of heart's absolute domination with invocation. When it occurs the devotee becomes totally annihilated by the invocation's illumination turning him as singular -purifying his essence with all sort of attractions and obstacles, and enabling him to pass through the material and spiritual worlds swiftly."

"As it is said: that the heart of a believer is the place especially reserved for the union with the God-Almighty. But so for as the heart's domain is occupied by the alien elements, God's Majesty and Exaltedness does not consider it befitting for His entry. However, once the herald of "there is no god" announces the cleanliness of heart's domain from alien elements, one may then expect the entry of the Lord of the Majesty and Splendor. As the Holy Quran says:

"So when thou art relieved still toil and strive to please thy Lord."
-the Holy Quran (94:7-8)

-Marsad al-ebad, p-150.

Therefore, in the light of above discussion it becomes clear that eminent gnostics while regarding invocation as one of the best means for undertaking gnostic journey, for its implementation have experienced and recommended various methods. The reason is that all invocation described therein assure the real aim behind them which is to cut off all connections from other than God and paying absolute attention towards God-Almighty. But their influence varies in proportion to the rank and degree of a devotee. What is the rank and position of a wayfarer, where does he stand upon the path, and what particular invocation will be suitable for him –are matters where the role of a competent teacher comes into picture.

In the books of traditions and supplications a lot of invocation and supplication have been narrated and for each one of them special rewards have been described accordingly. Over all invocations and supplications may be divided into two categories, namely: Independent and Conditional.

For some of the invocations particular timings, special conditions and a certain number have been prescribed and in these cases the wayfarer is supposed to perform them exactly in the same manner as prescribed by the

Infallible Imams (A) so that he earn the prescribed reward. But some of the invocations are independent and in those cases the devotee is free to select the suitable number for its recital and its timings in accordance to his circumstances, and conditions. Or, may consult his teacher and guide. Also, one may resort to the books of supplication and traditions.

Here it is important to emphasize the importance of the following matters:

1. First: A wayfarer must be aware of the fact that the real aim behind the invocation is to attain absolute concentration and heart's presence towards God-Almighty. Therefore, in selecting the timings, quantity and quality of invocation he should keep in mind the real aim and should continue recital, but whenever he feels tired, exhausted and disaffected he should discontinue and must start again at some appropriate time because the Commander of the Faithful Imam 'Ali (A) said:

"Sometimes the heart is. healthy and full of enthusiasm while at other times it is sick and disaffected, therefore, deeds must be performed when the heart is willing, otherwise, performance of a deed with a reluctant heart would result in heart's blindness."

-Bihar al-Anwar, vol. 70, p-61.

2.Second: It must be understood clearly that the real aim behind continuation of invocation and practicing asceticism is to attain self-perfection and God's Nearness which is not possible except through discharging due obligations. If a person is responsible for performance of some social and religious obligations, he must discharge them properly and while doing so should not remain negligent from God's Remembrance as well as recital of invocations to the extent he may do so. Also, he may again continue it in his free time, but if by taking the excuse of asceticism and continuation of invocation if he hides into seclusion and did not discharge his due obligations, then such deeds will not result in God is Nearness for him.

Obstacles of the Path

Starting a spiritual journey upon the road of perfection and attaining higher spiritual positions is not an easy and simple task rather is extremely difficult and complicated. A devotee has to encounter plenty of obstacles in his path and must struggle to remove them, otherwise, he would never be able to reach his Desired destination.

First Obstacle – Incompetence

The greatest obstacle for undertaking gnostic journey and attaining God's Nearness by a wayfarer is the incompetency of his self. A heart contaminated and darkened by sinning cannot become a center for the illumination of Divine light. When a human heart as a result of sinning turns into a Satan's commands center then how come God's favorite angels may descend into it?

Imam al-Sadiq (A) narrated a tradition from his father:

"For a human being there is nothing worst than sin because it wages war against heart until taking over its control. This condition of heart is called inverted or upside down heart."

-Bihar al-Anwar, vol. 73, p-312.

The heart of a sinner is an inverted heart, which forces him to move in the wrong direction. Then how could he move in the direction of God's

Nearness and could accept God's blessings and favors? Therefore, it is necessary for a wayfarer that before starting his journey to achieve self-purification and self-perfection, firstly he must try his best not to commit sins and only then he should engage himself into invocation and worship, otherwise his efforts and endeavor in invocation and worship will not result in his becoming near to God-Almighty.

Second Obstacle -Worldly Attachments

One of the greatest barrier is the attachments to worldly allurements such as desire of wealth and property, love of wife and children, attachment to house and other means of living, ambitions towards power and positions, attachments towards family, and even liking towards education and knowledge etc. are the types of attachments which prevent a human being from movement and migration towards God-Almighty.

A heart so much in love with perceptible things and is infatuated in them, how can detach itself so easily and may ascent towards the Upper-Heaven? A heart which is the command center for of worldly affairs, how could it become the illumination of Divine light. Apart from that in accordance to traditions the love of this world is the roots of all sins and transgressions, and a sinner can never ascent towards God's Nearness. Imam al-Sadiq (A) has said:

"*The love of world is the root of all evils.*"

-Bihar al-Anwar, vol. 73, p-90

The Holy Prophet (S) has said:

"*The first thing through which transgression against God-Almighty was done consisted of six characteristics: Love of world, love of position, love of women, love of eating, love of sleeping, and love of comforts.*"

-Bihar al-Anwar, vol. 73, p.94.

Jabir narrated that once he visited Imam al-Baqir (A) who said:

"*Oh Jabir my heart is sad and lull of grief 'May my soul be sacrificed upon you, what is the reason of your grief? I said. The Imam said: 'In whoever's heart the God's true and pure religion will enter, his heart would become detached to all* external attachments (other than God's)."

"Oh Jabir! what is world and its worth? Is it any thing else other than the mouthful you eat, the piece of dress you use to cover your body and the women you take for marriage ?"

"Oh Jabir! The believers do not trust the world and its life and do not regards themselves as safe from their transfer into the Hereafter."

"Oh Jabir! The Hereafter is the permanent abode of eternity while the world is a place of temporary abode and place of dying but the worldly ones are negligent of this reality except the true believers who are the people who think, deliberate, and take lessons from the world. Whatever, enters into their ears does not pre-ent them from God's Remembrance, and similarly possession of gold and wealth does not to make them negligent from God's worshiping , thus, they are the ones who earn the rewards of Hereafter because of their being aware about the religion."

-Bihar al-Anwar, vol. 73, p-36.

The Holy Prophet (S) said:

"A person never tastes the sweetness of faith until and unless he becomes indifferent to whatever has been eaten by him."

-Bihar al-Anwar, vol. 73, p-49.

Therefore, it is necessary for a wayfarer to completely detach his heart from such attractions so that movement and migration towards the higher exalted positions become possible for him. He should thoroughly cleanse his heart from thoughts and anxieties of worldly affairs so that they could be replaced by God's Remembrance.

However, it must be reminded that whatever has been condemned is -infatuation and intense attachment to worldly affairs -and not worldly affairs in themselves. A wayfarer, like any other human being for continuation of life needs housing, clothing, food, and life partner and in order to fulfill these requirements he has no choice except to work.

For the continuation of human race and to leave his offspring one must marry and for the sake of social life he has no choice except to accept social responsibilities. It is because of these considerations that none of them have been condemned in the Islamic canon law (*sharia*)³⁷. Instead if performed with the intention of God's Nearness (*qurb*), all of them are considered as worships bringing a person closer to God-Almighty. Because these things in themselves do not act as obstacles for movement, undertaking a gnostic journey, and engaging in God's Remembrance.

What acts as an obstacle for movement and invocation is infatuation and intense attachments to these affairs. If these affairs become the life's main aim and objective, thus, occupying his attention and thoughts completely in themselves then such a situation would result in his becoming negligent from God's Remembrance. Therefore in Islam money worshiping, women worshiping, and power and education worshiping are condemned because they prevent a man from migration and movement towards God-Almighty but the money, women, education, and position in themselves are not condemned.

Did not the Holy Prophet (S) Commander of the Faithful, Imam ' Ali (A), Imam al-Sajjad, and other Infallible Imams of Prophets (*Ahlul Bayt*) work, endeavor, and utilize the Divine bounties? This is one of the great advantage of Islam that for the World and Hereafter and their relevant affairs does not recognize any boundary and limitations.

Third Obstacle -Obedience of Passions

The Third obstacle is surrender to selfish whims, passions and carnal desires. Like the dark and thick smoke, self's whims and passions attack the heart's domain turning into a darkened heart, thus, lacking the decency for illumination of Divine light.

Whims and passion continuously pull the heart from one direction to another one, thus, never allowing him the opportunity to have a union with God-Almighty and developing some affection for Him. Day and night they try and endeavor to present their own passionate demands. Naturally, in

---

[37] Shariah, Divine law, a science which embraces every dimension of human conduct, including the political [Tr].

this situation who has the courage to think about migration and ascension towards the Celestial Kingdom of God-Almighty.

The God-Almighty has said in Holy Quran:

"And follow not desire that it beguile thee from the way of God."
-the Holy Quran (37:26)

The Commander of the Faithful Imam Ali (A) said:
"The most brave person is the one who could dominate over the passions of his self."
-Bihar al-Anwar, vol. 70, p-76.

Fourth Obstacle –Overeating

One of the main obstacles of the way for God's Remembrance and invocation is over-eating and being a slave of the belly. A person who strives day and night to arrange good and delicious food and fills his belly with different sorts of tasty foods, how could such a person will have union with God-Almighty, develop affection, and establish secret communications with Him? With a stomach full of food how could one may have a mood for worshiping and supplication? Some one who considers pleasure simply in eating and drinking, when would taste the sweetness of supplication with God-Almighty? It is because of these considerations that overeating has been condemned in Islam. Imam al-Sadiq (A) said to Abu-Basir.

"Stomach transgresses under the influence of over-eating. The most nearest situation between the God-Almighty and his servant is -when the stomach is empty and the worst situation is -when his stomach is full."
-Wasail al-Shi'a, vol. 16, p-405.

Imam al-Sadiq also said:
"God-Almighty considers over eating as something indecent."
-Wasail al-Shi'a, vol. 16, p-407.

The Holy Prophet (S) had said:
"Don't indulge in over-eating because it would quench the light of faith with-in

your hearts."
-al-Mustadrak, vol. 3, p-81.

Imam al-Sadiq (A) had said in a narration:

"For the heart of a believer there is nothing worst than over-eating, because it will cause hard-heartedness and seduction, while hunger happens to be the most delicious disk for a believer's soul and heart, and health for his body."
-al-Mustadarak, vol. 3, p-80.

The Commander of the Faithful Imam Ali (A) has said:

"When God-Almighty intends to reform the believer's affair, He bestows upon him three blessings: less sleep, less appetite, and less speech."
-al-Mustadarak, vol. 3 p-81.

He also said:

"Hunger is the best help for controlling self and breaking up chronic habits."
-al-Mustadarak, vol. 3 p-81.

There is a tradition narrated by Imam' Ali (A) that on the night of As-cent (*Mairaj*), God-Almighty said to the Holy Prophet (S):

"Oh Ahmad! How sweet and beautiful are the hunger, silence, and seclusion? 'Oh God! What is the advantage of hunger?' Asked the Holy Prophet (S). 'Wisdom, heart's tranquility, nearness to Me, continuous grief, righteous talks, thriftiness, and in difference at the time of ease and hardships, are the characteristics acquired by My servant as a result of hunger, silence, and seclusion.' Replied the God-Almighty."
-al-Mustadrak, vol. 3 p-82.

Of course, a wayfarer like other people for remaining alive and to have the required energy for worship requires food, but he should be careful to eat food just to fulfill his bodily requirements and should avoid over-eating strictly. Because, over-eating causes indigestion, lethargy and depression towards worship, hard heartedness, and negligence from God's Remembrance.

On the contrary moderation in eating and hunger result in one's feeling active and zealous for worship and attention towards God-Almighty. While, being hungry a human being is possessed with soul's purification, illumination and enjoyment which is not the case with a full stomach.

Therefore, it is extremely important that a wayfarer should eat only to the extent it is required for fulfillment of his bodily needs and especially should be hungry during invocation, worshiping, and supplication.

Fifth Obstacle - Unnecessary Talks

One of the obstacle which prevents a wayfarer from movement towards his ultimate desired goal, and intervene in achieving concentration and heart's presence, is useless and idle talks. God-Almighty has be-stowed upon him the power of speech in order to fulfill his genuine needs. If he used it to the extent it was needed then he has utilized this great blessing correctly. Apart from that because of excessive talking a persons thoughts became scattered and disturbed and therefore, cannot pay attention towards God-Almighty with heart's presence It is because of these considerations that too much talking and nonsense conversa-tions have been severely condemned in traditions. For example: The Holy Prophet (S) had said:

"Avoid speaking too much except while reciting invocations for God-Almighty, because, utterance of too many worlds other than God's Remem-brance causes hard-heartednessand the most distant apart people from the God-Almighty are the people with darkened heart."

-Bihar al-Anwar, vol. 71, p-281.

The Commander of the Faithful, Imam' Ali (A) said:

"Control your tongue and do count the words uttered by you in order to reduce your talk while engaging in an un-pious act."

-Bihar al-Anwar, vol. 71, p-281.

The Holy Prophet (S) said:

"There are three kind of talks, namely: useful, good and nonsense. The useful talks consist of God's invocation, healthy talks are the ones which are loved by God, and nonsense talks are spreading, rumors, and talking about the people behind their back."

-Bihar al-Anwar, vol. 71, p-289.

Also he said:

"Control your tongue because it is the best gift which you may present to the self; then he further elaborated: a person never tastes the reality of belief but to strictly control his tongue."

-Bihar al-Anwar, vol. 71, p-298.

Imam al-Ridha.[38] said:

"There are three things which indicate symptoms of intelligence and religious knowledge of jurisprudence: Patience, learning, and silence. And among them silence is the gate of wisdom, causes love, and is responsible for each blessing."

-Bihar al-Anwar, vol. 71, p-290.

The Commander of the Faithful Imam 'Ali (A) has said:

"The more one achieves perfection of reason the less he talks."

-Bihar al-Anwar, vol. 71, p-290.

Imam al-Sadiq (A) said:

"There is no worship superior than silence and going on foot towards the House of God for Hajj pilgrimage."

-Bihar of al-Anwar, vol. 71, p-278.

The Holy Prophet (S) said to Abu Dhar:

"I recommend you to practice silence, because it would keep Satan away from you. It helps a lot for the protection of your religion."

-Bihar al-Anwar, vol. 71, p-279.

Anyway, it is necessary for a wayfarer to control his tongue strictly, should

---

[38] Imam Ali ibn Musa al-Ridha (A): was born in Medina on Thursday, 11th Dhu'l qadah 148 A.H. He lived in a period when the Abbasids were faced with increasing difficulties because of Shiite revolts. After al-Mam'un the seventh Abbasid Caliph and a contemporary of Imam al-Ridha (A) murdered his brother Amin and assumed office, he thought he would solve the problems by naming Imam as his own successor hoping thus, to insure him in worldly affairs and turn the devotion of his follow-ers away from him. After encouragement, urging, and finally threats, Imam accepted on condition that he be excused from dismissals, appointments, and other involvement in matters of state. Making the most of this circumstance, the Imam extended guidance to the people, imparting priceless elucidation of Islamic culture and spiritual truths, which have survived in numbers roughly equal to those reaching us from the Commander of the Faithful Imam' Ali (A), and in greater number than those of any other Imam.

Finally after al-Ma' mum realized his mistake, for Shi'ism began to spread even more rapidly he is said to have poisoned him; he died at the age of 55 in Mashhad, Khorasan on Tuesday, 17th Safar 203 A.H.. He is buried in Mashhad Iran.

be serious in his talks and should avoid over-talking. In worldly affairs he should limit himself to the extent it is absolutely necessary, and instead should engage his tongue in recital of invocations, incantations, and in discussions of useful and important academic and social matters. The most celebrated mystic of our time, great professor Allameh Tabatabai (RA)[39] said:

> "I have witnessed the most precious effects of silence. Practice silence for forty days and nights speaking only when it is absolutely required, remaining en-gaged in meditations and invocations until attaining purity and enlightenment."

1. Sixth Obstacle -Love for Self (*Hubbe-Zat*)

Once a wayfarer succeeds in removing all the obstacles from his path and somehow manages to pass through all stages, then he has to be confronted

---

[39] Allameh Syed Muhammad Hussein Tabatabai: Was born into a family of scholars in Tabriz in 1271 A.H. Solar/1892 A.D. He lost his mother when he was 5 years old and his father at the age of nine. He studied his primary education over there for six years. In the year 1297/1918 he entered the field of religious and Arabic studies and was occupied with readings of texts until 1304/1925. In the year 1304/1425 he went to Najaf-e-Ashraf for higher religious studies where he studied Jurisprudence, mathematics, and Philosophy under the most eminent personalities of that period such as Ayatullah Abul Hasan Esfahani, Ayatullah Hojjat Kuhkamani, and Sayyed Hosayn Badkubi, and after finishing his curriculum returned to his native Tabriz in the year 1345/1935.

In the year 1325/1946 he settled in Qum where he continued his religious studies, teaching, and research activities until his demise in the year 1360/1981. Allahmeh Tabatabai in his Autobiography writes:

> "I forgot all that is fair and foul in the world and thought the sweet and bitter events equal. I withdrew from social contact with any except scholars; I cut back food and sleep and life's other necessities to the bare minimum and devoted the rest of my time and resources to scholarship and research. I would often spend the night in study until sunrise (especially in spring and summer), and I would always research the next day's lesson in advance, making whatever exertions were called for to solve any problem that arose so that by class time I would already have a clear understanding of the Professor's topic."

-Allameh S.M. H. Tabatabai, Islamic Teachings, p-14.

Allameh Tabatabai has written hundreds of the religious works, the famous among them is Commentary of the Holy Quran, (*Tafsir al-Mizan*) published in 20 volumes. In this work the Noble Quran is expounded in an unprecedented manner verse by verse. [Tr].

with the greatest barrier which is -love for self. Suddenly, he discovers that all actions, and deeds even worships were done for the sake of love for self. All his worshiping, asceticism, invocation, supplication, fasting, and prayer were performed for the sake of self and rewards of the Hereafter, resulting a net gain for his self. Such worships although will earn a person Paradise and eternal rewards but would not result in his ascent towards the most distinguished sublime spiritual positions of Invocations, Witnessing, and Countenance.

Without migrating from the positions of love for essence or love for self, a person would never be able to witness the unique and nonparallel beauty of the Lord of Glory and Majesty, and so for he does not tear off all the veils including the veil of self, he would not be able to develop the required capability of witnessing God's illumination.

Therefore, it is necessary for a wayfarer that through asceticism and struggle he must arrange his exit from the limited boundaries of love of essence by converting it into love of God and, thus, performing all deeds for His pleasure only, If he eats food, it is because of the fact that his eternal beloved has desires so. for the sake of his remaining alive, and if he worships, it is because of the reason. that he had considered God-Almighty as worth of being worshiped.

Such a person seeks neither this world nor the next one instead he is the seeker of God-Almighty. He does not want even to have miracles or special discoveries and except the real Creator does not have any other desire and objective. If he succeeds and passes through this crucial stage and even is able to give up his identity and personality than he may take up a giant step towards the threshold of Monotheism (*Towheed*), thus, ascending towards the most sublime spiritual positions of Witnessing, Countenance, and entering inside the Celestial Kingdom as described by the Holy Quran "Firmly established in the favor of a Mighty King." (the Holy Quran (54:55))

Seventh Obstacle -Indecisiveness

One of the great obstacle of the path and perhaps the most important one is the indecisiveness and lack of determination which prevents a person from starting his deeds. Satan and imperious-self in the beginning try their best to reflect matters relevant to gnostic journey and asceticism as insignificant and unnecessary. They endeavor to convince a person simply to engage in rituals without paying least attention towards heart's presence.

They would say: You don't have any other obligation except worshiping in a ritual manner. Why do you care about having heart's presence, attention, and invocation? If occasionally he though about these things, they will prevent him from his determination by utilizing hundred of tricks and treacheries, and sometimes they will reflect these matters before him as something so much difficult and complicated that he will become disappointed and hopeless.

> *But, a true devotee should resist the whispers of Satan and his imperious-self. By referring to Qur'anic-verses, traditions, and books of moral ethics and learning, he should make himself aware about the importance and need of spiritual migration, heart's presence, invocation, and witnessing the Supreme Reality. Once he discovers its real worth and see his own eternal salvation in it -he should move seriously, ignoring all whispers of hopelessness and disappointments telling his self: although, it is difficult but since my future salvation depends upon it I should better take action quickly, as God-Almighty has promised in the Holy Quran.* **"As for those who strive in us, We surely guide them to our paths."** *(the Holy Quran (29:69))*

Since, discussions regarding the explanation of first Method of attaining perfection and God's-Nearness became too lengthy, I apologize to my readers.

Second Means – Nourishment of Moral Virtues

One of the ways for gradual nourishment and perfection of self, spiritual migration, and attaining God's Nearness is to excel in moral virtues deeply rooted within human primordial nature. Good moral ethics are values which are incorporated within human Celestial Spirit and with their gradual nourishment the humanness of a human being attains perfection until finally ascending towards the exalted sublime position of God's Nearness. The Holy Essence of the Lord of the World is the fountainhead of all perfection; since, a human being also belongs to the Upper Heavens, through his pure, upright, and uncontaminated nature recognizes the human perfection which are in proportion to Heavenly Kingdom, naturally feels attracted towards them.

It is because of these considerations that all human beings at all times, regarding appreciation of good moral virtues namely: justice, sacrifice, righteousness, trust, benevolence, bravery, patience and perseverance, knowledge, defense of deprived, thanks, generosity, loyalty, reliance (upon God), hospitality, pardon and forgiveness, politeness, and social service etc. -are in agreement. The God-Almighty in Holy Quran said:

"And a soul and Him who perfected it, and inspired it (with

conscience of) what is wrong for it and (what is) right for it. He is indeed successful who causes it to grow. And he is indeed a failure who stunteth it."

-the Holy Quran (91: 7-10)

Moral virtues when repeated plant themselves firmly with in human self and like a habit become a part of human existence. It influences the self-building, what to become, and how to become of a human being. It is because of these considerations that special attention has been paid to-wards moral ethics in Islam, and they constitute a great portion of Islamic commands. there are hundreds and thousands of traditions which deal with ethics. Majority of Qur'anic verses consist of ethical commands; majority of the Qur'anic stories pursue moral objectives so much so that it could rightly be called as a book of moral ethics.

In principle, one of the great aim of Divine prophets had been self-purification and nourishment of. moral excellence. The Prophet of Islam too had clearly announced the objective behind his prophetic mission as perfection and nourishment of moral ethics and said:

"I have been appointed as prophet of God for the completion and perfection of moral ethics"

-al-Mustadrak, vol. 2 p-282.

Also, said:

"I recommend to you the importance of good moral conduct because, I have been appointed by God-Almighty to accomplish this very aim."

-Bihar al-Anwar, vol. 69, p-375.

Third Means – the Righteous Deeds

It may be derived from the Holy Quran that after the belief (*Iman*) the righteous deeds play the most important role in attaining self-perfection, God's Nearness, higher human ranks, and pure delightful life of the Next World. God-Almighty has said in the Holy Quran:

> "Whosoever doth right, whether male or female, and is a believer, him verily We shall quicken with good life and We shall pay them a recompense in proportion to the best of what they used to do."
> -the Holy Quran (16: 97)

And said:

> "But whoso cometh unto Him a believer, having done good works, for such are the high stations."
> -the Holy Quran (20:75)

And said:

> "And whoever hopeth for the meeting with his lord, let him to righteous deeds and make none share of the worship due unto his lord."

-the Holy Quran (18:110)

And said:

"Whoso desireth power should know that) all power belongeth to God. Unto Him good words ascend, and the pious deed doth He exalt."
-the Holy Quran (35:10)

The Glorious God in this verse explains that all power, prestige, and wealth belong to Him and the sacred word that is the clean and pure soul of a Monotheist (*Muahid*) and righteous belief in Monotheism (*Towheed*) will ascend towards God-Almighty, and this will be made possible through the righteous deeds.

The righteous deeds performed with pure intention and sincerity affect the doer's self thus, nourishing him for attaining perfection. The Holy Quran clearly explains that the pure and charming life of the Here-after and attainment of the most sublime spiritual position of God's Nearness and Countenance is possible only through the combination of belief and righteous deeds. The Holy Quran has emphasized the importance of righteous deeds a lot and regards it as the only means for achieving eternal salvation and prosperity. The value and worth of righteous deeds depends upon their being compatible with religious law and revelations.

Because the Creator of the men as well as of the world who is familiar with the special creation of human beings knows his path of perfection and salvation and therefore, accordingly has revealed it to the Holy Prophet (S) through the revelations so that he may present it to the people for their utilization. The God-Almighty said in Holy Quran:

"O you who believe, obey God and the messenger while he calleth you to that which quickeneth you."
-the Holy Quran (8:24)

The righteous deeds are the deeds that have been defined by religious law (*shariah*) as mandatory (*wajib*) or recommended (*mustahab*) deeds, and a wayfarer through their performance may undertake his spiritual migration leading him towards God's Nearness. This is the only way and all other ways are deviated and misleading and will never take a way-farer to his final destination. A wayfarer must be absolutely obedient to religious law and for his mystical journey should not follow any other path except the religious path and should avoid strictly engaging into invocations and incantations that do not have any authenticity in religious law.

Because, not only they do not take a wayfarer towards his destination instead, carry him farther apart from his destination since deviation from religious law is innovation and sin. To start with, a wayfarer should try his best to perform all religious obligatory obligations correctly in accordance with regulations, because, their renunciation will not result in attainment of higher spiritual positions, however seriously he may endeavor in performing recommended deeds and engaging into invocations and incantations.

During the second stage the recommended deeds and invocations might be included in the program. The wayfarer at this stage in accordance to his spiritual strength and personal capabilities may perform recommended deeds and the more he endeavors the greater will be the possibilities of his attaining higher spiritual positions. From the point of view of superiority, it should be pointed out that all recommended deeds are not equal rather some of them excel over others and with the result some of them could be more better and favorite, as have been mentioned in the books of supplication and traditions.

A wayfarer might select some supplications, prayers, invocations, and incantations from these books and then may engage himself on a regular basis. The more and precisely he performs them, the greater will be the purity and illumination of his soul, enabling him to ascend higher and higher up toward the exalted gnostic stations.

Here, we will point out to some of the righteous deeds and for the remaining ones the readers are advised to refer to other books but it should be reminded that mandatory deeds, recommended deeds, invocations, and supplications would be considered as righteous and favorite deeds only if they are performed with sincerity. The authenticity of a deed and its becoming favorite depends in proportion to the sincerity of the performer. From this consideration; firstly we must discuss sincerity (*ikhlas*), and I will describe some of the righteous deeds later on.

The Sincerity

The position of sincerity has been described as one of the highest stages of a wayfarer's gnostic journey and attainment of self-perfection. It is because of sincerity that the heart becomes center of illumination for Divine light, whereby wisdom and knowledge flowing through heart manifest themselves through appearing upon the tongue. The Holy Prophet (S) has said:

"Whoever devotes himself sincerely for a period of forty days for God-Almighty, streams of wisdom flowing from his heart will appear upon his tongue."

-Bihar al-Anwar, vol. 70. p-242.

The Commander of the Faithful Imam' Ali (A) said:

"Where are those who performed their deeds with sincerity for God-Almighty, andpurified their hearts so that they could absorb God's special attention to-wards them."

-Gharar al-Hukm, p-172.

Hadhrate Fatimah al-Zahra [40](S.A.) the daughter of the Holy Prophet (S) has said:

"Whoever sends pure and sincere worship for God-Almighty, He too reciprocates by bestowing upon Him His best favors."

-Bihar al-Anwar, vol. 70, p-249.

The Commander of the Faithful Imam 'Ali (A) has said:

"Pure hearts of believers are reserved for Glorious God's special attention, therefore, whoever purifies his heart will certainly be blessed with God's special attention."

-the Gharar al-Hukm, p-538.

The Holy Prophet (S) had narrated a tradition from Arch-Angel Gabriel who heard it from God-Almighty who said:

"That sincerity is a mystery from my mysteries and whoever is loved by me, I will deposit it in his heart."

-Bihar al-Anwar, vol. 70. p-249.

Sincerity consists of various grades and degrees, the most lowest grade of sincerity is that a believer should perform all his worships strictly for the sake of God-Almighty free from all traces of polytheism, hypocrisy, and ostentation. This much amount of sincerity is must for the correctness of worships, and without it the doer will not be able to receive God's Nearness. The worth of a deed depends upon pure intentions and sincerity, free from all traces of Polytheism and dissimulation. The Holy Prophet (S) has said:

"God-Almighty does not look at your faces and deeds rather looks inside your

---

[40] Fatimeh al-Zahra (S.A): The beloved daughter of the Prophet from Khadijah, Fatimah was born in Mecca on Friday, 20th Jumadath-than-iyah in the fifth year after the declaration of the prophethood (615 A.D.) She was so loved by the Prophet that he called her "a part of me." In 2 A.H. / 624 A.D. she married 'Ali ibn Abu Talib from whom she bore three sons, Hasan, Husayn and Muhsin (who died stillborn), and two daughters, Zaynab and Umme Kulthum. She was at the Prophet's bedside at the moment of his death and struggled for her husband's succession to the caliphate. She died at the age of 18 in Medina on 14th Jummaadi al awwl 11 A.H. (633 A.D.); and is buried in the graveyard of Jannatu'l Baqi in Medina. It is said that when she was born the whole sky became illuminated; therefore she is called al-Zahra', the "Radiant." She is the mother of the Shi'ite Imams and is considered the most holy of Muslim women.

hearts."

-Bihar al-Anwar, vol. 70, p. 248.

Imam al-Sadiq (A) has said:

"God-Almighty said: ' I am the best partner for You, and whosoever associates with me some one else in his deeds, then I will handover the entire deed to that associate, because I do not accept but pure and sincere deeds."

-Bihar al-Anwar, vol. 70, p-243.

Also, he said:

"On the Day of Judgment, God-Almighty will associate people in accordance with their intentions."

-Bihar al-Anwar, vol. 70, p-209.

The Commander of the Faithful Imam 'Ali (A) has said:

"How lucky is the one who worships and prays only for the sake of God-Almighty; does not engage his heart in whatsoever is seen by his eyes; does not forget God's Remembrance because of whatsoever enters into his ears,. and does not become envious in seeing things bestowed upon others."

-Bihar al-Anwar, vol. 70-229.

He also said:

"Sincerity in deeds is an indication of doer's salvation and prosperity."

Gharar al-Hukm, p-43.

A worship that is accepted by God-Almighty and earns perfection and His Nearness for the worshipper -is the worship free from all traces of self-conceit, dissimulation, Egotism, and ostentation offered for the sake of Him alone. The only criteria for acceptance of deeds is sincerity and devotion. The more is the degree of sincerity the greater would be the perfection and merit of the deed.

The worshippers may be grouped in to the following three categories:

1. The First Group: Consists of those who worship God-Almighty because of fear of Divine punishment and Hell's fire.
2. The Second Group: Consists of those who obey Divine commands for the sake of bounties of Paradise and rewards in the Hereafter.

Third Means – the Righteous Deeds

Although, worshiping with the above aims does not harm their correctness in any way and the doer will earn the eternal rewards and favors, because, the Holy Quran and traditions have very often utilized both of the above methods for the people's guidance.

Apart from that the Holy Prophet (S) himself, infallible Imams (A) of his Holy Progeny, and God's Favorite Saints too were afraid of Divine retributions, continuously cried for help and were eager and hopeful for Paradise and its bounties.

1. The Third Group: Consists of those who worship God-Almighty because they consider Him worthy of it and want to thank him for His Divine bounties and blessings. Such aim does not have any contradiction with sincerity -a criteria for the acceptance of deeds. Therefore, in traditions, in order to encourage people for God's obedience, His bounties and favors have been reminded, so that to show their appreciation, the human beings should obey His commandments. Even the Holy Prophet (S) himself and Infallible Imam (A) of his holy progeny sometimes in order to emphasize the importance and seriousness of worship said: *"Shouldn't I be a thankful servant?"*

Although, the deeds of all groups do get accepted, but among them it is the third group whose deeds carry special distinction because they are accompanied with a higher degree of sincerity. The Commander of the Faithful Imam 'Ali (A) has said:

"The worshiper of God-Almighty may be divided into following three groups: 1 First Group: Consists of those who worship God-Almighty for the sake of eternal rewards, which is like worshiping of merchants, (for the sake of profit).

1. *Second Group: Consists of those who worship God-Almighty because of the fear of God and retributions, which is like –the worshiping of slaves (for the sake of fear).*
2. *Third Group: Consists of those who worship God-Almighty because to*

express their appreciation and thanks for His bounties and favors which is like the worshiping of freeman." -Bihar al-Anwar, vol 70, p-196.
3. **The Fourth Group:** Consists of those who worships God-Almighty for the sake of attaining self-perfection and nourishment of their selves. Of course, perusal of this objective does not inflict any damage to the degree of sincerity and devotion that is the criteria for acceptance of deeds.
4. **The Fifth Group:** Consists of those who are the most favorite and distinguished servants of God-Almighty. Since they have recognized Him very well and consider Him as the Fountainhead of all Blessings and Perfection -Worship Him. Because, of their being aware of the Absolute and Infinite Power of the Lord of Splendor and Majesty, and since they have not discovered any other effective source of power except Him -consider Him alone worthy of worshiping, love Him and humiliate and humble themselves in front of His Exalted Glory, And this is called the highest degree of sincerity and devotion. Imam al-Sadiq (A) has said:

"There are three categories of worshipers: The first category consists of those who worship for the sake of eternal rewards which is the worshiping of greedy, because they are motivated due to greed.

The second category consists of those who worship because of fear of Hell's fire which is the worshiping of slaves, since their motivation is due to fear. But since I love God-Almighty -I worship Him, which is the worship of elders, and nobles whose motivation is tranquility and assurance. God-Almighty has said:

> *"And such are safe from fear that Day."*
> *-the Holy Quran (27:89)*

And further said:

> *"Say (O Muhammad, to mankind): If you love God, follow me, God will love you and forgive your sins."*
> *-the Holy Quran (3:31)*

Therefore, whosoever loves God-Almighty, He too loves him and (on the Day of Resurrection) he will be among those who have been blessed with peace and security"

-Bihar al-Anwar, vol. 70, p-197.

The Commander of the Faithful Imam' Ali (A) has said:

"Oh God! I worship you neither because of fear from the Hell's fire nor for the greed of Paradise's bounties, but, since 1 believe You are worthy of adoration and praise -I do worship you."

-Bihar al-Anwar, p-197.

All of the above mentioned groups are sincere and their deeds are accepted but still all of them do not hold a single rank, rather from the point of view of perfection they differ with each other -the fifth group possessing the most distinguished position.

It should be reminded here that the holder of distinguished ranks are not disqualified as for as the requirements of lower ranks are concerned, rather in addition to their being qualified for lower ranks they also possess higher distinguished credentials. The righteous and sincere slaves of God-Almighty, too are afraid of Him, are hopeful of His Mercy and Compassion, are thankful for His Bounties, and are anxious for attaining spiritual nearness with Him, but their motivation behind worship is not limited to only above things, instead, since they have discovered a better understanding of God-Almighty, they praise and worship Him.

Those distinguished and God's chosen human beings in spite of their attaining exalted spiritual positions have not given up the. lower positions, because, a wayfarer traveling upon the road of perfection when reaches relatively higher spiritual stations, also possesses the qualifications of lower stations which have been attained by him earlier in his spiritual journey.

Whatever was discussed so far was related to sincerity and devotion in worship, but sincerity is something which is not limited to worship only, rather a wayfarer gradually reaches to a point whereby he purifies himself as well his heart, for God-Almighty, cleansing the heart's dwelling from all sort of alien existence. So much so that all actions, deeds and thoughts, are assigned exclusively to God-Almighty, and the wayfarer does not perform any thing but for His pleasure. He is not afraid of other than God and does not trust other than Him, to the extent that even his friendship and enmity are done exclusively for the God's pleasure, and this is known as the highest degree of sincerity. The Commander of the Faithful Imam ' Ali (A) has said:

"How fortunate is the one whose deeds, knowledge, love, grudge, possession, renunciation speaking, and silence -all are reserved exclusively for God-Almighty."

-Gharar al-Hukm p-462.

Imam al-Sadiq has said:

"Whosoever loves, grudges, donates, and refrains exclusively for the sake of God-Almighty -is some one whose faith is perfect."

-Bihar al-Anwar, vol. 70, p-248.

Also, said:

"God-Almighty has not bestowed upon a servant any thing superior than -that there should not be anything in his heart except God-Almighty."

-Bihar al-Anwar, vol. 70 p-249.

The Commander of the Faithful Imam' Ali (A) says:

"Where are the hearts who have been donated to God-Almighty, and are committed exclusively for his obedience."

-Gharar al-Hukm, p-172.

When a wayfarer attains that privileged position, God-Almighty purifies him for Himself and through Divine Illumination, intuition, and revelations makes him immune against sins and transgressions. Such a human being is called God's devoted friend (*Mukhlis*) and they are the most distinguished servants of God-Almighty. The Holy Quran says:

"Lo! We purified them with a pure thought, remembrance of the Home (of the Hereafter)"
-the Holy Quran (37:46)

The Holy Quran says about Prophet Moses (A)

"And make mention in the scripture of Moses. Lo! He was chosen, and he was a messenger of (God), a Prophet. "

-the Holy Quran (19:51)

God's chosen devoted servants ultimately reach to a position whereby even Satan becomes disappointed in his efforts to make them deviated. The Holy Quran quotes Satan when he speaks to God-Almighty:

"He said: Then by Thy might, I surely will beguile them every one, save Thy single minded slaves among them."
-the Holy Quran (38: 82-83)

In the end it must be reminded that attaining such exalted position is not an easy and simple thing rather it requires self-purification, endeavors, and struggle in worshiping. The Commander of the Faithful, Imam' Ali (A) says:
"Sincerity and devotion are the fruits of worship."
-Gharar al-Hukm, p-17.

As has been described in traditions that engagements in worshiping and invocations continuously for a period of forty days and nights might be effective and useful for attaining inner purity enlightenment of soul, and the position of sincerity. But, this could not be accomplished in one single attempt rather should be attempted gradually after passing through various stages of sincerity.

Some Righteous Deeds

As was mentioned in earlier chapters of this books that the only path that could lead a wayfarer towards perfection and may help him in his ascend towards God's Nearness is obedience to revelations and following the path shown by Divine Prophets. The path which they followed themselves has been defined as performance of mandatory (*wajibat*) and recommended (*Nawafil wa Mustahabbat*) religious deeds which are called righteous deeds.

All mandatory and recommended righteous deeds incorporated into Islamic Cannon Law (*sharia*) and registered in the Holy Quran as well as in other books of traditions are called as righteous deeds. You may better identity them and might utilize them in following the righteous path. Here we will discuss some of righteous deeds as follows:

First -Obligatory Prayers

The Prayer is one of the best means for undertaking spiritual migration towards God-Almighty and attaining the exalted position of His-nearness. Imam al-Ridha (A) has said:

"The prayer is a means of attaining God's nearness for every righteous human being."

-al-Ka.fi, vol. 3, p-265.

Mu' awiyah bin Wahab asked Imam al-Sadiq (A)

"What is the best deed which brings human beings close to God-Almighty, and is also liked by Him ? The Imam replied: After enlightenment of God's Essence, I do not know any thing better than the 'prayer'. Did not you hear that God's righteous servant Prophet Jesus (A) has said: "God has recommended for me prayer and charity until I remain alive."

-al-Kafi, vol. 3, p-264.

Also, he said:

"The most esteemed and favorite deed before God-Almighty is -"Prayer" The Prayer is the last dying will of all prophets. How good it is that a human being takes a bath or performs ablution, then retires into a secluded corner where he is not seen by anyone and have the honor of performing genuflexion and prostration. When a servant bows himself down into prostration and prolonged it than Satan says:

"Oh! Woe upon me! this servant has obeyed God-almighty, while I transgressed and he has offered prostration which I refused."

-al-Kafi, vol. 3, p-264.

Imam al Ridha (A) has said:

"The most nearest position between the servant and God-Almighty is-the state of prostration [41] because God-Almighty has said:

"But prostrate thyself; and draw near (to God-Almighty)." -the Holy Quran (96: 19)

-al-Kafi Vol. 3, p-265.

Imam al-Sadiq (A) said:

---

[41] Prostration: Regarding prostration it is narrated that during one's entire life if one succeeds during a single prostration to achieve a real union with the Creator, it will compensate for all the past omissions. He would receive Divine blessings and would become immune from the satanic temptations forever. On the contrary if during prostration, which is the state of renunciation if his heart is preoccupied with any thing other than Him, he will be listed among the group of hypocrites and the misled. -the Profundities of Prayer, Ayatullah Sayyid Ali Khamenei, p. 5.

"When a human being stands for prayers,. God's Blessings descend upon him from the sky; the angels circle him around and one of them says., If this prayer-offerer would have known the worth of his prayer, he would never have broken his concentration (towards God) throughout the prayer."

-al-Kafi, vol. 3, p-265.

The Holy Prophet (S) has said:

"When a believer stands for prayer, God-Almighty looks at him until he finishes it, Hisblessing covers him from the sky; the angels circle him around and God-Almighty assigns an angel who says: 'Oh prayer offerer! If you would have known -who is looking at you and with whom are you communicating ? You would never have paid your attention towards any other thing, and you would never have been deviated from this position."

-al-Kafi, vol. 3, p-265.

Heart's Presence in Prayer

The Prayer is a celestial formula and Divine electuary, every part of which contains a hidden mystery. It is a means of love, communication, and remembrance of the Lord of the Universe. It is the best means of attaining perfection, spiritual ascension, and God's Nearness. According to Islamic traditions the prayer has been called -a believers heavenly journey (*Mairaj*) which protects him from moral indecencies.

It is such a pure sparkling stream of spirituality that whosoever enters into it five times a day will purify his soul from all sort of pollution and contamination. It is the greatest trust of the God-Almighty and is the criteria of acceptance of all other deeds. The prayer is such a mysterious heavenly formula, but subjected to its being alive and possessing spirit, which means heart's presence during prayer, paying attention towards God-Almighty, and being humble in front of Him.

The invocations, recitals of Qur'anic verses, genuflection, prostration, the witnessing, and salutations constitute the face and body of the prayer while the heart's presence and attention towards the Creator form its spirit. Since a body without a soul becomes a dead body lacking any characteristic, likewise a prayer offered without heart's presence, although satisfies as far as the performance of compulsory religious obligation is concerned, nevertheless, such a prayer does not help in ascending the prayer offerer towards higher spiritual positions. In principle, the greatest objective behind the establishment of prayer may be described as invocation recitals and engaging in God's Remembrance. God-Almighty said to the Holy Prophet (S):

> *"And establish worship for My Remembrance."*
> *-the Holy Quran (20:14)*

The Friday-Prayer has been described as an invocation in the Holy Quran:

> **"Oh ye who believe! When the call is heard for the prayer of the Day of Congregation, haste unto remembrance of God."**
> *-the Holy Quran (57: 9)*

The criteria for the acceptance of prayer is -the heart's presence, and whatever amount of heart's presence it may contain, the prayer will be accepted accordingly. It is because of this consideration that traditions have emphasized a lot about the importance of heart's presence in prayers.

For example:

The Holy Prophet (S) has said:

"Sometimes only half of the prayer gets accepted while at other times may be one-third, one fourth, one-fifth, and one-tenth of it will be accepted. Some of the prayers like an old wrapped cloth are pounded upon the offerer's head. As a matter of fact, only that portion of the prayer will be accepted from you, in which you have paid heartily attention towards God-Almighty."

-Bihar al-Anwar, vol. 84, p-260.

Imam al-Sadiq (A) said:

"When a servant stands of prayer, God-Almighty pays attention towards him and did not break it until the servant deviates from His-remembrance for the third time. When this happens, God-Almighty too turns his face away from the

prayer offerer."

-Bihar al-Anwar, vol. 84, p-241.

The Commander of the Faithful Imam 'Ali (A) says:

"Do not offer prayer in the state of drowsiness or napping; while offering prayer do not think about yourself; because, you are standing in the presence of God-Almighty. Indeed, only that portion of the prayer will be accepted from the servant in which he has paid heartiest attention towards God-Almighty."

-Bihar al-Anwar, vol. 84, p-239.

The Holy Prophet (S) has said:

"Each servant (of God), while standing in prayer pays attention towards other than Him, God-Almighty says: 'Oh my servant! Which way are you turning your face? Who is the one you are looking for? Do you seek a God and protect-or other than me? Are you looking for a benevolent other than me? While, I remain to be the Most Merciful among merciful, Most Compassionate among be nevolent and happens to be the Greatest Bestower. I will bestow upon you such a reward that could not be counted. Pay attention towards Me, because I and my angels are paying attention towards you."

"Thus, if the prayer offerer paid attention towards God-Almighty, his past sins are deleted. But again if he pays attention towards others (than God), he is reminded by God-Almighty like before. If he turns his attention towards prayer, his sins and negligence from prayer are pardoned and their effects are nullified."

"If for the third time he deviates his attention from the prayer, God-Almighty once more repeats his earlier warning, in case he paid attention towards the prayer, again his sins are pardoned. But if he deviated his attention away from the prayer for the fourth time, then God-Almighty and his angels turn their faces away from the prayer offerer and God-Almighty says to him: ' Now I have assigned you to the guardianship of someone who is liked by you."

-Bihar al-Anwar, vol. 84, p-244.

The value of prayer depends directly upon heart's presence and attention paid towards God-Almighty; to the extent heart's presence is achieved during prayer, it will be effective in attaining inner purification and God's-Nearness. It was not without reason that all Divine Prophets (A) Infallible Imams (A), and God's favorite saints paid so much atten-tion towards prayer.

About the Commander of the Faithful Imam' Ali (A) it has been written:

"*At the time of prayer his body used to tremble and the color of his face changed. They asked him the reason behind his agitation and fear. In reply he said: ' The time has arrived for returning of trust -which was offered to earth and heavens but they declined to assume this responsibility. But human being accepted this great trust. I am afraid that whether I would be able to discharge this heavy responsibility of returning this trust or not. "*

-Bihar al-Anwar, vol. 84, p-248.

About the Imam al-Baqir (A) and al-Sadiq (A) it has been narrated: *"At the time of prayer their faces used to turn pale and red with fear of God-Almighty; in their prayer they conversed with God-Almighty as though they are actually seeing him."*

-Bihar al-Anwar, vol. 84, p-248.

About Imam al-Sajjad (A) it has been narrated: *"When he stood for prayer the color of his face became pale with fear, and like a humble slave standing in front of his Master, his body parts trembled. His prayer was always used to be his parting prayer as though there will never going to be any other prayer offered by him after this one."*

-Bihar al-Anwar, vol. 84, p-250.

About the life of Fatimah al-Zahra (S.A.) the daughter of the holy Prophet (S) it has been narrated: *"Because, of the intensity of fear, during prayer even the number of her breaths could have been counted."*

-Bihar al-Anwar, vol. 84, p-258.

Regarding the life of Imam al-Hasan (A) it has been narrated: *"His body trembled during prayer. When he remembered Paradise and Hell, become so restless and agitated as though have been bitten by a snake. He requested Paradise from God-Almighty and sought His shelter from Hell."*

-Bihar al-Anwar, vol. 84, p-258.

"Ayesheh narrates about the Holy Prophet (S): while I was busy in talking with him, when the time of prayer arrived, suddenly be become so indifferent as though neither he recognizes us nor we do recognize him."

-Bihar al-Anwar, vol. 84. p.258.

About Imam al-Sajjad (A) it has been narrated:

"While he was in the middle of prayer his cloak rolled down from his shoulder but he remained unconscious about it. When he finished his prayer one of his companion asked: *'Oh son of the Holy Prophet (S) ! While you were offering prayer your clock rolled down but you did not pay attention to it.'*

"The Imam replied: *'Woe upon you! Do you know in front of whom I was standing ? Such awareness prevented me from paying attention towards my clock. Don't you understand that a servant's prayer is accepted only to the extent he pays attention towards God-Almighty during his prayer?"*

'Oh son of the Holy Prophet (S), Therefore, on this basis we all are going to be doomed?' Asked the companion. *'No! If you offer recommended prayers (Nawafil) God-Almighty through them will treat your compulsory prayers as completed."*

-Bihar al-Anwar, vol. 84, p-265.

"Regarding the Holy Prophet (S) it has been narrated that during prayer the color of his face changed completely, and a bubbling sound similar to the noises coming out from a boiling pot was heard coming out from his chest. When he stood for his prayer he was motionless like a piece of cloth fallen upon the ground."

-Bihar al-Anwar, vol. 84, p-248.

Degrees of Heart's Presence

Heart's presence consists of various ranks and degrees which differ from each other from the point of view of perfection. A wayfarer has to go through these various grades gradually so that he may ascent towards the higher spiritual positions of God's Nearness and Witnessing. It is a lengthy way containing various positions, whose introduction and explanation for some one deprived like me, who is looking from a distance and burning in regret -is not befitting. But some of these stages will be explained here in brief, which might be useful for wayfarers.

First Stage

This may be defined as a state in which the prayer offerer either through out the prayer or some part of it pays brief attention to the fact that he is standing before God-Almighty, speaks and converses with Him. However, at this stage he does not pay attention towards the meanings of words and does not understand the details of his conversation.

Second Stage

The second degree of heart's presence may be defined as a state in which the prayer offer apart from his being aware of the fact that he is standing before God-Almighty and is communicating with Him, also, pays attention towards the meanings of words and invocation and knows exactly what is he saying to God-Almighty. While announcing the worlds, simultaneously, he is also making his heart to understand its meaning like a mother who teaches her child how to pronounce a sentence as well as explains him its meanings.

Third Stage

The Third degree of heart's presence may be defined as a state in which the prayer offerer in addition of his being aware of the earlier stages, also comprehend very well the realities of Glorification, Adoration, Praise, Sanctification, Monotheism, and meanings of other invocations. Further, his understanding of the above is based upon logical arguments, pays attention towards them during prayer, understand very well as to what is he saying, what does he want, and with whom is he speaking?

Fourth Stage

The fourth stage of heart's presence may be defined as a state in which the prayer offerer, in addition of his being aware of the early stages, must also have influenced upon his inner essence the learning and meanings of invocations, and must have achieved the state of certainty (*yaqin*) and faith (*iman*). In that case the tongue follows the heart and since the heart believes in those realities pursues the tongue to undertake the recital of invocations.

Fifth Stage

The fifth stage of heart's presence may be defined as a state in which the prayer offerer in addition of his being aware of early stages has achieved the most sublime spiritual positions of revelation, intuition, and countenance. Through his esoteric eyes witnesses the Sacred Names and Characteristics of God-Almighty and does not see any thing except Him, even does not pay attention to himself his actions, deeds, and invocations.

He speaks with God-Almighty but is unconscious of the speaker and speech. He has given up his own existence and have become fascinated after witnessing the beauty of Lord's Holy Essence. Even at this stage there are ranks and degree varying in distinction relative to the status of the wayfarers. This stage is like an ocean of infinite depth and for some one deprived like me, it is better not to enter in it and leave it's description for those who deserve it:

"*Oh God! Please bestow upon us the sweetness of your invocations and the witnessing of your beauty.*"

Important Factors for Attaining Heart's Presence

In as much as heart's presence is important and worthwhile, in the same proportion its attainment is extremely difficult. No sooner a person starts his prayer Satan suddenly whispers in his heart pulling him from one side to another, and continuously engaging him into all sort of thoughts and memories.

The heart [42] engages himself into accounting, planning, reviewing past and future problems, solving academic problems; very often recollecting during prayers, topic which were forgotten by him completely and when he returns to himself discovers that the prayer is over. Even if in between he pays attention towards prayer he deviates immediately.

It is indeed sad and one must feel sorry about it! What should we do to dominate over this rebellious and playful self? How should we keep these scattered thoughts away from us during the prayer and keep our attention exclusively to remember God-Almighty. Those who have traveled this path and were able to receive Divine special favors can better guide us, and it would be better if the pen would have been in their hands. But, this helpless and veiled servant too would like to describe some points which may be useful in achieving heart's presence during prayer as follows:

---

[42] In his book "Sirr-us-Salat" (the Mysteries of Prayers), Imam Khomeini, describes the presence of heart, as follows:

"During prayers one must try to completely cut off the heart's preoccupation with worldly affairs. If a person is submerged in love and desires of this world, naturally his heart is busy continuously from one involvement to another. The heart behaves like a bird jumping from one branch to another. So for we have this tree of worldly ambitions or desires ("Hubb-e Duniya") in our heart, it will behave restless.

If by struggle, practice, efforts, and thinking about the severe consequences and losses, if one could succeed in cutting this tree of worldly ambitions or desires, then the heart will become reposed and peaceful. It will achieve spiritual perfection. At least the more one tries to free himself from worldly charms and temptations the more he succeeds in cutting the various branches of that tree in his heart, with the result, the presence of heart will be achieved in the same proportion."

Imam Khomeini further explains the term' love of this world' (Hubb-e-Duniya). "There are people who do not possess anything at all of this moral world, but still they could be the persons totally submerged in the love of this world. While on the contrary, one maybe one be like Prophet Sulaiman bin Dawood, (Solomon son of David) king of kings and possessing all the treasurers of this universe, but at the same time may not be a man of this world, completely detached from the lure of the world." [Tr].

Secluded Place

If one has to offer individual compulsory prayer or recommended prayer it is better to select an isolated free from noises and interference. The prayer's place should be free from pictures or any other object which might attract prayer offer's attention; should not be a public place, rather a secluded corner inside the home should be selected and prayer should always be offered over there. While, offering prayer, one should look at the place of prostration or may close his eyes, and among these two whichever he thinks is mere useful for heart's presence should be practiced.

It is advisable to offer prayer in a smaller room a near the wall so that the prayer offerer's view is restricted. While, offering congregational prayers one should look at the place of prostration and listen attentively to the recital of Qur'anic verses, if the congregational leader (*Imam*) is reciting them loudly.

Removal of Obstacles

Before the prayer all obstacles in attaining heart's presence must be removed and only then one should engage himself into prayer. e.g. If the prayer offerer needs to go to toilet, he must relieve himself first, and after performing required ablutions should engage himself into prayer. If he is not comfortable because of severe hunger and thrust, first he must satisfy his hunger and thirst by eating and drinking and then should offer his prayers.

Also, if because of over-eating he lacks the mood, he should wait a while till he feels ready for prayer. Similarly, if because of being extremely tired and exhausted or feeling sleeplessness, if he does not have the mood to offer prayer, he should first rest and sleep, and then should offer his prayer. If he is busy investigating something or is disturbed and agitated because of a tragic occurrence, he should try within the bounds of possibilities to eliminate the causes of concern before prayer .

One of the greatest obstacle is intense attachment to worldly allurements namely: Wealth and property, power and position, and woman and children. Severe attraction of these things causes prayer offerer's attention turns towards these things deviating from God-Almighty, during prayer. Therefore, the prayer offerer must seriously endeavor to cut off these attractions, so that heart's presence and attention towards God-Almighty become easier for him.

Strengthening of Faith

Man's attention towards God-Almighty depends in proportion to his knowledge and enlightenment relative to Him. If the faith has reached to the degree of certainty, has completely comprehended God's Majesty, Power, Presence, Dominion, and Knowledge, naturally will show humility and humbleness in front of him, and there would be no room left for negligence and forgetfulness. Some one who sees God's existence everywhere as his overseer, regards himself continuously before His presence, while standing in prayer -a place of talking with Him, will never be negligent from His remembrance.

Suppose, if one has to speak before a powerful king, he will naturally control all his senses, would know exactly what is he supposed to do, and what is he going to speak? So, if one recognizes God-Almighty with Splendor and Majesty, he would never be negligent of Him during pray-er. Therefore, a human being should endeavor for strengthening his faith and attaining perfect enlightenment so that he may achieve maximum heart's presence during his prayer. The Holy Prophet (S) has said:

"Worship God-Almighty as though you are actually seeing Him, and even if you do not see Him, He sees you."

-Nahjal-Fasahath, p-65.

Aban bin Toghlab said that I said to Imam al-Sadiq (A):

"I saw Ali Bin al-Hussein (A) offering prayer in such a manner that the color of his face changed. Please explain the reason. 'Yes! Because he recognized completely God-Almighty in front of whom he was standing in prayer.' Replied the Imam."

-Bihar al-Anwar, vol. 84, p-236.

Remembrance of Death

One thing which might be useful in achieving heart's presence is remembrance of death. If a person thinks about death, and pays attention to the fact that neither timings nor the circumstances of death's arrival are known, it may occur at any time, under any situation, even it is quite possible that this prayer might be the last one. In that case he would not offer prayer with negligence.

It is recommended that a prayer offerer should think about death before the prayer; should imagine that the moment of death has arrived; the death angel Israel for receiving the soul has already arrived, and it is only a limited time, say, an hour or few minutes have been left for him, after which his deeds' register will be closed forever, and he will be transferred to Eternal World.

Over there, his deeds will be scrutinized and the result would be either eternal prosperity and happy living near God's favorites or adversity, cruelty, punishment, and torture inside the Hell. By imagining and picturing dying one may better concentrate, may witness himself standing in front of God-Almighty, and thus may offer prayer with more humility and humbleness as his farewell prayer. Before beginning prayer create such conditions for yourself and then prolong it during entire length of prayer. Imam Al-Sadiq (A) said:

"Offer compulsory prayer during its time, like someone who is offering his farewell prayer, and is afraid that after this he will never have the opportunity to offer the prayer again. While offering the prayer, look at the place of prostration. If one realizes some one nearby is watching his prayer -he becomes more careful in offering his prayer. Know ! that you are standing in front of some one who sees you but is not seen by you."

-Bihar al-Anwar, vol. 84, p-233.

Readiness

After removing all obstacles around him, the prayer offerer should make himself ready for prayer by retiring into a suitable isolated place. Before standing he must remind himself about the Majesty and Infinite power of God-Almighty and his own weakness and incompetence. He must realize that he is standing in front of the Lords of worlds and is speaking to him. He is standing in front of such a Magnificent Power which surrounds everything even is aware of most secret affairs.

Imagine and manifest dying, accounting of deeds, Paradise, and Hell in your mind's eye; assign a higher probability that death might occur very soon, and even this very prayer could be the last prayer of his life. Prolonged these reflections until self became completely tamed and is in a mood to pay attention. Then with attention and hearts' presence recite the call for prayer-(adhan) and (aqameh) respectively, recite the following supplication and during its recital pay attention to its meaning.

(Allahumma elaika tawwajahato wa marzateka talabato wa thawabaka ibtaqhazzito wa beka amanto wa elaika tawwakalto allahuma salle ala Muhammadin wa aley Muhammad waftoh masamea qalbi lezekreka wa sabbatni ala deneka wa deney Nabiyeha wala tuzqe qalbi bada is hadeytani wa habli min ladunka rahamate inneka antal wahab.)

"Oh God! I seek Your refuge; desire whatever pleases Thou. Aspire to receive Your reward have faith in Thee and trust and rely upon You. Oh God! send salutations upon Muhammad (S) and his Holy progeny (A), open my heart's esoteric ears to Your invocation,. make me steadfast upon Your religion, and the religion of Your Prophet (S). Don't make my heart deviate after being blessed with Your guidance, and bestow upon me Your favors and blessings, verily! You are the most benevolent."

Then recite the following prayer:
(ya Mohsin qadatak al masiyee ya Mohsin ehsan al ati.)
"Oh Beneficent, verily bless me -the sinner; Oh Beneficent! bestow your favors upon me."

If after that one feels like having proper attention and humility he may say

Takbirateh al-Ahram by proclaiming, "God is Great" (*Allahu Akbar*) and may begin his prayer. But, if he feels that he is not yet ready, does not feel any change in his mood, should seek refuge [43] in God-Almighty from Satanic whispers and should repeat the earlier program till he gets ready.

At this moment with due attention and heart's presence should say Takbirateh al-Ahram while paying attention towards its meanings and may begin his prayer. But, he must pay attention as to whom is he talking and what is he saying? Be careful that tongue and heart coordinate each other and do not lie. Does he know the meanings of "God is Great" (Allahu Akbar) i.e. God is Greater than -that He could be described. He must pay attention correctly what is he saying? Does he really believe in it? Imam al-Sadiq (A) has said:

"When you stand facing Holy Mecca (Qiblah)[44] *with prayer intention -for-get the world and whatever it contains, people, and their affairs absolutely, make your heart free from every thing which prevents you from God's Remembrance and with esoteric eyes witness God's Majesty and Splendor. Recollect your stop-page in front of Him on the Day of Resurrection when each human being will make his earlier deposited deeds manifested, thus, returning towards God-Almighty.*

'During prayer be in a state of fear and hope, after making your proper intention and saying (Takbiratel al-Ahram, i.e. Allahu Akbar), whatever, the earth and sky may contain, consider it as small and insignificant, because when prayer offerer says it, God-Almighty looks in his heart, thus, if he had not paid atten-tion towards the reality of Takbirateh al-Ahram He says to him:

'Oh liar! Do you want to deceit me?' swear to my splendor and majesty that will deprive you .from My invocations pleasure and enjoyment of having private communications with Me."

-Bihar al-Anwar, vol. 84, p-230.

Of course preparation and getting readied before the prayer, during making intention and saying Takbirateh al-Ahram are extremely effective

---

[43] One should recite Esteaza:
 "I seek refuge in God-Almighty from .Satan -the damned one."

[44] Direction to which Muslims turn their face for Prayer. [Tr.]

in achieving heart's presence, but still more important than that, is the continuation of this state through out the prayer. If a slight negligence is shown, self immediately starts his action of flying from one side to another one, thus, breaking heart's presence and concentration.

Therefore, prayer offerer must watch his self carefully all along the prayer. He must tightly closed his hearts entrance towards all other than God and must prevent entries of scattered thoughts and memories should consider himself always standing in God's presence, should offer prayer as though he is actually talking with God-Almighty, bows down and prostrates in front of him; while reciting Qur'anic verses and invocations must pay attention towards their meanings; must realize what is he saying; with what Majestic Power is he speaking and should maintain this condition until the prayer is over. It is a difficult task but with efforts, endeavors, and seriousness it becomes easier. The God-Almighty has promised in the Holy Quran:

"And those who strive in Our (cause) -We will certainly guide them to Our paths."

-the Holy Quran (29:69)

If one does not succeed in the very first attempt instead of getting disappointed, he should become more determined and serious in trying again, until attaining domination over self gradually. The heart should be cleansed thoroughly from scattered thoughts and should be motivated to pay attention towards God-Almighty. If such thing is not possible within one day, few weeks and few months, he should not be disappoint because after all such a thing is possible. There were and still are many distinguished personalities who were able to achieve absolute heart's presence from the beginning till the end of prayer, and during prayer did not pay any attention towards other than God.

We would not be disappointed either from attaining such distinguished position and if achieving absolute perfection is not possible, we must try to attain at least whatever is attainable within the bounds of possibilities and should consider even this much as a great bounty.[45]

Second -Supererogatory Prayers (Nawafil)

Earlier it was mentioned that the Prayer happens to be the best means of spiritual migration, invocation, and God's Nearness. God-Almighty, who is absolutely more knowledgeable, as compared to any other person, about the special human creation, and their path of perfection, has defined prayer, and by means of prophets have handed it over to human beings -so that they may utilize it for their salvation and attaining perfection. The path of utilization from this means is always open. The prayer has not been limited to a certain fixed time, rather one may utilize from it at any time, any where and under all circumstances. Generally, the prayer may be classified into following two categories:

1. Mandatory or Compulsory Prayers (*Wajib*).
2. Supererogatory or Recommended Prayers (*Nawafil*).

There are six types of Mandatory or Compulsory Prayers:

1. Daily Prayer (*salat wajib*).
2. Sign Prayer (*salat ayat*), to be recited at the solar or lunar eclipse
3. Death Prayer (*Mayyit*).
4. Circumambulation Prayer during Hajj pilgrim (*Towwaf*).
5. Prayer which become mandatory upon one's taking an oath or making a solemn promise to God (*Nazr*).
6. Make up Prayer (*Qadha*). Daily prayers not offered by father become compulsory upon his eldest son, after his demise.

---

[45] In order to attain heart's presence during prayer we may utilize books which have been written about Mysteries of Prayer, like the book "Sirr-us-Salat" (Mysteries of Prayer) written by Divine Scholar and Great Leader of the Islamic Revolution, Imam Khomeini (R.A.) [Author].

Daily prayers are compulsory upon all adult Muslims after attaining puberty, but other compulsory prayers become compulsory during cer-tain periods under special circumstances. A person who desires to achieve salvation and perfection, as a very first step must perform all compulsory obligations strictly in their prescribed manner, and if performs them with heart's presence and devotion, become best means of achieving God's favor.

Quitting compulsory obligations and instead indulging into performance of recommended deeds will never result in achieving God's favor. If someone thinks, that by quitting compulsory obligation and by means of some recommended deeds, invocations, and incantations, he may complete his journey towards perfection and attaining higher spiritual positions- certainly he is making a mistake. But after performance of compulsory obligations, he may seek God's nearness by means of supererogatory prayers and other recommended deeds for attaining sublime spiritual positions.

There are plenty of supererogatory prayers (*nawafil*), and overall may be divided into two categories: Daily supererogatory prayers (*nawafil*) and other recommended prayers.

Daily Supererogatory Prayers consists of thirty four units (Rakats):

1. Supererogatory Prayer Noon (*Dhohr*) -8 units, (before compulsory (*Dhohr*) prayer, 4 times -2 units).
2. Supererogatory Prayer After-Noon (*Asr*) -8 units (before compulsory (*Asr*) Prayer, 4 times -2 units).
3. Supererogatory Prayer Evening (*Maghrib*) -4 units (after compulsory (*Maghrib*) Prayer, 2 times -2 units).
4. Supererogatory Prayer Night (*Isha*) -2 units (in sitting position, after compulsory (*Isha*) Prayer, and is regarded equivalent to one unit of standing prayer).
5. Supererogatory Prayer Morning (*Fajr*) -2 units (before compulsory (*Fajr*) Prayer).
6. Night Prayer (*Namaz-e-Shab* or *Salat al Lail*) -11 units.

Tradition books describe the importance of recital of daily supererogatory prayers; their effects and rewards have also been specified, and have been introduced as complimentary to compulsory prayers. But oth-er than daily supererogatory prayers other recommended prayers during certain special periods, places, and circumstances as well as their relevant rewards have also been described. The readers may study the details of different kinds of supererogatory prayers and recommended prayers and their advantages and rewards in the books of traditions and supplications[46] and may utilize them in your spiritual journey and attainment of self-perfection.

Apart from that prayer is desired and recommended at any time, every place and under all circumstances and a wayfarer may take its advantage. The path of taking advantage from this means remains always open. A human being at any time, any place, and under all conditions may be benefited from this great blessing and may establish a quick communication with God-Almighty. The Commander of the Faithful Imam .Ali (A) has said:

"Supererogatory Prayer (Nafilah) results in a believer's becoming near to God-Almighty."

-Bihar al-Anwar, vol. 87, p-36.

Imam al-Sadiq (A) said:

"Truly sometimes one half; or one third, or one fourth, or one fifth of prayer ascends upward (i.e. is accepted by God); only those portions of prayer ascend upwards which are accompanied by heart's presence; and because of this reason. We are assigned to recite supererogatory prayers so that through their means the shortcomings of daily prayers could be compensated."

-Bihar al-Anwar, vol. 87, p-28.

The Holy Prophet (S) has said:

"In order to become my beloved, my servant does not have any thing better than performing compulsory obligations-Through performance of recommended obligations (Nawafil) he becomes so much intimate with me that I become like his ears through which he hears; become as his eyes through which he sees; become as his tongue through which he talks,-become as his hands through which he

---

[46] Refer to Kulliyat Mafatteh al-Jinan of (late) Haj Sheik Abbas Qummi [Tr]

finds things,-and become as his feet through which he moves. If he beseech me I accept; if he desires some thing I bestow it upon him, I have never contradicted anything like contradiction in taking a believer's soul,-he is disgusted with death and I become disgusted seeing him unhappy."
   -Bihar al-Anwar, vol. 87, p-31

Third-Night Prayer (Namaz-e-Shab)

Among various recommended deeds (*Nawafil*) the Night Prayer carries special distinction, and the Holy Quran and traditions have made lots of emphasis and recommendations for its performance. God-Almighty says to Holy Prophet (S):

> "And some part of the night awake for it, a largess for thee. It may be that thy Lord will raise thee to a praised estate."
>   -the Holy Quran (17:79)

And in praise of God's Special Servants says:

> "And who spend the night before their Lord prostrate and standing."
>   -the Holy Quran (25:64)

And in defining believers characteristics says:

> "Who forsake their beds to cry unto their Lord in fear and hope, and spend of what we have bestowed up on them. No soul knoweth what is kept hidden for them of joy, as a reward for what they used to do."
>   -the Holy Quran (32:16-17)

The Holy Prophet (S) has said:
   "God-Almighty send revelation to world asking it to be indifferent towards

its admirers and to be in service to its forsakers. When a God's servant in the darkness of night engages himself in humming communications with his Creator, God-Almighty enlightens his heart."

"When he says: Oh God! Oh God! (Yarab! Yarab!) God-Almighty responds by replying -'yes my servant! Whatever you desire I will bestow it upon you, rely upon Me so that I make you self-sufficient'. Then God-Almighty says to His angels -'Look at my servant! How in the darkness of night is he busy in humming private communications with Me, while lovers of nonsense amusements are busy in pursuing their carnal desires and the ignorant ones are busy in sleep. Be you witness that I have forgiven my servant."

-Bihar al-Anwar, vol. 87, p-137.

The Holy Prophet (S) has said:

"The nobles of my nation (Ummah) are -the carriers of Holy Quran and night vigilants."

-Bihar al-Anwar, vol. 87, p-138.

And said:

"Angel Gabriel has made so much recommendation about night prayer to me, that I assume the righteous one of my nation (Ummah) will not sleep during night."

-Bihar al-Anwar, vol. 87, p-139.

And said:

"Two units of prayer in the middle of night is more beloved to me than the world and whatsoever it may contain."

-the Bahar al-Anwar, vol. 87, p-148.

Imam al-Sadiq (A) has said:

"Night Prayer makes face beautiful, conduct righteous, and (prayer offerer's) body performed; increases sustenance; pays debts; removes grief and increases shining of eyes."

-Bihar al-Anwar, vol. 87, p-153.

The Holy Prophet (S) said:

"Night Prayer is a means of pleasing God-Almighty and achieving friendship of His angels. It is a tradition and way of prophets; a light of seeing God and root of the faith (because it strengthens faith). Makes body relaxed and Satan agitated, it is arsenal against enemies; is a means for acceptance of prayer and deeds; increases Divine-Bounties for a human being; acts as an intercessor between prayer offerer and death's angel; it is the light and floor covering inside the grave as well as the defender to the questioning of two angels (Munkir and Nakir).

"Inside the grave it will become a companion and pilgrim of the prayer offerer till the Day of Resurrection. On the Judgment Day, it will provide a shadow for head; will become a crown upon head; a dress for body, a front light; and a barrier between prayer offerer and Hell's .fire. It will be a solid argument before God-Almighty for the believer, a means for making deeds heavier; a pass for crossing over the Sirat and a key of Paradise. Because, prayer consists of proclamation of God's Greatness (Takbir), Praise, Adoration, Worship, to show humility and humbleness in front of Him, respect, recital of the Holy Quran, and supplication. Indeed the prayer offered at its right time -is the most superior deed."

-Bihar al-Anwar, vol. 87, p-161.

There are many traditions and Quranic verses which describe the special importance assigned to Night Prayer. Its recital has been the traditions of prophets and God's favorite saints. The Holy Prophet (S) and the Infallible Imams (A) of his Holy Progeny have shown special interests and paid attention towards Night Prayer. God's favorite saints and mystics through their continuous engagements into Night Prayer, invocations, and supplications at dawn were able to attain exalted spiritual positions.

How beautiful and pleasing it is that a God's servant wakes up from sleep; leaves his soft and comfortable bed; makes ablutions, and in the darkness of night, while the others are busy in deep sleep, stands up before the Lord of the worlds; engages into humming communications with Him; and through this spiritual journey ascends towards Upper Heavens, thus, joining the angels of Celestial Kingdom in praising, worshipping, and adoring God-Almighty. At this moment, his heart becomes center of illumination of Divine light and with a heart fully saturated with God's desire ascends towards the most sublime spiritual position of God's Nearness.

Details of Night Prayer

The Night-Prayer consists of all together eleven units (Rakats) of prayer. The first eight units are offered as two units prayer (exactly like 2 units of Morning Prayer), repeated four times with the intention of Night-Prayer. After finishing these eight units, make intention for the (Prayer of Shafa)[47] and offer two units of prayer. In the end make intention of (Prayer of Witr) [48] and offer are unit of prayer with special instructions. There are special etiquettes and supplications for the Night Prayer that may be found in the books of traditions and supplications. [49]

Etiquette of Night-Prayer

The time of Night Prayer begins after midnight and the more nearer it gets to dawn the better it is. Whenever you are awakened for night prayer first of all relieve yourself from the call of nature, clean your teeth, make ablutions (*wadhu*), and make yourself perfumed.

The night prayer consists of 11 units (Rakats) as follows: 8 Rakat (4 times 2 rakat) Night Prayer 2 Rakat Prayer of Shafa 1 Rakat Prayer of Witr. The first eight rakats should be offered like 2 rakats of Morning prayer repeating four times with a salutation offered after every two Rakats. In the first Rakat recite Surah Opening:

(Bismillah ar Rahman nir Rahim; alhamadu lillahi Rab al alimin; ar Rahman nir Rahim,' Malike yom iddin,' iyyaka nabudu wa iyyaka nastayeen, ahede nassratal mustaqeem saratal lazina,' anamta aleyhim,' gharyil maqdhubeh alehim waladh dhuallin).

"In the Name of God the Beneficent and the Merciful", "Praise be

---

[47] **"By the Even and Odd (contrasted)."** -the Holy Quran (89:3) [Tr].

[48] Ibid.

[49] For the convenience of our readers the [Tr] has prepared "Etiquettes of Night-Prayer" abstracted from supplication books.

to God, Lord of the worlds,' the Beneficent, the Merciful," Owner of the day of Judg-ment,' Thee (alone) we worship, Thee alone we ask for help,' show us the straight path,' The path of those whom Thou hast favored,' Not (the path) of those who earn thine anger nor of those who go astray."
-the Holy Quran (1:1-7),

After reciting Surah Opening the prayer offerer may recite any other surah whatever he likes or may recite Surah "Sincerity" in all 8 Rakats:
(Bismillah ar Rahman nir Rahim,. qul ho wallahu ahad Allahus samad,. lam yalid walam yulad,' walam ya kun lahu kufu one ahad),

In the Name of God, the Beneficent and the Merciful
"Say: He is God, the One! God, the eternally besought of all! He begeteth not nor was begotten, And there is non comparable unto Him."
-the Holy Quran (112: 1-4)

In the second rakat of prayer like all others prayers, Qunoot is optional and recital of the following, three times is sufficient.
Subhan Allahi
"Glory to God"
Prayer of Shafa
After finishing eight Rakat of Night Prayer as described above, make intention of two rakats of prayer of Shafa as follows:
In the first Rakat after recital of Surah Opening recite Surah Nas (Mankind) as follows:
(Bismillah ar Rahman nir Rahim;
Qul auzu bi Rab bil nas,. Malik in nas ilahin nas,. Min sharril waswasil Khannas, Allazi yo vis viso fi sudoorin nase," Min al jinnate onenas.)
"In the name of Allah, the Beneficent, the Merciful"

"Say: I seek refuge in the Lord of mankind; The King of mankind,"

The God of mankind," from the evil of the sneaking whisperer; who whispereth in the hearts of mankind; of the jinn and of mankind."
-the Holy Quran (114:1-6)

In the second Rakat after recital of Surah Opening recite Surah Day Break as follows:

(Bismillah ar Rahman nir Rahim," Qui a uzu bi Rab bil falaq; min, sharrin ma khalaq, wa min sharre ghasiqin eza waqab, wa min sharrin naffasate fil uqad)

"In the name of Allah, the Beneficent, the Merciful."
"Say: I seek refuge in the Lord of Daybreak, from the evil of that which He created; from the evil of the darkness when it is intense; and from the evil of ma-lignant witchcraft and from the evil of envier when he envieth."
-the Holy Quran (113:1-5)

Prayer of Witr

After finishing two rakat of Prayer of Shaf'a, make intention of one Rakat of Witr Prayer as follows:

After recital of Surah Opening recite Surah Sincerity one time. Or, one may recite Surah Sincerity three times, Surah Day-Break one time and Surah Mankind one time, after Surah Opening. Having finished recital of the above raise your hands upward for Qunoot, and recite whatever you prefer or you may recite the following:

(Rabana atena fid dunia hasaneh wa fil akhre hasanah wa qena aza bin nar).

"Our Lord! Give unto us in the world that which is good and in the Hereafter that which is good, and guard us from the doom of Fire."
-the Holy Quran (2:201)

or, recite the following:

(Allahumma Kulle Waliyak al Hujjat ibnal Hasan Salawataka aleyhim wa ala abahe fi hazes saat wafi kulle saat walian wa hafiza wa qaiden wa nasera wa dalilan wa ayena hatta tuzkenahu arzaka toa wa tamat-teahufiha tavila, be rahameteka ya ar hamar rahimin.)

"Oh God! Protect Your Vicegerent (*Vali-e-Asr*), and send salutations upon him, and his Holy ancestors at this time as well as at all the times, (as our) Imam, guardian, supporter, and guide until such time; when you bestow upon him the honor of heading the (Divine) Government. And let the people be delighted in his reign, by bestowing success, and by extending his reign (as maximum as possible)."

Or recite the following:

(Rabana afrigh aleyna sabran wa sabbit iqdamana wa unsurna alal qomal kafiriin)

> *"Our Lord! Bestow on us endurance, make our foothold sure; and give us help against the disbelieving folk."*
> *-the Holy Quran (2:250)*

It is recommended that in the state of Qunoot one should try to cry and shed tears because, of remembering his past sins and transgressions, God-Almighty Day of Judgment and the Hell's fire. According to Islamic traditions, if one prays for forty believers God-Almighty grants his supplications. Therefore, in Qunoot it is recommended to ask God's

forgiveness for at least forty believers, (including your parents, relatives, neighbors, colleagues, scholars, martyrs etc.) in the following manner:

(Allahummaghfir)

Oh God! forgive (Mention the name of person, and repeat it for forty people) it has been narrated that the Holy Prophet (S) used to seek God is forgiveness seventy times. Therefore, while still maintaining your left hand in the state of Qunoot, and holding a rosary in your right hand recite the following seventy times:

(Astagh.frullahi rabi wa atubo elahe)

"Oh God! Forgive me and accept my repentance. The Holy Prophet (S) used to recite the following sentence seven times:

(Haza maqamal aize beka minan nar)

"Here is some one who has sought your shelter from the Hell's fire."

It has been narrated that Imam al-Sajjad (A) used to seek God's forgiveness three hundred times by reciting the following sentence:

(Al afoo)

"(Oh God!) Please Forgive!"

Therefore, while still holding left hand in the state of Qunoot, crying, shedding tears of regret and shame for past sins with the rosary in right hand, recite the above sentence three hundred times. After finishing it recite the following supplication only one time:

(Rubbe naqhfirli warhamni watoubli innaka antal tawwabul ghafoor urrahim.)

"Oh God! Please forgive me, be kind to me and accept my repentance. Indeed you are the one who accepts repentance, forgiver, and the most Merciful."

This completes the Qunoot of Witr prayer. After finishing Qunoot bow down into genuflection and prostration and finish the prayer in the usual manner like all other prayers with the recital of witnessing (*Tashahud*) and salutation (*salam*). Those readers who are not familiar with these Prayer rituals may refer to the Book: Profundities of Prayer written by:

Ayatullah Sayyid Ali Khamenei; Translated by S.H. Alamdar and Published by Ansariyan Publications, Qum.

Notes

1.

Fourth Means – Crusade (Jihad) and Martyrdom (Shahadat)

Crusade waged for the way of God-Almighty, extension of Islamic rule, proclamation of Monotheism (Towheed), defense of Islamic lands and governance of Quranic commands, combating against oppression and arrogance, and for the defense of deprived and oppressed -is considered as one of the great worship, which results in a crusader's achieving self-perfection and spiritual ascension towards God-Almighty. There are plenty of traditions and Quranic Verses which describe the special importance attached to crusade. e.g. : God-Almighty says in Holy Quran:

> "Those who believe and have left their homes and striven with their wealth and their lives in God's way are of much greater worth in God's sight. These are they who are triumphant."
> -the Holy Quran (9:20)

And said:

> "But he has bestowed on those who strive a great reward above the sedentary."
> -the Holy Quran (4:95)

The Holy Prophet (S) has said:

"There is a gate in the Paradise called as the "Gate of Crusaders." When the crusaders walk towards the Paradise, the gate opens and the crusaders with their swords hanging enter into Paradise passing through a grand welcome by angels, while the other people remain being held up for accounting of their deeds."

-Wasail al-Shi'a, vol. 11, p-5.

The Holy Prophet (S) said:

"For every virtue, there is an another higher virtue except when a human being sacrifices his life for the sake of God-Almighty. And in that case there exists nothing superior than that."

-Wasail al-Shi'a, vol. 11,p-10.

The Holy Prophet (S) said: "That God-Almighty bestows upon a martyr the following seven blessings;

1. "When the first drop of blood comes out his body all his sins are pardoned.
2. After martyrdom his head is placed upon the laps of two heavenly maids, who clean off dirt from his face and say greeting to you, and he too reciprocates their greetings.
3. They dress him in Heavenly clothes.
4. The store keeper of Paradise present him different kinds of perfumes and good smells, so that he may select whatever desires.
5. At the time of martyrdom his place in Paradise is shown to him.
6. After the martyrdom his soul is addressed -you are free to move in the Paradisewherever you desire.
7. A martyr is allowed to witness God's Beauty, which brings a special sort of comfort for every prophet and martyr."

-Wasail al-Shi'a, vol., 11,p-9.

God-Almighty says in Holy Quran:

"Lo! God hath bought .from the believers their lives and their wealth because the Garden will be theirs: They shall fight in the way of God and shall slay and be slain. It is a promise which is

> *binding on Him in Torah, the Gospel and the Holy Quran. Who fulfilleth his covenant better than God's? Rejoice in your bargain that you have made, for that is the supreme triumph."*
> -the Holy Quran (9:111)

The above mentioned verse is one of the most beautiful and tender verses of the Holy Quran in which the people have been encouraged to participate in struggle, with special delicacy and tenderness. In the be-ginning the verse says:

"*God has purchased of the believers their persons and their goods, and in re-turn gives them Paradise.*"

What a beautiful deal? The buyer is God-Almighty -the Lord of the Universe and Absolute Owner of all the riches. The believers are the sellers who believe in God-Almighty and Hereafter. And the thing being traded is -the eternal Paradise.

Then says:

God Almighty in Torah, Bible and Holy Quran -the three great Heavenly scriptures, has registered such promise.

Then says:

Do you know anyone else ?

Who is more faithful to his covenant than God ?

In the end God-Almighty gives glad tidings to believers about such a worthy deal and says:

That is the most supreme achievement.

The Holy Quran for a human being martyred in God's path confirms the highest position and says:

> *"Think not of those who are slain in God's way as dead. Nay they live finding their sustenance in the presence of their Lord."*
> -the Holy Quran (3:169)

The sentence in the presence of their Lord describes the supreme position assigned to a martyr. Human soul's remaining alive after death is not reserved for martyrs only, rather is applicable to all human beings. But the distinction of martyrs is the sentence: in the presence of their Lord. i.e. they will continue life -at the most superior positions, and will receive their sustenance at these positions, and naturally the sustenance received by them, will not be similar to the sustenance received by others.

Struggle in God's path and martyrdom are the most greatest and worthiest worships and a martyr through this distinguished means may attain the most subtle spiritual positions. What distinguishes this worship from other worships is its two dimensions, which may be described as follows:

1. First Dimension -The supreme Goal of the crusader:

The aim of a combatant is not to safeguard his own interest as well as the interest of his relatives. He is not a selfish or shortsighted person rather he is dedicated to achieve the objectives and goals desired by God-Almighty.

1. Second Dimension -The magnitude of sacrifice:

A combatant in order to undertake his spiritual journey, and for the sake of achieving his cherished goal i.e. the God-Almighty, invest his most valuable and dearest assets. If a human being offers some donation for a charity it does not mean more than that he has overlooked a certain portion of his wealth; similarly in case he worships, it does not mean more than that he has spent a certain amount of his time and energy; but a crusader overlooks every thing belonging to him; above every thing else he over looks his own life and surrender his entire existence to the God-Almighty with absolute sincerity. He closes his eyes from wealth, power, position, wife, children, and relatives, thus, suddenly surrendering his soul to God-Almighty.

The work done by gnostics and devoted individuals during their entire span of lives, may be accomplished by a crusader either all of it or even may be more than that in a very short time. The matter and materialistic world is too much confined for the exalted and enlightened spirit of a crusader, because of the same reason, like a formidable lion breaks his material cage, as a light winged pigeon flies over the vast illuminated Upper Heavens and from the most superior exalted positions ascends to-wards their beloved God-Almighty.

If other God's saints, gradually, during entire span of lives were able to attained the most distinguished spiritual positions namely -position of desire, love, witnessing a combatant martyr travels this one hundreds years distance in one single night and, thus, attains the most distinguished spiritual position of God's-countenance (*laqa*).

If other God's servants by means of invocations, incarnations, sitting and standing seek God's Nearness, a struggler of God's way through tolerance of wounds, pains, hardships, bullets, fragments of mortar shell, and ultimately by sacrificing his own soul attains God's Nearness; although, there is vast difference between these two.

The battle field possesses a special sort of purity, spirituality, and illumination; it is field of love, sacrifice, action, and enthusiasm; it is a field of competition for getting sacrificed in the beloved's path, and becoming alive for eternal life. The humming warm communications of the dwellers of trenchement with their beloved possess a special fervor of purity, illumination, and attraction whose examples cannot be seen even inside the mosques and temples.

Fifth Means – Benevolence and Service to Humanity

According to Islamic doctrine, God's worship and nearness neither can be summarized simply performance of prayer, fasting, Hajj, pilgrimages, invocations, and supplications, nor is limited to presence in mosques, temples, and tombs; instead, discharging social responsibilities, compassion, goodness, and serving God's servants, if done with the intention of God's nearness, are considered as most superior worships and could be-come a means for self-building, self-purification, and God's Nearness.

In Islam, devotion and undertaking spiritual journey towards God-Almighty do not necessarily require living in seclusion, rather could be done together with acceptance of social responsibilities as well as living a perfectly normal social life. Cooperation in righteous deeds and benevolence; goodness, endeavors in fulfilling the needs of believers and making them happier; defense of oppressed and deprived; taking care of the affairs of Muslims; solving their problems and extending a helping hand towards God's servants, from the Islamic point of view are considered a great worship whose reward is ten times higher than performance of a Hajj pilgrimage. Their exist hundreds of traditions narrated by the Holy Prophet (S) and Infallible Imams (A) which emphasize the importance of this matter. e.g.: the following has been narrated from Imam al-Sadiq (A) that God-Almighty said:

"My servants are my children, therefore, the most beloved persons before me are those who are kindest towards them and do their best in taking care of their needs."

-al-Kafi,vol. 2, p-199.

The Holy Prophet (S) has said:

"The people are God's children, therefore, the most beloved persons before God-Almighty are those whose benevolence reach to God's children, thus, making their families happier full of joy."

-al-Kafi, vol. 2p-164.

Imam al-Baqir (A) said:

"Smiling of a believer while encountering a fellow brother believer as well as solving his problems are accounted as righteous deeds. There is no worship more beloved before God-Almighty than making a believer joyful."

-Bihar al-Anwar, vol. 2, p-188.

Imam al-Sadiq (A) said:

"Whoever makes a believer happy has made me happy; whoever makes me happy has made the Holy Prophet (S) happy,. whoever has made the Holy Prophet (S) happy has made the God-Almighty happy; and whoever has made God-Almighty happy will enter into Paradise."

-Bihar al-Anwar vol. 74, p-413.

And said:

"Fulfillment of a believer's need before God-Almighty is more beloved than performance of Hajj pilgrimage for ten times each time spending ten thousands."

-al-Kafi,vol. 2, p-193.

And said:

"To strive for fulfillment of Muslim's need is better than circumambulating around the Holy Kaba seventy times."

-Bihar al-Anwar vol. 74, p-311.

And said:

"God-Almighty has created some of His special servants, that at the time of their needs, people take shelter in them. These are the ones who will be immune

from God's Punishment on the Judgment Day."

-Bihar al-Anwar, vol. 74, p-318.

Therefore, as described above, according to Islamic point of view -benevolence, goodness, helping God's servants and to solve their problems are considered as great worships. And if they are done with the intention of God's pleasure will become means for nourishment and perfection of self, spiritual migration and ascension towards God's Nearness.

Unfortunately, a majority of people lack the proper understanding of true Islam, and therefore, have been deprived from benefits of such a large and important part of Islamic worship. In their opinion worship-ping and undertaking spiritual journey towards God-Almighty is not possible, except, through prayer, fasting, pilgrimage, supplication, invocation, and incantations.

Sixth Means – Supplications (Dua)

The supplication (*dua*) is one of the best worship through which one may attain self-perfection and God's Nearness. Because of this reason God-Almighty has invited his servants to offer supplications. God-Almighty says in Holy Quran:

> "And your Lord hath said: Pray unto Me and I will hear your prayer. Lo!
> Than who scorn My service, they will enter Hell disgraced."
> -the Holy Quran (40:60)

And said:

> ("Oh mankind!) Call upon your Lord humbly and in secret. Lo! He loveth not aggressors."
> -the Holy Quran (7:55)

And said:

> "And when My Servants question thee concerning Me, then surely I am nigh. I answer the prayer of the suppliant when he crieth unto Me."

-the Holy Quran (2:186)

The Holy Prophet (S) has said:

"The supplication (Dua) is the soul of the worship."

-Sahih Tirmidhi, vol. 2, p-266.

Imam al-Sadiq (A) has said:

"Supplication is worship, because God-Almighty says: ' You must continue to seek God-Almighty and should never say: It is all done."

-al-Kafi, vol. 2. p-407.

And said:

"You should never quit supplication in all circumstances, because you will never find any other substitute like supplication in attaining God's-Nearness. Even, for insignificant [50] and minor affairs one must supplicate, and because of their being insignificant supplication should not be abandoned, because, after all the Master of petty affairs happens to be the same Master of large affairs."

-al-Kafi, vol. 2, p-467.

God's Servant must supplicate because his entire existence needs God-Almighty. Because, a human being in essence is absolutely poor, needy, and dependent; and in case he becomes deprived of God's blessings even for an instant, he will be destroyed as though he was never existed. Whatever, reaches to a servant is bestowed from God-Almighty, therefore, a servants should admit this primordial dependency by his tongue and should confirm his poverty, servitude, and needs, through his practical actions, which is the real meaning of worship.

At the time of supplication a human being remembers God-Almighty, establish humming communications with him, and like a humble servant with tearful eyes presents his needs before the God-Almighty the Owner of Absolute Riches. By abandoning his hopes from the world of poverty and wants, he establishes his link with the Most Supreme Source of all Blessings and Perfection.

---

[50] Even if one need's an insignificant thing like shoe's laces, one must pray and ask God-Almighty [Tr].

Flying upward from the world of poverty, he succeeds in witnessing the Beauty of God's Essence, through his esoteric eyes. The state of supplication and humming private communications with God-Almighty is one of the most pleasurable and beautiful condition of a servant which will never be exchanged for any price by God's saints.

Refer to al-Sahifah al-Sajjadiyyah [51] and other supplication books and study the details of humming communications of Infallible Imams (A) of the Prophet's Holy Progeny. Establishing communications with God-Almighty and hoping that He will accept the supplications, brings tranquility, and assurance for the suppliant's heart. If a human being, while facing lives hardships for solution of his problems and difficulties, does

not seek refuge in God-Almighty, then how could he show perseverance against them and have assurance for continuation of his life?

Supplication is a believer's arsenal through which he struggles against disappointments and despairs, and seeks help from a hidden super natural power for solution of his difficulties and problems. The Divine-Prophets and Infallible Imams (A) always utilized this arsenal and have recommended it strongly for believers. Imam al-Ridha (A) said to his companions.

---

[51] Al-Sahifah Al-Sajjadiyyah: includes certain supplications quoted from Imam Zain al-Abidin 'Ali b. Hussain b. 'Ali ibn Abi Talib (A). He is one of the Imams belonging to the household of the Prophet whom Allah has kept pure and free of defilement. The Imam was the fourth in line of the Imams of the Prophet's household. Imam' Ali ibn al-Husain (A), was born in the year 38 A.H. or, perhaps as is conjectured, a little before that and lived for a period of 57 years.

Imam al-Shafi considered Imam" Ali ibn al-Husain (A) as the most supreme jurist of all the people of Medina" Abd al-Malik bin Marwan said to him, "in the area of religious sciences, in devotion and piety, you have been granted that which no one before you has had other than your ancestors". Further Umar bin ' Abd al-Aziz said, "The light of this life, ' the beauty of Islam is Zain al-Abidin" Al-Sahifah Al-Sajjadiyyah represents and stands out as a profound social work of the time and a reflection of a supreme endeavor to meet the exigencies of spiritual ordeals facing the society at the time of the Imam. But beyond this it is a profound collection of supplications in the divine tradition, a unique compilation which will remain throughout the ages as a gift to mankind, a work of moral in-spiration for worldly conduct and a torch of guidance. Human begins will constantly remain in need of this heavenly souvenir; and the need increases whenever Satan comes to increase the allurements of the world for people, and by its fascination to keep them in bondage [Tr].

"Use the arsenal of Prophets." What is the arsenal of prophets? He was asked. "Supplication". Replied the Imam."

-al-Kafi, vol. 2, p-468.

Imam al-Baqir (A) said:

"God-Almighty, among .the believers loves the one, who supplicates a lot; and I recommend you to supplicate specially at the time of dawn until sun-rise, be-cause, at this time the gates of Heaven are opened; people's sustenance is distrib-uted and their great wants are granted."

-al-Kafi vol. 2, p-478.

The Holy Prophet (S) has said:

"Supplication is believer's arsenal; is the pillar of religion and light of the earth and sky."

-al-Kafi, vol. 2, p-468.

Supplication is a worship rather is the soul of all worships and brings eternal rewards. It is a believers ascension to Heavenly Kingdom, makes the supplicant's spirit perfected and nourished and helps suppliant to at-tain God's Nearness. The Commander of the Faithful Imam' Ali (A) said:

"Supplication is the key of prosperity; the best supplication is the supplication which comes out .from pure chests and pious hearts; supplication or hymns with God-Almighty results in salvation; and through means of sincerity one is saved from adversities and wickedness, therefore, when hardships become intense one should seek refuge in God-Almighty."

-al-Kafi, vol. 2, p-468.

Therefore, supplication is a worship that if done properly in accordance with relevant conditions will result in suppliant's attaining self-perfection and God's Nearness, and these results certainly depends upon the rank and degree of the supplication. Because, of this reason a Lord's servant at any place, under any circumstances should never be negligent from this great worship, since a supplication is never going to be ineffective, although it may not produce immediate and apparent results. It is possible that sometimes the grant of suppliant's wants might be delayed; or may be they will not be fulfilled in this world; but even this is not without wisdom; because, occasionally a believer's demand are not in his real interest and a

Sixth Means - Supplications (Dua)

Wise God knows better what is really good for his servant.

Therefore, a servant should always stretch his hands before the Almighty Omnipotent God, and should supplicate for his wants. If it is deemed appropriate his wants will be granted in this world. But, sometimes God-Almighty thinks it appropriate to delay the grant of his servant so that he does more intensive humming communication. with Him, .thus, attaining higher exalted spiritual positions. Sometimes, divine expediency dictates that his grant should not be granted in this world so that he should remain continuously engaged in God's Remembrance, and receive a much better reward in the next world. The Holy Prophet (S) said:

"May God-Almighty bless the servant who seeks his needs from God-Almighty and pleads for their fulfillment through supplications whether his wants are granted or not. Then he recited the following verse:

"It may be that in prayer unto my Lord, I shall not be unblessed."
-the HolyQuran (19:48)

-al-Kafi vol. 2 p-475.

Imam al-Sadiq (A) said:

"Sometimes a believer supplicates for a need before God-Almighty; but, He orders His Angels to delay the grant of servant's needs, because, He loves to hear his voice and supplication more. Then on the Day of Judgment says to him: ' Oh My servant! You called me but I delayed your request, now in return I will bestow upon you such and such reward and so and so supplication. ' Hearing it the servant would say: I wish none of myneeds would have been granted in the world. ' He says so because he sees the excellent rewards of Hereafter."

-al-Kafi, vol. 2, p-490.

And said:

"Be careful about the etiquettes of supplication, and pay attention as to which personality are you talking, how do you beseech Him, and for what purpose is He implored?

"Think about the Majesty and Splendor of God-Almighty, and look inside your heart and know that He is aware of whatever is contained therein,. He knows

about your heart's secrets and the truth and falsehood hidden therein. Be careful, to identify correctly the path of your salvation or misfortune lest you re-quest a thing from God-Almighty which contains your destruction while you imagine your salvation in it. The God-Almighty said in Holy Quran:

> "Man Prayeth for evil as he prayeth for good, for man was ever hasty."
> -the Holy Quran(17:11)

"Therefore, think correctly regarding what do you want from God-Almighty and for what purpose is it required. A supplication will be accepted only if you exert absolute concentration of your entire existence towards God-Almighty,. melting your heart while witnessing His presence; abandoning all your dispos-als, and absolute surrender of all affairs with sincerity to God-Almighty. So, if you did not act in accordance to above mentioned conditions of supplication do not look forward for its acceptance.

"Because, God-Almighty is aware of all your secrets and mysteries. Perhaps you beseech God-Almighty for something, while you know that your intention is opposite to your request."
 -Haqayaqi-Faiz, p-244.

Seventh Means – Fasting (Sawm)

Fasting is one of the greatest worship which exerts tremendous influence in one's efforts for self-perfection, self purification, and self building. There are many traditions which describe the special distinction assigned to fasting. Following are few examples: The Holy Prophet (S) has said:

"*The Fasting is a shield for protection against Hell's fire.*"

vol. 7, p-289.

Imam al-Sadiq (A) said:

-Wasail al-Shi'a,

"*God-Almighty said: ' Fasting is for Me and I bestow its reward upon the fast observer.*"

-Wasail al-Shi'a, vol. 7, p-290.

And said:

"*The fast observer moves an enjoys inside the Garden of Paradise, and angels pray for him until the fast breaking time.*"

-Wasail al-Shi'a, vol., 7, p-296.

The Holy Prophet (S) has said:

"*Whoever observes one recommended fast for the sake of reward, forgiveness for him becomes compulsory.*"

-Wasail al-Shi'a, vol. 7, p-293.

Imam al-Sadiq (A) has said:

"The sleep of a fast observer is regarded as worship; his silence is considered as praise, his deeds are accepted and his supplications are granted."
-Wasail al-Shi'a, vol. 7, p-294.

The Holy Prophet (S) has said:

"God-Almighty said: 'For all righteous deeds of servants there is a reward from ten times to seven hundred time, but since, fasting is specially reserved for me -I will bestow its reward. Therefore. only God-Almighty knows the reward of fasting."
-Wasail al-Shi'a,vol. 7, p-295.

Fasting. is a special worship which is a combination of two parts i.e. negation and confrontation. The first part consists of self-Restraint and renunciation of drinking, eating, and sexual pleasures, which are legitimate pleasures, as well as not to tell a lie about God-Almighty and Holy Prophet (S) and some other affairs which have been described in details in Jurisprudential books.

The second part consists of devotion, intention, and desire to seek God's Nearness, which in reality are tantamount to soul of this worship. The reality of fasting consists of self-restraint and voluntary relinquishment of material pleasures namely -Eating, drinking, sexual intercourse, and not to tell a lie about God-Almighty and Holy Prophet (S), with the intention of God's Nearness.

The definition of a fast as given in the books of Jurisprudence is — that if some one with the intention of God's Nearness renounced the affairs namely -eating, drinking, sexual intercourse, discharge of seamen, telling a lie about God-Almighty and Holy Prophet (S), to take a dive inside water, remaining in the state of impurity as a result of a wet dream -his fast is correct and does not require to take a make up (*qadha*) fast or pay ransom (*kuffara*). This fast is known as the fast of common people.

But, in traditions the scope of self-restraint have not been limited to the above mentioned limits rather it covers much wider dimensions. In traditions it has been mentioned that simply abandonment of eating and drinking is not enough, instead a real fast observer is the one who prevents all his limbs and body parts from sins. i.e. the eyes should be prevented from the sins relevant to the eyes, as well as prevent ears, tongue, hands, and feet from their relevant sins. Such fast belongs to God's special servants.

Further, superior than this is the fasting of the most special ones (*khawwas*) in which case the observer of the fast apart from abandoning eating, drinking as well as renunciation of all sins also disengages his heart from all sort of scattered thinking which prevent him from God's Remembrance. He should continuously engage himself in God's remembrance and should know that He is seeing all his actions. As God's guest he should make himself readied for His countenance. For example let us refer to the following tradition: Imam al-Sadiq (A) said:

"Fasting is not achieved simply by renunciation of eating and drinking. When you observe fast your eyes, ears, tongue, stomach, and sexual parts should also be fasting with you. While in the state of fasting prevent your hands and sexual parts from sinning, should remain silent continuously except for speaking something good and useful or to the extent it is required to communicate with your house servant."

-Wasail al-Shi'a, vol. 7, p-118.

Also said:

"The dignity and prestige of fasting should be understood by you wry clearly. As much as possible, maintain silence except for God's Remembrance. It should not be such that the day of your fasting should be similar to the day in which you are not observing fast."

-Wasail al-Shi'a, vol. 7, p-117.

The Holy Prophet (S) said in a sermon:

"Whosoever observes fasting during Holy month of Ramadhan while maintaining silence and preventing his ears, eyes, tongue, sexual organs, and other body parts from lying, backbiting, and other forbidden acts, with the intention of achieving God's Nearness, God-Almighty will bestow upon him His Nearness, so that he will become a companion of Prophet Abraham (A) -God's chosen friend."

-Wasail al-Shi'a, vol. 7, p-117.

Imam al-Sadiq (A) said:

"Fasting does not mean only renunciation of eating and drinking rather it has conditions which must be followed strictly in order to have a complete and perfect

fast which means internal silence. Did not you hear the reply of Mary daughter of Imran who said to the people:

"'*I have vowed a fast for God-Almighty, therefore, today will speak to none i.e. since, I am fasting therefore must be quiet.*' *So, when you observe fast protect your tongue from lying; don't be angry; don't curse, don't be rude; don't argue and dispute; due to ignorance don't reject or be indecent to each other, don't be negligent from God's remembrance; continuously practice silence, in-tellection, patience and keep distance from the wicked people. Assign importance to the Hereafter; must look forward for the day when God's Promise will be fulfilled; and collect some provisions for God's countenance.*

"*Poise dignity, humbleness, humility, and fear like a servant who is afraid of his master, should be practiced; should remain in the state of hope and fear. If you cleansed and purified your heart from faults; your inner self from conceit and treachery; your body from pollution, renounced every thing other than God; accepted His Guardianship through fasting, and preventing inner and outer self from performance of God's forbidden things; respected God's rights by remaining afraid outwardly and inwardly because of His presence,. during fasting donated your self to God-Almighty, purified and cleansed heart for God-Almighty and assigned him to act in accordance to His commands.*

"*If you observed fast in a manner described above, then indeed you really are a true fast observer and have discharged your duty well. But in as much as you deviated from the above criteria, your fast be considered as deficient and incomplete in the same proportion. Because, fasting is not limited only to renunciation of eating and drinking rather God-Almighty has made fasting a veil for other actions and sayings which make fasting canceled. Therefore, how small is the number of fast observers and how large is the number of hungry ones.*"

-Wasail al-Shi'a, vol. 7, p-119.

Role of Fasting in Self-Building

Fasting is one of the most important and valuable worship, which if, observed in accordance to its special etiquettes and conditions, and maintaining the same degree of quality as required by sacred Islamic canon

Seventh Means – Fasting (Sawm)

law (*sharia*), will exert tremendous impact upon the self-building, self-perfection, and self-purification efforts.

Fasting is extremely influential during the stages of purification of self from sins and other moral indecencies and making it readied for perfection, decoration and utilization of Divine Illuminations. A fast observer through renunciation of sins controls, subdues, and ultimately forces the imperious-self into submission. The duration of fasting is a period of quitting sins and practicing self-asceticism -a period of struggling with self, and practicing self-restraint.

During this period a fast observer not only purity and cleanse his self from sins and other moral abjectnesses, but even abandons his legitimate pleasures such as eating and drinking, and through these means makes his self purified and illuminated. Because, hunger results in attaining internal purification and more attention towards God-Almighty. A human being, white hungry very often possesses a feeling of contentment or Joy[52] but lacks such mood when his stomach is full.

In summary, fasting is very effective in acquiring piety, and because, of this consideration the Holy Quran has defined acquiring piety as the main objective behind the fasting.

> *"O ye believe! Fasting is presented for you, even as it was prescribed for those before you, that ye may ward off (evil)."*
> *-the Holy Quran (2:183)*

The one who observes fast during the Holy month of Ramadhan, because, of fasting prevents himself from engaging into sins and other moral abjectnesses through out the month, would succeed in dominating his self and therefore, may continue this habit of renunciation of sins even after the Holy month.

So for whatever has been described was related to the influence of fasting

---

[52] Those who have observed fasting during Holy Month of Ramdhan or have observed recommended fasts may appreciate these feelings [Tr].

in purifying self from sins and other moral indecencies. But also from the point of view of positive dimensions it is very influential in achieving self-purification, decoration of inner self and God's Nearness which will be described briefly as follows:

1. Fasting i.e. self-restraint and renunciation of special acts which break the fast -is a worship, which if observed with sincerity and intention of God's Nearness, results in nourishment and perfection of self and God's Nearness like other worships.
2. By renunciation of legitimate pleasures and quitting sins the fast observer's heart gets cleansed and polished, becomes free from all scattered thoughts and memories of other than God and through this means earns the decency of absorbing the Divine blessings and illuminations. In this stage God's special blessings and favors are bestowed upon him and, thus, with Divine rapture ascends towards God's countenance. It is because of these reasons that it has been mentioned in the traditions that breathing and sleeping of a fast observer merit the reward of a worship.
3. The days of fasting are the best times for worship, prayer, supplication, Qur'anic-recital, invocation and charitable deeds; because, during this period self is relatively better prepared for heart's presence, devotion and attention towards God-Almighty as compared to any other period. The Holy Month of Ramadhan have been called as the best times, spring of worship (specially recital of the Holy Quran) and the most appropriate opportunity for paying attention to wards God-Almighty.

Because, of this reason the special virtues of the Holy Month of Ra-madhan and worshiping during it, have been emphasized a lot in the books of Islamic traditions. For example; when the Holy Month of Ra-madhan arrived, Imam al-Sadiq (A) emphasized its importance to his children and said:

"Endeavor in worship because in this month people's sustenance is distributed and their demises are registered, those who will be returned to God-Almighty are

decided in this month, In this month there is a special "Night of Power" (Qadr), the worshiping in which excels the worshiping of one thou-sands months."

-Wasail al-Shi'a, vol. 7, p-221.

The Commander of the Faithful Imam 'Ali (A) said:

"Oh people! During the Holy Month of Ramadhan read a lot of supplication and seek God's pardon (Esteghfar) because, by means of supplications the calamities are removed from you and by means of asking God's pardon your sins are forgiven."

-Wasail al-Shi'a, vol. 7, p-223.

Also he said that one day the Holy Prophet delivered a sermon in which he said:

"Oh people! The month of God with blessing mercy and pardon has came to you, a month which is the best month among all months before God-Almighty, its days are the best days, its nights are the best nights and its hours are the best hours. It is month in which you have been invited by God-Almighty for a feast, and have been selected as the recipient of this special favor. Your breathings merit the reward of praise, while your sleeping in this month earns the reward of a worship. In this month your deeds are accepted and prayers are granted."

"Therefore, with true intention and pure hearts beseech God-Almighty to bestow upon you His special favor to be able to observe fasting and recite the Holy Qur'an. Because, the most unfortunate and wretched one is the one who remains deprived from God's pardon during this great month. With your thrust and hunger remind yourself about the thrust and hunger of the Day of Judg-ment; pay charity to poor and destitute people, pay respect to elders; be kind towards youngsters, and observe the bonds of relationship with your kith and kins."

"Watch your tongues, cover your eyes from seeing forbidden objects and prevent your ears from hearing forbidden affairs. Be kind to the orphans of the people so that the others are kind towards your orphans. Repent for your sins and at the time of prayer raise your hands upward, because, these hours are the best hours in which God-Almighty looks towards mankind with mercy and com-passion. Their hymns are granted, their cries are heard. Whatever they ask is bestowed upon them and their prayers are fulfilled."

"Oh people! Your (selves) are mortgaged against your deeds and therefore, by means of repentance make yourself free. Your back has become too much heavy due to sins; by prolongation of your prostration make yourself light burdened. Know that! God-Almighty has taken the oath of his Majesty and Splendor that he will not punish those who offers prayers and bows down in prostration, and on the Day of Judgment will not scare them through the Hell's fire."

"Oh people! whoever in this month will make arrangements for the fast-breaking (iftar) of a believer will be bestowed upon the reward equal to freeing of a slave and all of his past sins shall be pardoned. He was asked: 'Oh prophet of God! But all of us are not in a position to arrange the fast-breaking of a fast-observer. The Prophet replied: 'Protect yourself from the Hell's fire and offer fast-breaking even if it happens to be a piece of date with a glass of sharbet."

"Oh people! whoever makes his conduct better in this month, on the Judgment Day will be bestowed upon the permit for crossing over the Sirat. Whoever will open the knots of difficulties of people Is affairs in this month, God-Almighty on the Judgment Day will make the accounting of his deeds easier."

Whoever makes people immune from his mischief, God-Almighty on the Judgment Day will make him immune from his wrath. Whoever treats an orphan with respect, on the Judgment Day, God-Almighty will treat him with honor. Whoever takes care to strengthen family bonds with relatives, God-Almighty will extend His blessing upon him on the Judgment Day, and whoever will cut off his family ties, God-Almighty too will deprive him from His blessing on the Judgment Day."

"Whoever offers supererogatory prayers in this month, God-Almighty will register for him immunity from the fire. Whoever performs a compulsory deed in this month, will be bestowed the reward of seventy compulsory deeds performed in other months. Whoever offers a lots of salutation upon me in this month, on the Judgment Day, God-Almighty will make the balance of his righteous deeds heavier. Whoever recites one single verse of the Holy Qur'an during this month will be bestowed the reward of finishing the entire Holy Quran in other months."

"Oh people! The gates of Paradise are opened in this month, beseech God-Almighty that it should not be closed upon you. The Doors of Hell are closed, and ask God-Almighty that they are not opened upon you. The devils are chained in this month, ask God-Almighty not to allow them to take over your control."

"Imam' Ali (A) said: 'Oh Prophet of God! which one is the best deed during this

Seventh Means –Fasting (Sawm)

month?' The Holy Prophet (S) replied: 'Oh Abul Hasan! The most supreme deed in this month is piety and renunciation of Divine forbidden acts."
-Wasail al-Shi'a, vol. 7, p-227.

As is evident from the above narration that the Holy Month of Ramadhan is a month full of blessings and special virtues. It is a month of worship, self-building, supplications, night prayer, and self-perfection. worshiping in this month is bestowed rewards many times of the reward of worship performed in other months. Even the sleeping and breathings of a believer are given the reward of a worship. In this month the gates of the Paradise are opened while the Hell's doors are closed.

God's angels continuously invite the people towards God's worship, especially at the dawn and on the night of Power (*Lailatul Qadr*) in which worshiping and night-vigil are superior than the prayer of thousands months.[53] God-Almighty in this month have granted an audience invit-ing all the believers for a Divine feast; the invitation of which have been brought by the messengers.

The host is the Most Merciful and Most compassionate God-Almighty, the God's most favorite angels are the servants and the believers are the guests. The table spread of Divine blessings containing all sorts of re-wards and favors has been provided. From all dimensions, the Divine special blessings and favors –which cannot be seen by eyes, ears are helpless to hear about them, and human hearts cannot even imagine them are readied to be awarded upon the guests in accordance to their merits, worthiness, and absorbing capabilities.

If we are negligent, we will feel sorry and regret on the Day of Judgment, whereby feeling sorry and being regretful will not be of any advantage. The special acts and supplications of the Holy Month of Ramadhan are described in the book –Mafateeh al-Jinan by late Haj Abbas Qummi as well as in books of supplications; and with sincerity, attention, and heart's presence utilize them for spiritual migration and attaining God's Nearness.

In the end, it must be reminded that other worships too, like prayer,

---

[53] **"The Night of Power is better than a thousand months."** -the Holy Quran (97:3) [Tr].

fasting, invocations, and supplications might be useful and effective in self-building and nourishment and perfection of the self. But for the sake of brevity it would not be appropriate to provide their detailed explanation and description in this book.

A Mystical Poem (Ghazal-e-Irfani) of Imam Khomeini (R.A.)

(Added by [Tr].) Since the present book: Self-Building of Ayatullah Ibrahim Amini deals with Islamic Mysticism, I thought it appropriate to include here the translation of a famous mystical poem of Imam Khomeini (R.A.) [54] -the most celebrated gnostics of our times -as a gift to our readers. These verses were composed by the late Imam (R.A.) a little before when he permanently

---

[54] Imam Ruhollah Mousavi Khomeini: Was born on the 20th Jamadi-ul-Thani 1281 A.H. (1902 AD in Khomein (Isfahan Province), in Iran. His father was Sayyid Mostafa Khomeini, a well-known and beloved scholar of his day, martyred by the agents of Reza Khan (the father of the deposed Shah). His father left three sons and three daughters. Imam Khomeini was the youngest in the family. Imam Khomeini lost both his tutors, his mother and aunt at the age of 15.

The Father and Founder of the Islamic Revolution in Iran studied Islamic sciences under the guidance of his elder brother Ayatollah Pasandideh. Ayatollah Khomeini also underwent special instructions with the help of Sheik Abdul-Karim Ha'eri Yazdi in 1922. When Ayatollah Ha'eri Yazdi passed away in 1937, Imam Khomeini was established as a genius scholar of high distinction.

Imam Khomeini was well versed in Islamic Jurisprudence, Philosophy, Mysticism, and Astronomy. In the earliest" Fatwa" issued by Imam Khomeini in 1963, he condemned the shah's regime for its complete subordination to foreign powers specifically the United States. He further criticized the deposed Shah for maintaining close political, economic, military, and intelligence ties with Israel and his anti-Islamic policies.

joined his beloved God-Almighty, leaving this temporary abode -with a tranquil, and contented heart, a spirit full of joy, and a conscience hopeful (of receiving) God' s forgiveness. The following are the mystical verses:

Man beh khale labat-e-doost giraftar shudom. Chashme bimar too ra didam wa bimar shudam.

Oh my beloved! After witnessing your Infinite Beauty (*) I become entangled.

Seeing, the manifestation of Your Glory, I become saturated with joy and ecstasy.

[*] During the spiritual migration or gnostic journey (*ser wa salook*), away farer (*salik*) gradually succeeds in witnessing divine illumination which are revealed to him intermittently. i.e. He witnesses at certain instants then it disappears. How such things occur are beyond description and those who have experienced it are helpless to explain it to others.

Ibn abi al-Hadid Moatazali writes:

"Whatever the most celebrated gnostics have said has been obtained from the Commander of the Faithful Imam' Ali (A). He says: 'Sheikh Abu Ali Sina and Qashiri, whatever about the status of wayfarer and his journey have said is quoted from the words of Imam' Ali (A) Following is an example: Sheikh Abu Ali Sina has said:

'When a wayfarer in his determination reaches to a certain limit pleasant ecstasies from Divine illumination becomes manifested for him like the lightening

---

Imam Khomeini was first arrested after the uprising on June 1963 and finally exiled to Turkey. In October 1965, Imam Khomeini moved to the Holy City of Najaf (Iraq). From Najaf, Imam Khomeini continued to issue fatwas (religious guidance). The deposed Shah who hoped that by sending Imam Khomeini to an exile, he would succeed in preventing the Imam's influence and totally diminishing his popularity. The Shah was frustrated. Throughout the fourteen years of the exile in Najaf, Imam Khomeini continued his ceaseless campaign.

The success of Islamic Revolution of Iran springs out from his untiring endeavors in awakening and directing the Ummah. It was in December 1978, when one of the greatest of all the demonstrations took place. It can be said to be an exceptional demonstration in the history of the world. This demonstration paved the way for the escape of the Shah, his final overthrow and ultimate triumph of the Islamic Revolution.

sparks which shines and become silenced. This state has been called by the learned mystics as a situation whereby a wayfarer is confronted with the joy of union and pain of separation (with the beloved) alternately. i.e. After the illumination is silenced the wayfarer is filled with grief and pain. The more deeper a wayfarer goes into asceticism this situation becomes further intense.'

-Share Isharat, vol.3 p-384.

And these are the meanings of this first verse.

Farigh az Khud shudam wa koos anal haq bezadam. Hamchu Mansoor kharidar sare dar shudam.

I forget my own existence [55] and proclaimed the slogan -'I am the truth', and like the Mansoor Hallaj volunteered my self for hanging [56].

Ghame dildar fakandeh ast be janam sharari, ke bejan amadam wa shorahe bazar shudam.

The agony and pain of your love has burnt[57] my entire existence. That I become fed up with my own self; and my affairs become the talks of the town[58]

---

[55] When the gnostic journey of a wayfarer ends his interior becomes a mirror of God-Almighty whereby real pleasures descend upon him. At this stage he feels happy and joyful with himself, because he sees something special within his innerself. Sometimes the gnostic looks at God-Almighty while at other times he looks at him, thus, finding himself wavering between these two views. Eventually, he reaches to a point where his ownself disappears and he sees only God-Almighty, which are the meanings of "forgetting my own existence". In gnostic terms this stage is also called being annihilated in God-Almighty (*fana fillah*).

[56] Means being patient, offering resistance, tolerating difficulties, and hardships, and becoming a target of acquisation by the people for the sake of God-Almighty. And that is the way Imam Khomeini (R.A) was, who suffered a imprisonment, exiles, pains, and suffering for the sake of his beloved.

[57] There is a narration from the Commander of the Faithful Imam' Ali (A):
"*God's love never passes over a thing without getting it burnt.*"

[58] The becoming the talks of the town may be explained in the light of the following tradition quoted from the Holy Prophet (S):
"*When God-Almighty loves a person from my Ummah He fills the hearts of His favorite distinguished saints, spirits of angels and other Heavenly creatures with his love so that all of them love him. How fortunate is he ? How fortunate is he ? He will have the right of intercession on the Day of Judgment. So for as a servant is not liked by God-Almighty he does not become famous.*"

Dare meykhana gooshaid beravim shabo rooz, ke man is masjido wa az madrase bezar shudam.

"Let the doors of tavern [59] be opened, and let us go there day and night.

Because, I become disgusted with, the Mosque [60] as well as from the School.

Jame zohdo riya kardam wa bar tan kardam, kharqe pir kharabati wa hashyar shudam.

"I took off the dress of ascesticm and dissimulation." [61]

-Faiz Kashani, al Muhajatul Baiza, 7-8.

[59] The tavern here means the spiritual position of God's Nearness attained through performance of recommended (*nawafil*). In accordance with authentic narrations, after attaining such a position, God-Almighty becomes the ears and eyes of the servant. The eyes and ears are for seeing and listening and what pleasure could be greater for a person than seeing and listening through those special eyes and ears.

[60] Here the Mosque and School mean worships which lack the conditions required for attaining God's Nearness or they might indicate the preliminaries required for starting the gnostic journey of a wayfarer. Islam being one of. the most perfect and comprehensive divine religion consists of degrees and stages containing exoteric and esoteric affairs. In order to understand its mysteries the condition of confidentiality (*mahram*) is essential which is only possible through deeds, struggle, abstinence, and guidance of Prophet's Infallible Household (A) (Ahlul Bayt).

The school, books and class are preliminaries for understanding, un-derstanding is preliminary for action and action is preliminary for ac-quiring confidentially (*mahram*).

Sayyid Bin Taoos a great Shiite scholar in his will to his son:

"My son! If you deal with God-Almighty through the path of truth and reality, He will make your heart like a mirror in which the knowledge which God-Almighty desires for you could be seen, because according to the traditions of the Holy Prophet (S) it has been mentioned that a believ-er looks at Divine illumination."

-Kashf al-Mohajateh, p-136.

In nutshell, it could be said that the book and school which could not elevate a person to the level of Sayyid bin Taoos or Imam Khomeini (R.A.) -one should not be blamed for being disgusted with them which are the meanings of this verse.

[61] Means relinquishment of moral indecencies like deceit etc., renun-ciation of worldly attachments, and reaching to the real asceticism which makes a wayfarer worthy of receiving Divine mysteries and sublime realities.

And become awakened[62] after wearing the robe of a tavern's haunter."

Waiz shahar, ke az pind khud azaram dad, Az dome rinde mai allodeh madad kar shudam.

"The town's preacher [63] with his preaching made me uncomfortable[64]

Therefore, I sought refuge[65] in some on who was inwardly upright but outwardly lewd."

Beguzarid ke az butkadeh yadi be kunam, Man ke ba daste bute malkada bedar shudam.

Let me allow to remember the temple's[66] sweet memories. Where I was awakened [67] from the sweet touch of my beloved's hand.

The above translation and commentary of Imam's mystical poetry was a difficult task indeed for some one like me, but thanks God that it has been accomplished. I have utilized the most common mystical terms and phrases which are most conventional among gnostics. However, it must be admitted that Imam Khomeini's level of mysticism (*irfan*) is far higher that its interpretation could be limited to such conventional mystical boundaries.

---

[62] Renunciation of world and its allurements and possession of real piety and ascesticm result in association with the Holy Prophet (S) and his Infallible Household (A) in this world and Hereafter, which are the meanings of becoming awakened.

[63] Means the pseudo-preachers who prevent people from nearing the real pious scholars, thus, depriving them from being benefited from their sacred existence.

[64] Means restrictions imposed by them cheap talks and illogical arguments.

[65] Taking shelter with those perfect and pious models who are intoxicated with God is love. The indication here means towards the learned teachers of Imam Khomeini (R.A.).

[66] Means the Celestial Kingdom and the Celestial Lights representing the sacred existence of Holy Prophet (S) and his Household Ahlul Bayt (A) who are the infinite and absolute source of blessing and guidance for the mankind.

[67] Means acceptance of receiving the blessing guidance through the sacred light of the Holy Prophet and his Holy House Hold (A)

Supplication of the Holy Month of Sha'ban (Munajat-e-Shabanyeh)

1. The supplication of the Holy Month of Sha'ban-the famous (*Munajat-e-Shabanyeh*) narrated by the Commander of the Faithful Imam 'Ali (A) and other infallible Imams of Prophet (S)'s Ahlul Bayt, is one of the most precious mystic supplication. Imam Khomeini (R.A.) the most perfect gnostic of our times, in his repeated speeches have emphasized the special spiritual importance of this precious supplication. Those who are blessed with Divine grace of keeping themselves continuously engaged in supplications and God's remembrance loves this supplication a lot, and because of this supplication eagerly await for the arrival of the Holy Month of Sha'ban.

This supplication contains vest sublime themes especially the etiquettes and manners of servanthood; the manners of how to face the God-Almighty; how to beseech Him; how to tell him about heart's secrets; how to open tongue for offering apologies and how to remain hopeful. Also, in these supplications the meanings of interpretation of God's Countenance (*Laqa*), God's Witnessing (*Shahood*) God's Nearness, (*Qurb*) have been described in a delicate manner, which do not leave any doubt or confusion for those wayfarers, who are still double minded, and who do not want to believe. Regarding self-awareness which is preliminary for God's learning (*Marefah*), this supplication contains most meaningful and surprising points.

Since the recital of this supplication, especially, during the Holy Month of Sha'ban as well as throughout the year for the wayfarers of spiritual migration have been strongly recommended, I feel it appropriate to present its English translation for the utilization of dear readers. For the convenience of those readers who do not know how to read Arabic, its pronunciation in English has been included.

1. Added by [Tr].

Allahumma salle ala Muhammadin wa ale Muhammad," wasma , duai eza dawatoka; wasma' nedai eza nadetoka," wa aqbbil alliya eza najetoka faqad harabto elaika," wa waqfato baina yadeka" Mustakinan laka muttazzare an elaika" rajeyan lema ladaika thawabi; wa ta'lama ma .fi nafsi," wa takhboro hajali; wa ta'refo zamiri wala yakhfa alaika amro munqallbi," wa maswaya wama' orido an obdea behi," min manteqi wa atafawawhu behi min talebeti; wa arjuho leaqebati," wa qad jorat maqade roka aliya. Ya sayyidi! fima yakuno minni ila akhire umri, min savi rati wa ala niyati," wa bejadeka la abide ghairaka zeyadati," wa naqsi wa nafi wa zarri.

Elahi inharamtani faman zallazi yarzuqni wa in khzaltani taman lazi yansurni. Elahi auzobeka min ghzabeka wa huloole sakhteka. Elahi in kunto ghaira mustahilin le rahmanteka fa anta ahlun an tajuda aliya befazle sa'teka" Elahi kaanni benalsi waqefatun bena yadeka," wa qad azzallaha husno tavakoli alaka faqulta ma anta ahlohu; wa tughmadtani be afuwaka. Elahi in afowta faman owla minka bezaleka; wa in kana qad dna ajali,. wa lam yodneni minka amali faqad ja 'Itol iqrara bezarbe elaika wasilati. Elahi! Qadjurto ala nafsi fin nazare lahafalahal waslo in lam taghfir laha. Elahi lam uazal birroka aliya ayama hayatifala taqta'a birraka anni fi mamati. Elahi kaifa ayasa min husane nazereka li ba'da mamati,. wa anta lam tawalleni lllal jamila fi hayati. Elahi tawwala min amri ma anta ahlohu wa ud aliya befazleka ala muznebin qad ghamarahu jahalahu. Elahi qad satarta aliya zunuban fid duniya, wa ana ahwaju ila saterha aliya minka fil ukhra izlam tuzjhirha leahdin min ebadekassaleheen. Fala tafzahani yomal qayamatch ala ra 'usil ashade. Elahi judoka basata amali wa afvoka aftalo min amali. Elahi fasurrani be leqaika yoma taqzi fehay baina ebadeka. Elahi etezari elaika etezaro man lam yastaqhney unqaboole uzrehi faqbal uzri ya akrama mone tazara elaihil musioona.

Elahi la turudda hajati wala tukhaiyyeb tama'i wala taqta'a minka rajai wa amali. Elahi la ard ta havani lam tahdini walou ardta fazihati, lam to afini. Elahi ma azunnoka tarud doni fi hajatin qad afneto umri fi zalabeha minka. Elahi falakal hamdo abadan daiman sarmodan yazido wala yabido kama tohibbo wa torza. Elahi in akhaz tani be jurmi akhaztoke be afweka wa in akhastana be zunobi akhastoka be maghferateka wa in udkhaltanin nara alamto ahleha anni ohibboka.

Elahi in kanna saqhora fi jambe ta'ateka amalifaqad kaborafi jambe rajaika amali. Elahi kaifa unqalabo min indeka bil khaibate mahruman wa qad kana husno zanni be judeka untaqlebani bin najate marhuman. Elahi wa qad afneto umri fi shir ratis sah ve unka wa ablato shababi fi sakratit taba odimneka. Elahi falam asteqiz aiyyamaqh terari beka wa rukoni ela sabil sakhateka. Elahi wa ana abdoka wabno abdeka qaimun baina yadaika mutawasselun be karameka elaika.

Elahi ana abdun ata nassalo elaika mimma kunto owajehoka behi min qil latis tehyai min nazareka wa utlobul afwa minka ezil afwo natun lekarameka. Elahi lam ya kunli holum fa untaqila behi un maseyateka illa fi waqtin aiqastani le mahabbeteka wa kama ard ta unakuna kunto fa shakartoka be idkhali fi karameka wale tathire galbi min ousakhil ghaflate unka. Elahin zur eliyya nazara man na daitaho fa ajabaka wastamal-taho bema wao nateka fa ataka ya qariban la yabodo ani mughtarre behi wa ya javadan la yabkhalo amman raja thawabaho.

Elahi hubli qalban yudnihe minka shoukohu wa lisanan yurfa'a elaika sidqohu wa nazaran yoqarrebohu minka haqohu. Elahi inna man ta'rrafa beka ghairo majhulin man la azabeka ghairo maqhzulin wa man aqbalta alaihe gnairo mamtukin. Elahi inna manin tahahoj beka lamustonirun wa inna mane tasama beka lamastajirun wa qad luz to beka. Ya Elahi fala tukhaiyab zanni min rahmateka wala tahjubni unrafateka. Elahi ogmeni fi ahle wa vilayateka moqama man raja izziyadata min mahab-bateka. Elahi wal himni walahan be zekreka ila zekreka wa himmati fi rohe najahe asmaika wa mahlle qudseka. Elahi beka alaika illa alhaqtani be mahalle ahle ta ateka wal maswassalehe min marzateka fa inni la aqde ro le nafsi alafan wala amleko laha nafan.

Elahi abdohaz zaiful muznebo wa mamlukokal munibo fala tajalni min man sarafta unho wajhaka wa hajabahu sahwoho on afweka. Elahi hubli kamala[inqtai elaika wa unre absara qulobena be ziae Zare ha elaika hatta takhreqa absarul qulobe hujoban noore fata sela ila ma'dinil azamate wa tasira arwahona muallaqatan be izze qudseka. Elahi qojalni mimman nadetahu fa ajabaka wala khat ta ho fasa eqa le jalaleka fana jetaho sirrun wa amela laka jahran.

Elahi lam ossallit ala hosne zanni qunotal ayase walan qat' a rajai min jamile karameka. Elahi in kanatil khatoya qad asqatatni ladeka fasfah anni be hosne tavvakuli alaika. Elahi in khat tatrniz zunobo min makareme lutfeka faqad nabbah nani el yaqino ila kareme atfeka. Elahi in anamatnil ghaflato aniestedade lil qaika faqad nabbah hatnil ma'refato bekaramil alyaka. Elahi inda'ani ilan nare azimo aqabekafaqad da'ani ilaljannate jazilo thawabeka. Elahi falaka asalo wa elaika abtahilo wa ar-ghabo wa as aloka untosal leya ala Muhammadin wa ale Muhammadin wa un taj alani mimman yodimo zik ra ka wala yan qoso ah da ka wala yaqh folo un shukreka wala yes takhifo be amreka-Elahi wal hiqni be noore ezzekal abhaje fa' akuna laka arefan wa un sevaka munharifan wa minka khaifan moraqeban ya zaljalale wal ikrame wa sallallaho ala Muhammadin rasulehi wa alehit tahirina wa sallama tasliman kasira.

"In the Name of God the Beneficent the Merciful"

"Oh God! Send salutation upon Muhammad and His Holy Progeny and since, I beseech You (please) grant my prayer; whenever I cry,-please listen to my cry; whenever I supplicate You please pay attention towards my condition; Because, I have taken refuge in You, am standing before Thy Threshold in a state of grief, entangled with hardships shedding tears, while still remaining hopeful of Your mercy and compassion-Thou are Knowledgeable about my heart; is aware of my needs, knows thoroughly about myself; and there is nothing hidden from You as far as my affairs of this world and next worlds are concerned."

"And whatever I bring upon my tongue to speak about my needs as well as regarding my being hopeful in Thee for my eternal salvation-Thou know every thing about it-Oh my Master! Thou will governs all the hidden and apparent affairs of my life till its very last breath; whatever profit or loss reaches to me, it is from Thee and not from other than Thee-Oh God! If Thou deprive me than who else is there to provide my sustenance ? If Thou make me abject then who else is there to support me? Oh God!! I take refuge in Thee from Thy wrath and the severity of punishment-Oh God! If I don't deserve to receive Your blessing–Thou possesses the decency of bestowing forgiveness upon me with Thy infinite mercy and compassion."

"Oh God! As though I am standing before Thy sacred threshold; my good faith and trust in Thee has already spreaded the shadow of mercy upon my head,-whatever was befitting from Thy magnanimity and benevolence, Thou have done with me accordingly, forgiveness and bless-ing has surrounded my entire existence-Oh God! If Thou pardon me who else is more befitting than Thee ?"

"And In case my death is near and my deeds did not earn Thy nearness, Then I will present my admittance of sins as a means to receive Thy forgiveness. O God! I do admit that I have oppressed my self: then woe be upon the self: if you do not bestow forgiveness upon him. Oh God ! Thy beneficence and merci surrounded me throughout my living; there-fore, do not deprive me from Thy grace in my dying. Oh God! how can I be disappointed from receiving Thy Favors, after death, because during my entire life I have not seen any thing from Thee except compassion ?"

"Oh God! Be my guardian and supervisor over my affairs the way it is befitting of Thee (not what I deserve) pay attention with Thy benevolence and merci towards me -a sinner who has been overtaken completely by his ignorance. Oh God! Indeed thou have covered all my sins in this world; I need their cover-up in the Hereafter much more than the covering of this world, because, Thou were kind and did not expose them to anyone of your descent servants; therefore, on the Day of Judgment do not insult and expose me in front of all the humanity."

"Oh God! Thy mercy and compassion have increased my hopes, because Thy forgiveness is for better than my deeds. Oh God! On the Day when Thou will issue the final verdict for Thy servants, make me happy with Thou countenance. Oh God! I beseech Thou for forgiveness like some one who really is in need of acceptance of his repentance, therefore, accept my excuse, oh Beneficent! Who is besought by the sinners for atonement. Oh my Master! Do not turn down my request; do not deprive me from remaining hopeful of Your forgiveness," through the grace of Thy magnanimity do not cut off any hope and desire.

"Oh God! If thou had the intention of seeing me despised, would never blessed me with Thy guidance; if Thou had intended seeing me contemptible, would not have blessed me with health and happiness. Oh God! I can never believe it that Thou will turn down my request for which I have spent an entire life beseeching Thee for its grant. Oh God! Thou are the only one worthy of praise and adoration -the eternal and continuous praise always increasing and never ending, only if it could receive Thy pleasure and acceptance.

"Oh God! If Thou will remonstrate me for my offenses I will seek refuge in Thy forgiveness," if Thou will take me to task against my sins, I will take Thee to task for Thy forgiveness, if Thou will send me to Hell will inform its inmates that I loved Thee. Oh God! If my deeds are insinificant, but as compared to them my hope and desire in Thy magnanimity and benevolence is too much. Oh God! How can I return deprived and disappointed from Thy magnanimous kingdom, while remaining quite hopeful about Thy compassion and merci, that thou will be kind to me, and would include me among the rescued ones.

"Oh God! I have spend my entire life in ignorance, negligence, and forgetfulness from Thee, wasted my youth drunken into passions being ignorant of Thee. Oh God! I did not awake, because of being too proud to receive Thy forgiveness, and in this manner I followed the path of Your wrath and rage. Oh God! I am your humble servant and son of your servant who is now standing before Thee, pleading for Thy mercy and compassion as a means of my salvation.

"Oh God! I am your servant who has came to Thy threshold as ashamed and apologetic, I seek forgiveness and pardon for all my sins and transgressions, which were committed by me due to my lack of modesty from Thy presence, because bestowing forgiveness is the characteristic of Thy magnanimity. Oh God! I do not have the power of relinquishing sins except that Thou awaken me with love and kindness. Or, if thou desire that I should become the way Thou want me to be,' must be thankful to Thee for spreading Thy compassion and cleansing and purifying my heart from the filthiness of negligence.

"Oh God! With Thy Magnanimity treat me like some one to whom Thou invited -he accepted, and Thou asked him for obedience –he obeyed. Oh near one who is never away from Thy lovers, Oh Beneficent and Merciful who never acts miserly towards those who are hopeful of Thy favors. Oh God! Bless with a heart eager and anxious of Thy nearness, a tongue which should keep itself engaged in sending the words of truth upward towards Thee, and an insight which should bring me closer to Thee.

"Oh God! Whoever is known by thee cannot remain unknown; whoever takes refuge in Thee can never be despised, whoever received Thy attention would never become servant of anyone else, whoever followed Thy path become enlightened, whoever sought Thy shelter become secured. And I have taken refuge in Thee, therefore, Oh God! Don't disappoint me from Thy blessings and do not deprive me from receiving Thy grace and favors."

"Oh God! Consider me among Thy favorite saints and bestow upon me the rank of some one who strives to receive Thy love as much as possible. Oh God! Reveal upon me the sweetness and pleasure of engaging into Thy remembrance continuously, bless me with the courage to seek pleasure, victory, and dependence in Thy Sacred Names and Exalted Essence. Oh God! I swear You by Thy Own Exalted Essence and the right which Thou possess over the creation to include me among the obedient ones and bestow upon me a descent position of Your pleasure and consent, because I am totally incompetent and neither can defend my self while encountering an evil nor can increase any profit for myself Oh God! I am a helpless servant and repentant sinner full of defects and faults, therefore, do not include me among those who earned your displeasure and because of their negligence become deprived of Thy forgiveness.

"Oh God! bestow upon me perfect attention towards Thee; open the esoteric eyes of my hearts so that they could witness Thy glory and piercing through the veils of celestial lights may connect them with the Absolute Source of Majesty; let our souls achieve the union with Thy Exalted Holy Essence. Oh God! consider me as some one to whom Thou called he accepted Thy invitation, when Thou paid attention toward him became infatuated due to Thy glory and splendor and Thou confided in him secretly he accepted it explicitly.

'Oh God! Don't impose hopelessness and sorrow upon my good expectations towards Thee, do not cut off my hopes from your generosity. Oh God! If my offenses have made me low and abjected before Thee, pardon me for the sake of my reliance and good faith in Thy forgiveness. Oh God! If my sins have made me distant apart from Thy mercy and compassion, my belief reminds me about Thy magnanimity. Oh God! If ignorance and negligence have caused me to remain unprepared for Thy countenance, Thy bounties and blessings make me aware. Oh God! If Thy wrath and punishment will send me to Hell's fire, Thy generosity and reward have invited me towards the eternal Paradise.

"Oh God! Therefore, whatever I need I beseech Thee; cry and shed tears with hope, desire and anxiety before Thy Holy Threshold; I request Thee to send salutations upon Muhammad and His Holy Progeny; include me among the ones who are busy in Thy remembrance continuously; never break their commitments with Thee; don't forget thanking Thee even for an instant; and don't treat Thy commands lightly."

"Oh God! Enlighten my existence with the illumination of thou Sacred Essence whose cheerfulness and joy is far superior than any other pleasure, so that I become absorbed in Thee completely, getting cut off from others, fearing Thee and paying attention towards Thy commands. Oh Thou possessor of splendor and majesty and salutations of God and lots of greetings be upon Muhammad and his Holy Progeny"

A Prayer

[68] Oh Lord! Be kind to us. Bestow upon us Your love and knowledge and guide us from darkness towards illumination. If You Yourself make us know You, we would certainly love You, because, we would love You. Your Love would burn whatever falsehood, ignorance and arrogance there exist; rather the fire of Your love will burn down whatever veils exist between You and us. We would become the way -you want Your friends to be.

Oh our Lord, Master. Creator, God and Bestower of bounties. We have inflicted tyranny upon ourselves. Admit our sins and before the Day of Judgment cry: *Is there a way to get out of the Hell* ?[69] With Your mercy and compassion we have rested all our hopes upon You so that on the Judgment Day we are not doomed to utter the above cry and do not combine for us the suffering of this world and Hereafter.

---

[68] Added by [Tr].
[69] The Holy Quran (40: 12)

www.ingramcontent.com/pod-product-compliance
Lightning Source LLC
LaVergne TN
LVHW091704070526
838199LV00050B/2281